HAND BOOK OF STATIONERY, PAPER CONVERTING AND PACKAGING INDUSTRIES

A complete hand book on Stationery, Paper Converting and Packaging Industries covering various manufacturing technologies and processes alongwith their machineries & raw materials sources of different paper converting, stationery and packaging industries which are having tremendous demand now-a-days as well as having a very bright future scope.

By:

EIRI Technocrats

&

SUDHIR GUPTA

Recipient of Udyog Rattan Award

and

15 years experienced Industrial consultant.

PUBLICATION DIVISION

ENGINEERS INDIA RESEARCH INSTITUTE

4449, Nai Sarak, Main Road, New Delhi - 110 006 (INDIA)

Phones : 291 8117, 291 6431, 292 0361 ✱ Fax : 91-11-291 6431

Printed & Published by

ENGINEERS INDIA RESEARCH INSTITUTE

Regd. Office : 4449, Nai Sarak, Main Road, New Delhi - 110 006 (INDIA)
Phones : 291 8117, 291 6431, 292 0361 ● Fax : 91-11-291 6431

Distributed by

SMALL INDUSTRY RESEARCH INSTITUTE

New Delhi (INDIA)

ISBN : 81-86732-09-8

Printed in New Delhi (India)

Rs. 400

Printed & Published by **Sudhir Gupta** for **'Engineers India Research Institute'**, and Laser Type Set by **Dharmender** at Engineers India Research Institute, and Printed at 'Kumar Offset Press', 251/8, Padam Nagar, New Delhi - 110 007

PREFACE

The Stationery, Paper Converting and Packaging Industries are now-a-days in India are increasingly day-by- day because of various utilities of these kinds of products. New technologies, methods and processes are being developed gradually. The packaging industries have captured a complete market in India as well as in abroad countries.

We have recently broughtout a valuable and informative book on Paper Converting, Stationery and Packaging Industries which is fully informative with the informations of PVC Insulation tape, Ammonia paper, Lead pencil, Tracing paper, Stickers, Artist colours, Ball point pen, refill and inks, BOPP adhesive tapes, Exercise note-book and register, Carbon paper, Computer stationery, Corrugated sheet board and boxes, Duplicating ink, Paper envelopes, Fountain pens, Gummed tape, Laminations, Tags, labels & seals, Office paste, Paper bags, Paper cones & tubes, Rubber stamp pad & ink, Table offset & DTP, Sealing wax, Staple pin, Staplers and Gem clips with Paper pins, Water proof ink, Wax crayons etc. and many other lucrative projects with their technologies are covered in a single volume.

The book is indispensable for all those who are in venture of the complete informations about stationery, paper converting and packaging industries.

Director
ENGINEERS INDIA RESEARCH INSTITUTE
Nai Sarak, New Delhi.

CONTENTS

1

AMMONIA PAPER

INTRODUCTION

Ammonia paper is nothing but ammonium compounds coated on specially kind of paper. It is also known as blue print paper and mostly used for making copies of original illustration may be figure, diagram, graphs, flow sheet etc. Normally these papers are used for making copies for these and project work done by students and researches as this is very cheap and good looking.

Practically all blueprint paper made today has as the basic light sensitive-compound ferric ammonium oxalate, while the colour forming compound is a mixture of sodium and potassium ferricyanide known to the trade as Redsol. As a preservative, an oxalate or citrate is generally used. The printing speed of the sensitized paper may be varied from slow to fastsimply by varying the amount of Redsol in the formula.

USES AND APPLICATION

1. It is the paper most widely used for getting subsequent copies of an original illustration.
2. It is available in every stationary shop, schools, colleges, universities and other higher academic institutes.
3. It is the only cheapest paper available in the market for getting copies, thus preferred by most of the colleges, researchers, and scholars.
4. It is very simple in processing.
5. The blueprint comes out very clear and bright. 6. As many as copies may be taken out with one illustration.
6. There is only one big disadvantage of these copies is that original illustration has to be made on a so called butter or tracing paper with drawing ink (black).

MANUFACTURINGPROCESS

The common blueprint papers have been made using many formulae, but practically all of them are simple variations of the original process suggested by Sir John Herschel. He discovered in 1840 that ferrc salts when exposed to light in the presence of organic matter, were reduced to the ferrous state. His experiment involved the use of a ferric salt coated paper which was then exposed and the paper treated which was then exposed and the paper treated with potassium ferricyanide to develop the image.

The ferrous salt produced during the exposure period reacts with the ferricyanide to give blue ferrous ferricyanide. This undergoes molecular rearrangement to form ferric ferrocyanide or fernbull's blue and the soluble ferric ferroycyanide which still remains on the exposed portions is removed by washing with water.

In actual practice there is much divergence from this basic reaction. Ferric ammonium citrate and ferric ammonium oxalate are used as the light sensitive salts, either alone or in combination, and are coated on the base sheet along with potassium ferricyanid

A typical formula is as follows:

	Parts by weight
Ferric ammonium citrate	125
Potassium Ferricyanide	45
Water	1000

Such a coated sheet must be dried in the darkness since the chemicals are photoreactive in the wet state. Such a paper is comparatively slow printing and will not age too satisfactorily. The addition of oxalic acid has been suggested but although it shortens the required exposure time, it also has a degrading effect on the paper and reduces the quality of the blue colour. Citric acid has been added to help improve the clarity of the white.

SUPPLIERS OF RAW MATERIALS

Base Paper:

Andhra Pradesh Pulp & Paper Mills Ltd.,
Rayamundry (A.P).

Basant paper Mills,
2nd floor Camac Sheet,
Calcutta.

Potassium Ferricyanide:

Maharashtra Fine Chemicals,
813, Bhawani Peth,
Poona - 2

Ferric Ammonium citrate:

Dr. Paul Lohmann (India) Ltd.,
145/1, Jessore Road,
Calcutta - 700 055

SUPPLIERS OF PLANT & MACHINERIES

Mixers:

Jayems Engineering Co. Ltd.
139, M. Connaught Circus
2nd Floor, New Delhi - 110 001
Phone: 332 4146, 332 3680

Coating Machine & Dryer:

Panchand Kushaldas & Sons,
11-B Noble Charmers, 1st Floor
Ghoga Street, Mumbai - 400 001

Niwa Machinery Company Limited,
12-4-6, Chome, Omari-Nishi-Otwku,
Tokyo (JAPAN)

PLANT ECONOMICS OF AMMONIA PAPER

Rated Plant Capacity = 1.50 Ton/Day

COST OF LAND & BUILDING

(Total land area required 250 sq. mtr.)	Rs.	1,48,750.00

LIST OF PLANT & MACHINERY

1. Mixer for mixing ferric ammonia citrate and potassium ferricyanide
2. Coating machine
3. Dryer
4. Other miscellaneous equipments and ancilliaries

LIST OF RAW MATERIALS

1. Ferric ammonium oxalate
2. Potassium ferricyanide
3. Base paper
4. Packing material (waterproof paper)
5. Miscellaneous

FIXED CAPITAL

Land & Building	Rs.	6,98,750.00
Plant & Machinery	Rs.	1,93,000.00
Other Fixed Assets	Rs.	88,000.00
TOTAL	**Rs.**	**9,79,750.00**

TOTAL WORKING CAPITAL/MONTH

Raw Material	Rs.	4,19,200.00
Salary & Wages	Rs.	37,375.00
Utilities & Overheads	Rs.	45,010.00
TOTAL	**Rs.**	**5,01,585.00**

TOTAL CAPITAL INVESTMENT

Total Fixed Capital	Rs.	9,79,750.00
Total Working Capital for 3 Months	Rs.	15,04;755.00
TOTAL	**Rs.**	**24,84,505.00**

TURN OVER/ANNUM

Ammonia Paper 450 Ton	Rs.	90,00,000.00

PROFIT = RECEIPTS - COST OF PRODUCTION

= 90,00,000.00 - 66,59,611.10

= 23,40,388.90

PROFIT SALES RATIO = Profit/Sales x 100 = **26.00 %**

RATE OF RETURN = Operating Profit/T.C.I. x 100 = **94.20 %**

BREAKEVEN POINT (B.E.P.) = 30.68 %

2

ARTIST COLOURS

INTRODUCTION

Artist colours are a range of colours used for commercial work. They are not actual inks but belong to the paint class, except that they are water based and conventional dyes and pigments are used. They come as paste or solid blocks and are meant for commercial work by artists :-

Poster Colours:- Poster colours, also known as "Poster Inks" or "poster paints" are closely related to drawing inks, except that they are thicker in composition and alike to paints. They are commonly used for art work by desingners, art school etc. These inks (or paints) are formulated on shellac borax base and are coloured with finely dispersed pigment pastes. These inks are semi viscous opaque in character essentially consist of a water soluble or dispersable binder, plasticizer and preservative. A wide range of colours are aimed at.

Two formulations are possible, either based on shellac- Borax, or without the use of the above resin. The first type is known as aqueous pigment pastes.

Formula (Aq. ink) :-

Pigment powder	20
Castor Oil	3
(dispersing agent - sandoz)	
Resocol V (sandoz)	15
Carboxyl methyl cellulose 2% solution	25
Water	35
Phenol	2

For inks based on shellac - Borax, base, the following formula is used.

Formula :-

Pigment paste	10-15	parts
Bleach shellac borax base	30	”
Water	60	”
Phenol	1	”

Castor Oil can be used for better dispersion & Resocol can be used for homogenity of solution.

The popular sheds are :-

1.	Maganta	2.	Mauve
3.	Cobalt blue	4.	Prussion blue
5.	Ceruullean blue	6.	Light green
7.	Medium green	8.	Deep green
9.	Ultra arine blue	10.	Turquoise green
11.	Dark green	12.	Chrome yellow
13.	Lemon	14.	Yellow ochre
15.	Orange	16.	Gremson lake
17.	Scarlst lake	18.	Scarlet lake
19.	Vermmillon	20.	Carmine
21.	Pink	22.	Burnt siona
23.	Burnt anbre	24.	Vandyke brown
25.	Grey	26.	Black
27.	White		

Water Colours :-

Artist colours are either water based on oil based paint coloured with acid dyes or pigments. For high quality, work referred as ‘tempera’ colours, where the coating are expected last for long perwards only selected fast pigment pastes can be used.

For lower quality “student colours” and allied materials, the technical properties of the colouring matter used are not critical and higher choice of selection is available.

Water Paints :-

These are made in powder, paste, black or tablet form.

Powder paints consists of a mixture of binder (dextrin) dry ground with a pigment (usually a colour lake or toner) in the ratio of 1:4 by weight. When used the powder paint is diluted with water to any desired consistency.

Paste paints are suppllied in tubes. They consists of a coloured piigments and an extender dispersing agent usually an anionic type is used to assist dispersion for the purpose. The binder is a material gum, plasticised with glycerine. The following extuders can be used :-

Bartytes	Barium sulphate.
Blanc fixe.	
Alumina	(aluminium hydroxide)
Paris white	(Calcium carbonate)
Mineral white	(calcium sulphate)
China clay	(aluminium silicate)

The extender is suitably selected to suit the opacity and viscosity of the paint.

MANUFACTURING PROCESS

For making wax crayons the clays and colours are throughly mixed and the mixture is added to the molten was a stearic acid with stirring. The homogeneous wax is then poured in the moulds. The cast crayons of 12 different colours are then packed in colourful card board boxed for sale.

Commercial water coloures are made in paste and block on tablet form. Body pigments with clays and binding materials along with requeste quantity of water are throughly mixed in a mixer or pot mill. Paste so obtained is pressed. Tablets are then packed in the boxes.

For making oil colours, colours (pigments and dyes along with extender binders such as double boiled linseed oil, tung oil etc.) are properly mixed in a kneader (horizontal type) and then passed through a triple roll mill. After 4-5 passes, the product is filled in tubes by paste filling machine and then packed. For making poster colours, the clays, colours (pigments & dyes) along with the binders are mixed in the mixer and then ground in the pot mill for obtaining homogenous paste. The paste so obtained is filled in bottles with the help of filling machine. Six bottles of different colours are packed in the card board box for sale.

Poster Colours :-

2% solution of CMC is prepared in cold water. CMC on soaking overnight in cold water goes into solution easily. Vigorous agitation is done while adding the CMC other wise lumps are formed and agitation is also necessary after soaking. Add now carton OI phenol ground with pigment paste to this solution. If foaming is observed, use 0.1% to 02%. Anti-mussol (de-foaming agent, sandoz) liquid the consistency of the ink can be adjusted by either thickening solutions or water resocol V is used to prevent the ink from separation or flocculation. It acts as a binder ink from separation or floculation. It acts as a binder between the pigments and the thickner namely CMC solution.

Mixing :-

Mixing involves blending the pigments and other raw materials intimately so that the pigments are almost completely wetted out, any air in the mixture is displaced and cluster of particles are reduced from large lumps to small aggregates.

Efficiently mixed inks are fairly uniform in colour and consistently wet particles somewhat smaller then pin heads can be distinguished by the eye.

The 3 roll mill has long been the main machine for dispersing stiff paste inks.

With mixer, great care must be taken not to add to much pigment to the vehicle, so that the mix does not become too stiff for the power available. The resistance to stirring varies and often increases at the start and attains a maximum at some point during and not necessarily at the end of the operation. Care must be taken to minimise contamination due to dusting if necessary by enclosing the mixtures in separate compartments which are separately pented from outside when the mixing operation is completed a ocprechtative sample of the mix grind on a lab. 3 roll mill & tested against a standard ink for colour match, tinctorial strength and consistency. Any addition in dry colour to recttify the shade or strength to adjust the body is made to the mixer. After further mixing the entire batch of mixed ink is sent to the mill room for grinding and when this operation is completed, it should compare favourable with the standard ink.

PRINCIPLES OF FORMULATIONS

Following parameters are imported.

1. Colour matching
2. Grinding
3. Consistency
4. Drying time
5. Length of ink
6. Printed appearance
7. Machine peerformance etc.

Quality control & Testing :-

The following para meters are important (physical tests).

1. Fineness of grind
2. Consistency
3. Drying time
4. Strength by reduction
5. Length
6. Tack
7. Shade & colour
8. Particle size
9. Texture
10. Coverage
11. Livering & Storage aviailability
12. Bulking value

SUPPLIERS OF RAW MATERIALS

Carbon Black:

Bhagat ji Chemical,
31/2, Anand Parbat- Ind Area,
New Delhi - 110 015
Ph : 5751097

Iron Oxide (Red):

Cyanamides & Pigments Ltd.,
43, Chowringheee Road,
Calcutta - 16.

Ultramarine Blue:

Ultramarine & Pigments Ltd.,
Baldola Bhawan, 117,
Maharshi Karve Road,
Mumbai - 400 020

Prussian Blue:

Goodlas Nerolac paints Ltd.,
Forbes Building,
Charanjit Rai Marg,
Fort, Mumbai - 400 001

Zinc Oxide:

Anil Rubber Co.,
1443/5, Iqbal Market,
Sadar Bazar, Delhi - 110 006
Ph: 520 486

Lead Sulphate:

National Chemical Corporation,
No.9, deevkaran Mansion,
Pathakwadi, Shamaldas Gandhi Marg,
Mumbai - 400 002

Zinc Sulphate:

Pinkto Chemicals,
7, Amratala Street,
Calcutta - 7.

Tinainum Di-Oxide:

Reema Marketing (P) Ltd.
2280/19, Gali Hingabeg,
Tilak Bazar,
Delhi - 110 006
Ph : 2928844

Dehydrated Castor Oil:

Himalaya Oil & Soap Industries
Plot No. A - 54,
MIDC, Badllapur,
Kulgaon - 421 503
Distt. Thane. (M.S.)

Oils:

Shriram Foods & Fertiliser Industries
Vanaspati Marketing Department
6th Floor, Kanchenjunga,
18, Barakhamba Road,
New Delhi - 110 001
Phone : 331 5524

Organic Dyes Pigments & Their Emulsions:

Madhur Chemicals,
936/13, Narang Chambers,
1st Floor, Gali Teliyan,
Tilak Bazar,
Delhi - 110 006
Ph. 593142, 291655, 2523389

Dryers:

Jayems Engineering Co. Ltd.,
139, M. Connaught Circus,
2nd Floor,
New Delhi - 110001
Phone : 332 4146, 332 3680

Synthetic Resins, Emulsions & Vernishes:

Parekh Dye Chemical Industries (P) Ltd.,
Mafatlal House,
2nd Floor,
Backbay Reclamation,
Mumbai - 400 020

Natural Gums, Resins, Starch, Dextrin etc.:

The Anil Starch Products Ltd.,
P.B. No. 1062,
Anil Road
Ahmedabad -2.

Carboxy Methyl Cellulose, Agar & Polyvinyl Alcohol:

Cellulose Products of India Ltd.,
P.o. Kathwada Maize Products,
Dist. Ahmedabad.

SUPPLIERS OF PLANT & MACHINERY

Bhasker Enterprises
70/1/1, Mangolpur Kalan,
Delhi - 110083

Triple Roll:

Jayems Engineering Co. Ltd.,
139-M, Connaught Circus,
2nd Floor, New Delhi - 110001
Phone : 332 4146, 332 3680

Planetary Mixer:

Sehgal Industrial Works
T - 1698, Malkaganj Road,
Subzi Mandi,
Delhi - 110007
Phone : 2520381, 233823.

Weighing Machine:

J.S. Enterprises,
B-3, Mukerjee Tower,
Delhi - 110009
Ph. - 72 14 503

Tube Filling Machines:

H.B. Mechanical & Engineering Works
355/28, Tri Nagar,
Onkar Nagar - B,
Delhi - 110035
Phone : 722 4505

PLANT ECONOMICS OF ARTIST COLOURS

Rated Plant Capacity = 250.00 Kgs./Day

COST OF LAND & BUILDING

(Total land area required 500 sq. mtr.) Rs. 8,25,000.00

LIST OF PLANT & MACHINERY

1. Planetary mixer
2. Triple roll mill, each with feed roll, complete with take off apron
3. Containers
4. Tube filling machine
5. Weighting machine
6. Tabletting press
7. Misc. equipments & devices like counter balances, stainless steel drums, testing appartus

LIST OF RAW MATERIALS

1. Pigment
2. Paint medium
3. Banc fixe
4. Other misc. raw materials like disspersing agent etc.
5. Label, packing tubes, boxes etc.

FIXED CAPITAL

Land & Building	Rs.	8,25,000.00
Plant & Machinery	Rs.	4,01,000.00
Other Fixed Assets	Rs.	1,14,000.00
TOTAL	**Rs.**	**13,40,000.00**

TOTAL WORKING CAPITAL/MONTH

Raw Material	Rs.	1,34,875.00
Salary & Wages	Rs.	38,061.00
Utilities & Overheads	Rs.	74,000.00
TOTAL	**Rs.**	**2,46,936.00**

TOTAL CAPITAL INVESTMENT

Total Fixed Capital	Rs.	13,40,000.00
Total Working Capital for 3 Months	Rs.	7,40,808.00
TOTAL	**Rs.**	**20,80,808.00**

TURNOVER/ANNUM

Receipt from the sale of 13800 box one box containing 144 tubes

TOTAL Rs. 44,85,000.00

PROFIT = RECEIPTS - COST OF PRODUCTION

= 44,85,000.00 - 34,78,532.44

= 10,06,467.56

PROFIT SALES RATIO = Profit/Sales x 100 = **22.32 %**

RATE OF RETURN = Operating Profit/T.C.I. x 100 = **48.37 %**

BREAK EVEN POINT (B.E.P.) = 51.09 %

3

BALL POINT PEN REFILLS

INTRODUCTION

In modern time ball pen refills are being produced from plastic materials and is having bright future in specially India. Previously ball pen refills were manufactured from conventional metals like Copper, Aluminium alloys but now a days plastic has taken its place due to several inherent advantages of plastic over conventional metals and plastic is replacing metal very fast.

In the recent year there has been a tremendous demand of ball point pens. It is widely used right from the top executives to the school going students. The only and the most important feature of these pens are that they are economical and are easy to use. Economical in away that they cost far lower than the ordinary fountain pen. These are the two feature which make this item absolutely in dispensable another reason for that sudden growth in demand and consumption of the item is due to the governments policy to enhance education standards in the country. The Government is trying best to promote education thereby giving a face lift in the education standard. As a result there has been a tremendous growth in this area.

Ball pen refill is stocked by big stationery merchants, general merchants and even road side small shops. The demand is on the rise everyday.

USES AND PROPERTIES

The ball point pen ink is quite different from other type of writing inks. This ball point pen ink has some specific properties which are described below:

1. The ink is high viscous which cannot come out of the refill unless the refill is used for writing.
2. The ink does not come itself out of refill.

3. It writes after reveral intervals and does not change on any stage.
4. It does not spoil up to one or more years if properly preserved.

Main application of ball pen refills as clear from the fact is in refills of different sizes of ball pens. These are very convenient and much cheaper in cost compared to metallic refills this product have now monopolised the market without any completion from other marterials.

B. I. S. SPECIFICATIONS

IS : 3707 - 1984 : Ball point pen Refills (Second Revision)
IS : 10560 - 1983 : Jotter ball pen Refills

IMPORTANT DETAILS

MATERIALS:

Tube (Ink Container) :- Tube shall be made of either any plastic or metal. When made of plasic, the material shall be sufficiently hard and rigid and shall have low moisture absorption. When made of metal, the material shall be rigid and shall have no visible defects or sharp edges.

Writing Tip :- This shall be made from brass or nickel copper alloy or stainless steel or any other non-corrosive material having some hardness characteristic or higher than that of brass.

Ball :- Ball shall be made of stainless steel or tungsten carbide. The hardness of the ball shall be between 650 to 750 HV.

Ink :- The ink shall be solvent based. It shall contain no undissolved particles of dye or agglomerates of undispersed pigments. The inkl shall be of such quality as to ensure a smooth and continuous writing.

Dimensions :- Refills shall be made according to dimensions given unless otherwise agreed to between the supplier and the purchaser. The diameter of the ball shall be between 0.50 to 1.20 mm as agreed to between the purchaser and the supplier.

Requirements :- The refill shall be so made as to be straight and concentric with its ball. The refills shall have either a collar or a crimping at a distance from the ball end. The refills shall be accurately made so that they are completely interchangeable with the ball point pens unless otherwise agreed to between the purchaser and the supplier.

The tube shall be filled with ink and shall not react with it. Colour of the ink shall normally be black, blue, green or red. The ink shall not overflow the barrel or leak around the ball. The refill during disuse shall not ooze out ink when held with ball point tip upward and downward and shall not result in smudginess and discontinuity in writing. The ball shall be so mounted as to have free rotation to enable smooth writing but shall not be loosely fitted nor loosen in use. The tip holding the ball shall be worked over so that its edge shall be smooth and not have any feathers, fins, etc, that would scratch the paper while writing.

The refill containing 0.3 g of ink shall write a continuous line of 1,000 minimum for refill having ball diameter above 0.80 mm and 1,200 m minimum for refill having ball diameter up to 0.80 mm.

TESTS:

Smoothness of Writing (Routine) Test :- Each refill shall be used to draw 50 to 60 continuous loops on a sheet of white supercalendered printing paper within a period of 15 seconds. The loops shall be continuous without excess deposit of ink and shall be uniform in colour. Writing shall be smooth and refill shall not scratch the paper.

Writing Characteristics (Type) Test :- The refill shall be tested on a sheet of white super-calendered printing paper of cream laid or cream wove paper by writing numerous fast as well as slow letters, flourishes, ovals, reversals, angles, etc. The writing shall be such that it has complete continuity without excess deposit of ink or variation in intensity or line getting split up.

Starting Test :- The refill shall be made ot draw a few lines or letters on a sheet of paper to ensure continuous writing. The refill shall then be kept in the vertical position with the writing tip upward for 30 minutes. The refill shall now be tested on a white super-calendered printing paper or cream laid or cream wove paper by drawing at least four lines, starting exactly from the margin, with normal writing pressure. The refill shall start marking the first line from a distance of not more than 15 mm and the subsequent line shall start immediately from the margin where they are drawn.

Length of Writing (Machine Writing) :-

Apparatus:-

a. *Standard Paper :-* The paper shall be white super-calendered printing paper or cream laid or cream wove papaer.

b. *Standard Test Machine :-* A mechanical writing machine designed to give continuous writing while rotaing the pens simultaneously:

1. On their axis, and
2. with speed setting of 110 mm/secone

The pens shall be fixed in such a way that they move freely up and down in their holders at a writing pressure or 125 ± 2 grams. The acute angle betwwen the paper and the pens shall be 80 ± 2 degrees. A paper-feed, mechanism shall feed the rolled paper automatically through the test machine. A revolution counter indicating the number of metres written during the test shall be fitted.

Writing Test :- Remove the protective coating, if any, from the balls of the refills under test. Write lines and turns by hand with each test sample until writing commences. Place the pens in the standarad test machine and start the writing and start the writing test. Stop the machine after each 500 metres of writing and, using a clean cloth, remove accumulated ink and paper dust from the writing tips. Mark the standard paper at points along its length to indicate each 500 metres of writing. Continue the test until each test sample ceases to write a continuous line. Reserve the test papers for assessment of length and continuity of writing. Any interruption of continuity due to any necessary adjustment in the mechanism or change of paper rolls shall be neglected.

Smearing Test :- After writing a few lines or letters on a sheet of white super-calendered printing paper or cream laid or cream wove paper and waiting for 5 seconds, the writing shall be rubbed lightly with hand. The ink shall have been dried, so that it could not be smeared. Further there shall be no feathering or spreading or strike through the paper.

Test for Resistance to Water :- Ten different letters shall be writen with the refill on a sheet of cream laid or cream wove paper. The paper shall then be immersed in water maintained at a temperature 25 ± 2°C for 24 hours. The paper shall then be removed and allowed to dry and then be examined. The letters shall remain legible.

Corrosion Resistance Test :- The metal parts of the refill shall be dippped in a boiling 10 percent (w/w) aqueous solution of sodium chloride for a period of 15 minutes. After removal from this solution they shall be immersed in 10 percent (w/w) aqueous solution of sodium chloride at room temperature of 2 hours. They shall then be removed, washed with clean water, wiped with a soft cloth and allowed to dry for 24 hours at room temperature. The metal parts shall not show any visible signs of corrosion.

Accelerated Ageing Test :- The refills shall be suspended point down and subjected successively to each of the following conditions:

Exposure	Time (Hours)	Temperature	Relative Humidity (Percentage)
I	168	60 ± 1°C	85-90
II	48	-2 ± 1°C	-

At the end of the test the refill shall satisfy the writing test and the ink shall not have leaked nor its colour changed or after the test.

Storage Test :- The refills shall be kept under normal storage for not less than six months from the time of manufacture. After this period they shall not have lost the writing characteristics and shall again satisfy the requirements

Marking:-

The refills shall be marked with the manufacturer's name or registered trade-mark, batch number and year of manufacture.

Ball point pen refills may also be marked with the ISI Certification Mark.

Packing :-

The refills shall be packed as agreed to between the purchaser and the supplier.

Packing shall be printed to give the following information:

a. Manufacturer's name or registered trade-mark,
b. Year of manufacture,
c. Batch number, and
d. Colour of ink.

MANUFACTURING PROCESS

Ball Pen Refills comprise mainly of the following four parts

1. Tube (Ink Container)
2. Writing Tip
3. Ball
4. Ink

The refills are prepared from poly vinyl chloride (PVC) by the straight extrusion process. The dia of the tube is 3 mm & the extruder of this diameter is used for this purpose.

First of all the ingredients are compounded in the compounding unit as per formulation given below:-

1.	PVC Resin	55%
2.	Plasticizer such as dio-octylphthalate chlorinated paratin waxe	5%
3.	Stabilizer	3%
4.	Epoxy platicizer	10%
5.	Fillers	20%
6.	Pigments	0.5%
7.	Lubricants	4.5%
8.	U.V. Stabilizers	2%
		100%

After the compounding is complete, the material is feed into the hopper of the extruder where the tube of 3 mm dia is prepared which is cut on the top to the desired length normally loan & packed.

Ink Filling (Manufacture of Final Refills) :-

Filling of ink is a great problem. this problem is due to narrow diameter of the tube. Viscosity of the ink is high and it can not flow into the tube by gravity flow. There are two ways to fill the ink into the tube, one is to lower the viscosity of ink by simple heating and other way is to fill the ink with quite a high pressure. Later way is preferred as simple a heating of the ink spoils the quality of ink and also may damage the PVC Tube.

For high pressure ink filling, the ink is pressed into the tube from one end. For applying a pressure to the ink a piston cylinder arrangement is used. Ink is filled into the cylinder and piston is pushed into it. Tube is fixed at the outlet of cylinder. Up to a certain length, the ink is filled and the tube is next put at the mouth. This whole process can be also done by manually. The tubes of a specific length are put in the carrier and the finished riffle comes out. It is always kept in mind that printing is done before ink filling. Heated metal letter are used for printing. Ball point is fixed at the end from which the ink is filled. After this we fix the metal on the top of HDPE tube which is main cover of ball point pen.

After the final refill is formed the refill is stamped by a stamping machine & followed by punching.

PLANT & MACHINERY SUPPLIERS

Bhupendra Engg.Works,
B-83, Okhla Phase-I,
New Delhi - 110020
Ph:6813710

Ganton (P) Ltd.,
G-77, Himalaya House,
Curzon Road,
New Delhi.

RAW MATERIAL SUPPLIERS

Indian plastic Ltd.,
Chemical Division,
Polsan Bridge,
Kandivli,
Mumbai - 400067

Nuchem Plastic Ltd.,
54, Indl. Area,
Faridabad.

PLANT ECONOMICS OF BALL POINT PEN REFILLS

Rated Plant Capacity = 4000.00 Nos./Day

COST OF LAND & BUILDING

(Total land area required 70 sq. mtr.) Rs. 1,54,000.00

LIST OF PLANT & MACHINERY

1. Extruder of diametre 3 mm with other accessories.
2. Dies
3. Punching machine
4. Ink filling machine
5. Hot stamping machine
6. Nozzle fixer
7. Miscelleneous (water pumps etc)
8. Water cooling tank
9. Cater pillar cum cutter unit

LIST OF RAW MATERIALS

1. PVC Granules
2. Plasticizes, Stabilizers, filler etc.
3. Ink
4. Nozzel (Brass)
5. Miscelleneous.

FIXED CAPITAL

Land & Building	Rs.	1,54,000.00
Plant & Machinery	Rs.	1,00,000.00
Other Fixed Assets	Rs.	40,000.00
TOTAL	**Rs.**	**2,94,000.00**

TOTAL WORKING CAPITAL/MONTH

Raw Material	Rs.	30,500.00
Salary & Wages	Rs.	25,468.00
Utilities & Overheads	Rs.	11,400.00
TOTAL	**Rs.**	**67,368.00**

TOTAL CAPITAL INVESTMENT

Total Fixed Capital	Rs.	2,94,000.00
Total Working Capital for 3 Months	Rs.	2,02,104.00
TOTAL	**Rs.**	**4,96,104.00**

TURN OVER/ANNUM

By sale of 12,00,000 Refills	Rs.	12,00,000.00

PROFIT = RECEIPTS - COST OF PRODUCTION

= 12,00,000.00 - 9,30,798.22

= 2,69,201.78

PROFIT SALES RATIO = Profit/Sales x 100 = **22.31 %**

RATE OF RETURN = Operating Profit/T.C.I. x 100 = **54.26 %**

BREAK EVEN POINT (B.E.P.) = 52.57 %

4

BALL POINT PEN, REFILLS & INK

INTRODUCTION

Ball pens are manufactured generally from plastic in different varieties with demand of different classes of people. Majority of people in India like medium class Ball pens. Writing stationery in used today include such writing tools as fountain pens, ball pens etc. Now-a-days ball pens are more convenient and popular because these are most suitable and preferred by all to make duplicate or triplicate copies of bills etc. The main part of ball point pen is refills which is made of high viscous liquid.

The ball pen refill making unit consists of small machines which can be installed even in house without creating any nuisance to the residents or neighbours. The machines can be easily operated even by small boys and girls or by household members with a few minutes practice. Following instructions will be supplied with a unit. The prices are so economical that an entrepreneur with hard work can be cover up the cost of unit with the sale of two months production.

USES, APPLICATION AND PROPERTIES

1. The ball point pen ink is only used in ball point pen refills by filling in the tubes.
2. The ball point pen refills are in extensive use in every home, industrial house, commercial establishment school, school and colleges, and every shop etc.
3. The following are the properties for wide use of ball point pen refills and inks.

   (a) The ink pot is eliminated in using this refill.
   (b) It writes fluently and does not scratch the paper.
   (c) Once the ball point pen ink writes, the writing cannot be rubbed or removed.
   (d) It gives a very shining and attractive writing.

(e) It is fine media for duplicate bills.
(f) By supplying slight pressure, the ball point pen refills can give clear and legible 3-4 copies of any document. If rice paper is used, about 5-6 copies can be obtained.
(g) It does not give any leaking and writes only when desired.
(h) Impressions made by these refills are permanent and durable.
(i) Ink remains wet for quite a long time.

Due to above advantage, the ball point pen refills and inks are very popular sed every where. Other advantage is that refill cost is not much and can be afforded y almost every class of people.

The ball point pen ink is quite different from other type of writing inks. This all point pen ink has some specific properties which are described below:

1) The ink is high viscous which cannot come out of the refill unless the refill is used for writing.
2) The ink does not come itself out of refill.
3) It writes after several intervals and does not change on any stage.
4) It does not spoil up to one or more years if properly preserved.

RAW MATERIALS REQUIREMENT

The main raw material for ball point ink making is oleic acid, mineral oil and dyestuffs. Any wax free mineral oil can be used for the purpose, but the commonly used mineral oil is light colour wax free distilled mineral oil obtained from naphthene crude such as coastal crude which should have the following specification.

Viscosity	-	100°F
Specific gravity	-	0.912 and 25°C

Oleic acid is used as fatty acid in ball point pen ink. In place of oleic acid, the mixture of unsaturated oleic, lenolic and lenolic acids can also be used.

Regarding dyestuff, it is in the form of fine poser and is used in ball point ink making. It is available in different colour and shades and is selected depending upon the ink colour to the manufactured. The oil soluble dyestuff are used in this industry.

Raw materials for the manufacture of refills are plastic tube inks of various colours, ball points. All these items are manufactured in the factory. For making the tubes plastic (PVC) is purchased from outside and for making the ink various ingredients are procured from their respect manufacturers. Ball points are either procured from outside or are manufactured in the factory. The selection of plastic or PVC depends upon the desired quality of the tube. Sometimes instead by plastic tube, metallic (brass) tubes are used. These metallic tubes do not require any separate ball point. The quantitatives requirements of raw material is given below. All the estimation are on theoretical basis. These requirements may change according to the circumstance.

Basis	-	10,000 Plastic Refills per Day
HDPE	-	90 kgs.
Plastic or PVC	-	20 kgs. + 20 kgs. = 40 kgs.
Ball Point	-	10,000 Nos.
Ink	-	10 Kgs.

PROCESS FLOW SHEET

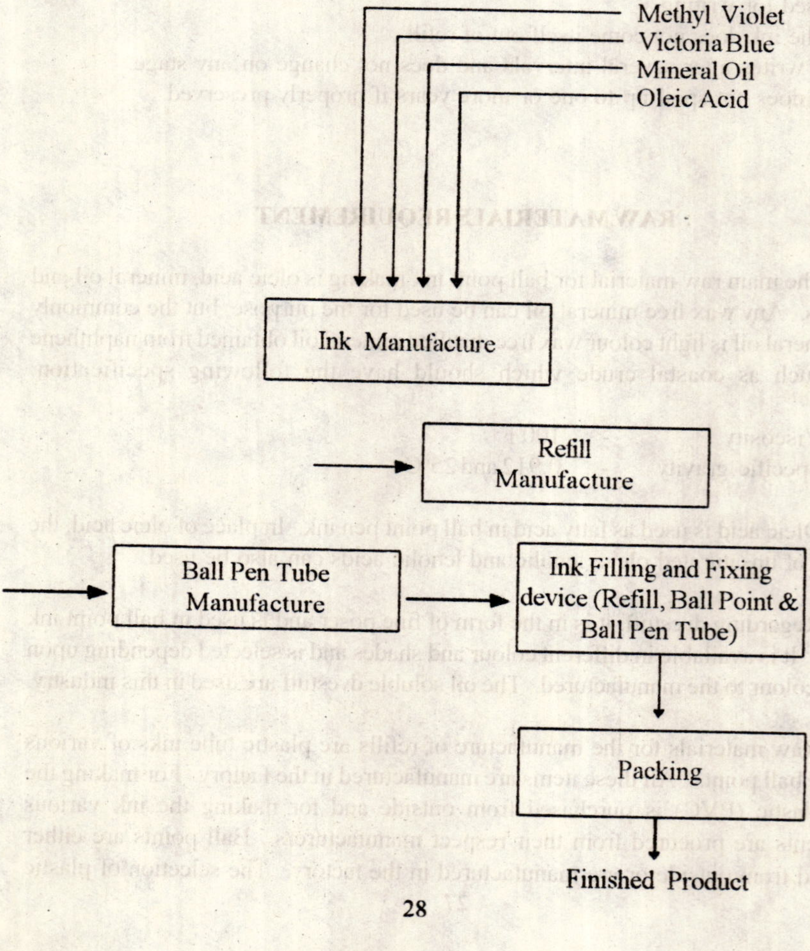

MANUFACTURINGPROCESS

The ball point pens are manufactured by injection moulding machine. Injection moulding is one of the most important process used in manufacturing of plastic goods. Injection moulding is a multi-step process, came out usually in a single machine, in which a thermoplastic is melted or plasticised and injected into a mold forming a cavity of the shape and size of the desired article. The mold is kept a temperature below the solidifying point of the plastic, causing the injected plasticised mass to take the form of the mold cavity and after a sufficiently long cooling time the mold is opened and the article ejected. The injection moulding process comprises four stages, each of which must be closely controlled and regulated to obtain good quality moldings. These stages are

1. Plasticizing
2. Injection
3. After filling and
4. Cooling and mold release.

Plasticizing:-

The resin is fed from the hopper of the molding machine and heated & softened to make it plastic in a heated cylinder. To achieve a suitable state of plasticization, which will ensure a good quality products, requires close control of temp. of the cylinder and the residence time of the resin in the cylinder. During this operation, the resin compound is conveyed from one end to the other end of the cylinder and is heated, melted and plasticised during the operation.

Injection:-

In the stage a correct amount of plasticised melt is injected from the plasticizing cylinder into the relatively cold mold, while closed under controlled pressure. The amount of material injected into a mold is controlled by the machine feed mechanism on position or plunger type molding machine.

After Filling:-

The solidification of the plasticised melt begins in the cold mold soon after its injection in the mold from the walls of the mold. The injected materials is kept under pressure for some time to ensure adequate filling to the mold and prevent the back flow of the polymer and to compensate for the decrease in volume due to solidification. The quality of article very much depends upon the temperature and pressure of the material in the mold cavity at the moment it starts solidifying in the gate. When the mold is being filled, the temperature of the plasticised melt starts falling.

Cooling & Could Release:-

Some further time is allowed to elapse for cooling of the molded article in the mould until it is sufficiently rigid to be ejected with out any risk of deformation taking place subsequently, control of mold temperature is also important if the quality of the article is to be maintained uniform and consistent throughout the entire range.

The refills are prepared from poly vinyl chloride (PVC) by the straight extrusion process. The dia of the tube is 3 mm & the extruder of this diameter is used for this purpose.

1. **Cylinder Temperature:**

Appearance of melted plastic is issued from the nozzle is to be noted carefully as success in moulding depends largely on it. It is guide to cylinder temperature. Moulding temperature varies to the type of materials is in use and it runs from 120°C to 290°C.

2. **Injection Pressure:**

The injection pressure can be positively and directly controlled by the operator. If forces the material into the mould and desired quantity of melted plastic comes out from the cylinders.

3. **Temperature of Mould:**

The mould temp. will also influence pressure required to fill a mould. If mould temp. is 100°C, the materials may freeze and stop the flow of materials into the mould before it is completely filled, while filling the mould with too hot materials will require and excessively long time to cool the moulded articles to the point it become sufficiently rigid to eject from the mould.

Manufacturing of Filling Ink:

Filling ink contains organic material and vehicles. For vehicle long chain unsaturated fatty acids is more suitable. On mixing, all the ingredients in proper proportions the ink for filling is produced. The ink of the ball point riffle is of special type and viscous such that it can not come out without writing. Ball point pen ink consists of coloured organic compound and a base. This base may be any mineral oil. The most important characteristic of the oil that it should be wax free.

SUPPLIERS OF PLANT & MACHINERIES

Injection Moulding Machines:

Brimco Plastic Machinery Pvt. Ltd.,
55, Brimco House,
Govt. Industrial Estate,
Charkop, Kandivli (West),
Mumbai - 400 067

Klockner Windsor India Ltd.,
E6, U2 Road,
Magle Industrial Estate,
Thane - 400 064
Maharashtra

Dies:-

Ajay Engineering Works,
Doodhwali Pole,
Ghokanta Road,
Ahmedabad - 1.

Ink Filling Machines:

Amiri Metal Industries,
Railway Station Shamil,
Dist:- Muzaffarnagar - U.P.

Atlar Engineering Works,
8, Diwan Hall,
Chandni Chowk,
Delhi.

SUPPLIERS OF RAW MATERIALS

Fatty Acids:-

Swastic Oil Mills,
P.N.B. House,
18-D, Brabourne Road,
Calcutta.

Oleinc Acid:-

Yanelhi Prakash Investment Corporation Private Limited
Alice Building,
Dr. P.N. Road,
Mumbai - 400 001

Methyl Violet:-

Anand Industries,
Rajroot Road,
Junagarh.

PVC Reffils Tube & Other Parts:-

Advance Process Works,
18, M.K. Broas Industrial Estate,
Zari-Mari, Kurla Andheri Road,
Andheri (E),
Mumbai -- 400 072

H.D.P.E.:-

Polyolefines Industries Ltd.,
Mafatlal House,
Backbay Reclamation,
Mumbai - 400 001

Plasticizers:-

Indofil Chemicals Co.,
Nirlon House,
Dr. Annie Besant Road,
Mumbai - 400 025

Nozzle Manufacturers:-

Golden Switch Pvt. Ltd.,
5618, Besant Road,
Pahar Ganj,
New Delhi.

SUPPLIERS OF REFILL MACHINERY

Riyat Engineering Works,
86-E/1, Krishna Nagar,
Near Shafdarjang Enclave.

Nidhi Enterprises,
5 Block Gita Colony,
Delhi - 110 031

PLANT ECONOMICS OF
BALL POINT PEN, REFILLS & INK

Rated Plant Capacity = 8000.00 Nos./Day
= 2400000.00 Nos./Annum

COST OF LAND & BUILDING

(Total land area required 500 sq. mtr.) Rs. 6,95,000.00

LIST OF PLANT & MACHINERY

1. Injection moulding machine, 3/4 02, 3/8 Oz and 1/4 oZ.
2. Buffing machine
3. Dies
4. Punching machine
5. Ink filling machine
6. Centrifuge machine
7. Hot stamping machine
8. Nozzle inserting machine
9. Testing equipment
10. Weighing machine platform type

LIST OF RAW MATERIALS

1. HDPE (High Density Polyethene)
2. Refill tube 800 kg.
3. Plasticizers, stabilizer, fitters
4. Ink
5. Nozzle
6. Metals for ball pens
7. Others

FIXED CAPITAL

Land & Building	Rs.	6,95,000.00
Plant & Machinery	Rs.	61,500.00
Other Fixed Assets	Rs.	80,000.00
TOTAL	**Rs.**	**8,36,500.00**

TOTAL WORKING CAPITAL/MONTH

Raw Material	Rs.	84,000.00
Salary & Wages	Rs.	31,500.00
Utilities & Overheads	Rs.	15,400.00
TOTAL	**Rs.**	**1,30,900.00**

TOTAL CAPITAL INVESTMENT

Total Fixed Capital	Rs.	8,36,500.00
Total Working Capital for 3 Months	Rs.	3,92,700.00
TOTAL	**Rs.**	**12,29,200.00**

TURNOVER/ANNUM

By sale receipt of 24,00,000 Ball Point Pen

TOTAL	**Rs.**	**30,00,000.00**

PROFIT = RECEIPTS - COST OF PRODUCTION

= 30,00,000.00 - 18,87,590.00

= 11,12,410.00

PROFIT SALES RATIO = Profit/Sales x 100 = **37.08 %**

RATE OF RETURN = Operating Profit/T.C.I. x 100 = **90.00 %**

BREAK EVEN POINT (B.E.P.) = 33.13 %

5

BALL PEN REFILL INK

INTRODUCTION

The manufacture of ball-point pen inks is occasionally undertaken by printing ink makers, although these inks are used for writing purposes and not for printing.

These inks are highly concentrated dye solutions in non-drying oils which have to fulfill certain special conditions to ensure that the pen continues to function properly until the ink reservoir is reasonably exhausted. The ink flows on to the paper through a narrow circular gap between the balis and the top of the pen, and careful filtration is necessary to ensure that no grit or undissolved dye is present which would cause the orifice to become blocked. Viscosity must be maintained within narrow specified limits, and the ink must be waterproof and dry by rapid penetration into the paper, while remaining fluid in the pen.

The inks are formulated from non-drying vegetable oils such as castor, or solvents such as the higher Glycols in which oil-soluble dyestuffs are dissolved. The dyestuffs are usually oleates or linoleates of the basic dye range, but solublised dyes in the phthalocyanine series are also employed as are nigrosines and indulins.

PROPERTIES

The ink used for ball point pen refill should have the following properties.

1. It should not dry while present in the refill.
2. It should have proper flowability.
3. It should not solidify at least for 2 years.
4. Its drying time should be appropriate after writing on the paper.
5. It should be resistant to water andresistant to chemical bleach.
6. The ink should not fade up in presence of lights.

USES AND APPLICATIONS

The ball point ink is used in refills, jotter refills and any other refills which are used for writing purposes.

The various available colours of refill inks are viz, black, blue, indigo, red, orange, violet, green, pink, purple, parrot green, scarlet, lemon yellow and other shade.

B. I. S. SPECIFICATIONS

IS : 5805 (1993) - Ink for ball point pen refill.

BALL PEN INKS FORMULATIONS AND PROCESSES

A ball pen refill is expected to accomplish for more writing than a fountain pen reservoir. The pen must not leak even at high altitudes. The ink must have adequate surface tension characteristics, it must flow freely from the pen but must not spread on the paper. The pen must be water resistant and write without smudging under wet conditions, it must be light fast and withstand prolonged exposure. The medium must dry on the paper but not in the pen.

Oil based ball pen inks are used in the reservoir at a consistency of about fifty poises, forces of gravity is mainly responsible for their ability to until and the ball pen will not wrist at all if the reservoir is held beneath the rotating ball.

Waxoline pigments are often used dispersed in a medium containing a large amount of ricinoleic acid are some hexylene glycol. The waxoline dye readily dissolves in rinrio!eic acid on the water-bath waxoline pigments are used at about 20% pigmentation and can be ground into the medium on a three roll mill

Martin (Brit. pat 652, 359, 1947) gives suitable formulations.

Cold Climate Ball Pen Ink :-

	Percent
Oil soluble dyes	15
Resin	25
Castor oil	20
Ricinoleic acid	30
Diethylene glycol Mono butyl ether	10
	100

Tropical Climate Ball Pen Ink :-

	Percent
Oil soluble dyes	15
Resin	35
Castor oil	25
Ricinoleic acid	25
	100

Success depends to a fair extent on the tempt at which the ink will be used. It is common experience that same ball point pens have to be warmed on a cold morning before the ink will flow. During wear the ball gap increases and the ink tends to leak and stain.

The hands and articles of clothing, Fehling and resin (British part 634, 564, 1945) showed that if the ball point ink column is divided in to two, with two inks of the same density to stop mixing, but the upper ink of higher viscosity such as 50 poise compared with 5 poise.

The tendency of the ink to leak at the ball gap during wear is appreciably decreased. Inks would form a basic dye dispersed in fatty acid media are fugitive compared with modern permanent aqueous inks, and since fatty acid is non drying transfers can be taken months after origins.

Quick-drying ball pen inks based on resins is alcohol type solvents came into vogue, but they do not write well on grassy, glazed waxed surfaces, nor over oil and water, as the rotating ball picks up deposits from the surfaces which are incompatible with the ink. They give patchy letters due to ink films of charging thickness and colour density. They do not write easily as the media lack the lubricating nature of oil based vehicles.

The solvents are moderately water miscible, consequently the inks absorbs water vapor and ionize to a much greater extent than oil based inks causing more corrosion.

The quick-drying inks are slightly acetic, pH - 5 - 6, while the oil-based inks are nearly neutral pH 6-7. The quick drying ink reservoirs normally retract excess ink which prevents any leakage due to seepage outside the refill, but if the ball is used to dryness the ink seal at the ball breaks and air is introduced which neutralizes the pressure difference at both ends of the refill causing erratic writing and if the refill is held up word a back leak occurs.

Ball pen inks of improved light fastness can be obtained by changing to amine deriatives of acid dyes, are colour based on copper phthalocyanine tetrasulphonic acid suitable media are made from the alhydes and glycol-soluble waxes dispersed in glycol ether solvents. Urea or other soluble dilucent in the colour seem to dissolve preferentially carrying up 35% of the dye stuff into the vehicle in the forms of colloidal dispersing which results in better dispersed as well as more light resistant inks. US Patent 2623, 827 describes thixotropic emulsions which can be cast into soft sticks and inserted into ball pen reservoirs.

These inks became fluid when in contact with the rotating metallic ball. Croda Ltd. have published the formulations of a blue thixotropic emulsion ink. The crill additive is a sorbitol ester non ionic surface active agent which controls. The spreading & consistency of the ink.

PLANT ECONOMICS OF BALL PEN REFILL INK

Rated Plant Capacity = 300.00 Kgs./Day
Black Ink - 50 Kgs/Day
Blue Ink - 150 Kgs/Day
Red Ink - 50 Kgs/Day
Green Ink - 50 Kgs/Day

COST OF LAND & BUILDING

(Total land area required 500 sq. mtr.) Rs. 9,25,000.00

LIST OF PLANT & MACHINERY

1. Stainless mixing tank with stirrer and motor
2. Triple roll mill
3. Storage tank
4. Laboratory testing equipments
5. Pumps, valves, tanks, fittings, motors etc.

LIST OF RAW MATERIALS

1. Resin
2. Castor oil
3. Ricinoleic acid
4. Carbon black
5. Oil soluble dyes, red, blue, green.
6. Packaging material

FIXED CAPITAL

Land & Building	Rs.	9,25,000.00
Plant & Machinery	Rs.	7,40,000.00
Other Fixed Assets	Rs.	3,55,000.00
TOTAL	**Rs.**	**20,20,000.00**

TOTAL WORKING CAPITAL/MONTH

Raw Material	Rs.	5,16,700.00
Salary & Wages	Rs.	45,061.00
Utilities & Overheads	Rs.	87,700.00
TOTAL	**Rs.**	**6,49,461.00**

TOTAL CAPITAL INVESTMENT

Total Fixed Capital	Rs.	20,20,000.00
Total Working Capital for 3 Months	Rs.	19,48,383.00
TOTAL	**Rs.**	**39,68,383.00**

TURNOVER/ANNUM

By sale of 90000 kgs. Rs. 1,23,00,000.00

PROFIT = RECEIPTS - COST OF PRODUCTION

= 1,23,00,000.00 - 87,81,791.77

= 35,18,208.23

PROFIT SALES RATIO = Profit/Sales x 100 = **28.60 %**

RATE OF RETURN = Operating Profit/T.C.I. x 100 = **88.66 %**

BREAKEVEN POINT (B.E.P.) = 31.58 %

6

B.O.P.P. ADHESIVE TAPES

INTRODUCTION

B.O.P.P Insulation tape is a narrow flexible band. B.O.P.P insulation tapes are made in a number of different types and sizes to suit specific electrical insulation requirements as well as certain other dictated by environment in which the electrical equipment would be used. Insulation tapes must be temperature resistant, oil resistant and so on. B.O.P.P insulation tapes are made of cotton textile fabric, silk, PVC or woven asbestos. In certain cases paper gum tapes are also used. Pressure sensitive PVC tapes and black cotton textile fabric adhesive tapes are, however , most commonly used. Moreover, PVC insulation tapes are mainly emphasized due to its advanced technology of manufacture and better quality as compared to others. Furthermore, BOPP film insulation tapes are latest technological development in the field of electrical insulation tapes. Due to its better tensile strength.

USES & APPLICATIONS

B.O.P.P as the name implies Insulation tapes are mainly used for insulating purposes. However, other uses & applications are serialize here. The following are the main applications of pressure sensitive tapes.

1. Masking : It means the protection of a portion of a surface during spray painting
2. Stenciling : During the painting of numbers and names on surfaces a portion of the surface is protected by means of adhesives tape.
3. Protection : Prevention of corrosion or accretion of metals wood plastics etc. During the process of manufacture of protected by means of adhesive tapes.
4. Packaging : Bags, packages, and boxes etc. are closed by means of such adhesive tapes.
5. Cracks or openings are scaled by means of the pressure sensitive adhesive tapes.

6. Holding : Keeping door etc. of the refrigerations, stoves, or any other such types articles closed during shipment is achieved by the use of such adhesive tapes.
7. Identification & Marking : Pipelines, cables, wires etc. are marketed by such adhesive tapes of different colours for identifications.
8. Insulating : Coils of electric motors are protected against electrolytic corrosion by covering with such adhesive tapes.
9. Reinforcing : Leather and fabrics etc. are reinforced by means of such tapes in the manufacture of bags belts, and shoes etc.

PRESENT MANUFACTURERS

Wonder Polymers Pvt. Ltd.,
201, Aradhana Bhawan,
2nd Floor,
Azad Pur Complex,
Delhi-110033
Ph: 7113046, 7113063, 7223459
Brand: **SUNTAPE**

M.P. Industries
A-21, Panchwati,
G.T. Karnal Road,
Delhi-110033
Ph: 7233535, 7213489
Fax: 91-11-7226794
Brand: **MAPSA**

Morgan Industries Limited,
39, Basant Lok,
Vasant Vihar,
New Delhi-110057
PH: 6885502, 6885503
Fax: 679425
Brand: **MAGIC**

Taipack Limited,
40, Hanuman Lane Flat No.4,
Connaught Place,
New Delhi-110001
Ph: 345166, 353697
Fax: 011-3746338

FORMULATION

Latex Crepe	:	100
Zinc Oxide	:	100
Hydrogenated Resin	:	60
B-naphthol	:	1
Heptane or other solvent	:	450

MANUFACTURING PROCESS

The process of manufacture of BOPP Insulation/Adhesive tapes is as follows :-

1. Unwinding of films from spools.
2. Adhesive coating an film.
3. Drying of adhesive on film.
4. Silicon spraying
5. Rewinding
6. Slitting
7. Group
8. Metering
9. Testing
10. Packing

The Bopp insulation tapes can be manufactured primarily by two ways -

1. Making of Plastic film by extrusion by the relative resins & then adhesive coating on the extruded films.

2. By direct coating of adhesives on film. In this report, 2nd method has been followed as such from market that are wounded on a spool & direct adhesive different width of BOPP are available with various thickness. But here, BOPP film of thickness 0.03-0.05 mm is taken. The width of film is 2 ft. The film is unwind from spool & fed to adhesive coating chamber, Prior to feeding, BOPP films to adhesive coating chamber, the adhesive should be prepared as follows:

PREPARATION OF ADHESIVE MASS :-

Pressure sensitive adhesives can be solvent based or water based (emulsion) acrylic based adhesive are used for P'tzttc tapes and are usually prepared in emulsion form as they possess the correct balance of adhesive and cohesive properties. These are prepared by conventional emulsion polymerization technique. Rubber lattices may also be utilized for preparing rubber emulsion adhesive. However, other additives must be added in emulsion form or otherwise consultation of the looted will occur. Wetting agents improve wetting and consequent adhesion on non-ferrous surface. Often chemicals are also added to control the viscosity of the latex for proper application, such chemicals being gum tragacanth, karya gum, methyl cellulose, polyvinyl alcohol or acetate.

The tackifier resin can be emulsified readily by dissolving oleic acid in the resin solution can reducing the viscosity of the resin by adding a little toluene or xylene and emulsifying in potassium hydroxide solution, occasionally containing ammonium caseinate, utilizing a colloid or homogenizing mixture. Proper selection of the adhesive for application to a particular backing material for a particular end use is extremely critical. As for example vinyl film backing in electrical industry is usually stretched considerable during wrapping operating and refractive pull of the backing subjects the adhesive to a shearing stress.

The adhesive must posses good instantaneous bonding ability and must have sufficient shear resistance furthermore, improper formulation will make plasticizer migrate from the tape impairing tack and cohesive strength of the adhesive.

This is the reason for which acrylate copolymers are often used in vinyl backing to avoid plasticizer migration.

ADHESIVE COAT:

On the BOPP film, firstly a primer coat of any one of the above two formulation is applied, and then an adhesive coat of any one of the following tree formulations is applied.

Adhesive Coat Formulation :	**Parts**
1. Nonyl phenol ethylene oxide condensite (97% by wt. of exymethylene unit)	22.4
2. Sodium acetate	1.0
3. Water	465.0
4. Sodium meta bisulphites	0.9
5. Ammonium persulfate	0.45
6. Vinyl acetate	83.6
7. 2-Ethyl hexyl acrylate	352.0
8. Acrylic acid	4.4

APPLICATION OF COATING

The application of primer coating and adhesive coating is done as follows . The emulsions of primer coat and adhesive coat are taken in two batch. A rotating disc fitted on an axis is dipped in each bath. The top position of the disc touches a small pulley which pulls the tape from the rolls.

Gravure Coating:

Adhesive coating on BOPP film is done with Gravure coaters. Gravure coater employ an ingrained cylinder, running in a trough of coating material, to meter the transfer of coating to the web. The engraved roll is doctored with a thin blade to ensure that on even amount of coating is left in the engraved cell. Direct gravure coater consist of two rolls only. The engraved roll transfers the coating directly to the web at the nip formed by the engraved roll and a rubber backing roll. This has the disadvantage that unless there is good flow out of the coating, the engraved pattern is good flow out of the coating. The engraved pattern is transferred to the web. This is eliminated by using a three roll system as in the off set gravure process.

Silicon Spraying:

Silicon may be applied by spraying . The principle distinction in spray-gun design depends on the method used to obtain atomization of the coating liquids.

Airless Spraying:

In airless spraying the coating is delivered to the nozzle under very high pressure and atomization results from dispersion in air as it leaves the nozzle.

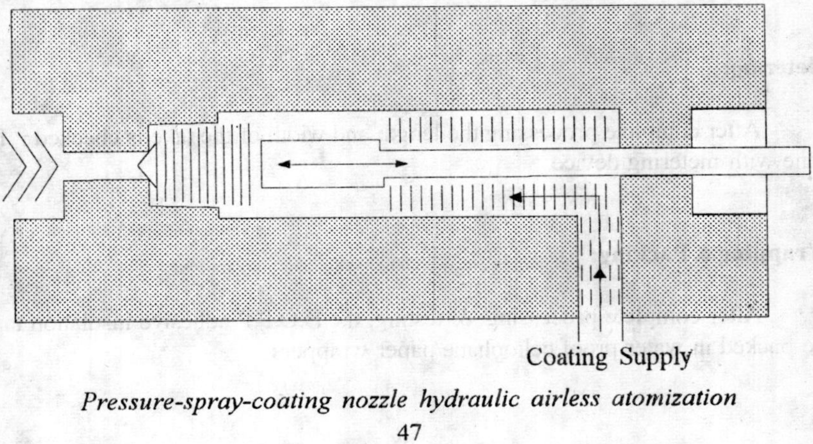

Pressure-spray-coating nozzle hydraulic airless atomization

Winding on Card Board:

The winding of tapes is more difficult than the winding of natural or synthetic monofilaments because of the added complication of possible twisting. This can reduce the tensile strength by 15-20% and must, therefore, be avoided.

Slitting:

In principle, there are two ways to produce film tapes :

1. Cutting of undrown film using a bar equipped with razor blade like knows and stretching the resulting film ribbons lying side by side.

2. Monaxial stretching of the film over its whole width and slitting the width tape affer wards from the stretched film.

Both methods are applied in the practice , they demand somewhat different technologies, & lead to tapes with differing property characteristics. The film is slit into tape f sufficient width (3/4) so what the stretched and oriented tapes will be or required dinner. Slotting is usually carried out using a sitter bar containing razor-like blades. During slitting the film should be under controlled tension for accurate cutting & this is best achieved by sitting the sitter bar close to a roll of drag bar.

Group Slitting:

Group slitting in the sense of slitting in a combination of different width such as 3/4",1/2", & 1/4" and so on. Since the width of start film is 2 foot the slitting can be done in the parallel sequence of 3/4" width which is required . However, with these 2 ft. start width a group slitting of 3/4" x 1/2" x 1/4" can be done.

Metering:

After complete processing the length and width of the take is checked . It is done with metering device.

Wrapping & Packing:

After complete processing & testing, the B.O.P.P adhesive insulation tapes are packed in water proof cellophane/paper wrappers.

ADDRESSES OF PLANT AND MACHINERY SUPPLIERS

Machinery for Tape Plant:-

Brimco Plastic Machinery Pvt. Ltd.,
Brimco House,
55, Industrial Estate,
Kandivli (West),
Mumbai - 400067
Gram : Brimseal

Kailash Engineering Works ,
5/31, Kirti Nagar,
Industrial Area,
New Delhi - 110015

Slitting & Winding Machine:-

Sud & Waren (P) Ltd,
Plot No. 72.,
Sector 6,
Faridabad ,
Haryana.

ADDRESSES OF RAW MATERIAL SUPPLIERS

BOPP Film:-

Bhor Industries Ltd,
16, Apollo Street,
Mumbai -400001

Branch Office :
4/24, Asaf Ali Road,
New Delhi - 110017

Casmo Films Ltd,
30, Community Centre,
Saket, New Delhi - 110017

PLANT ECONOMICS OF
B.O.P.P. PRESSURE SELF ADHESIVE TAPE

Rated Plant Capacity = 6000.00 Sq. Mtr./Day

COST OF LAND & BUILDING

(Total land area required 1000 sq. mtr.) Rs. 14,25,000.00

LIST OF PLANT & MACHINERY

1. BOPP tape making machine 30" complete with adhesive coating unit,heat, drying chamber
2. Slitting machine
3. Slitting scoring machine
4. Polythene packet sealing machine

LIST OF RAW MATERIALS

1. BOPP film (30 micron)
2. Pressure sensitive adhesive
3. Packing materials rolls, cartons, films etc.

FIXED CAPITAL

Land & Building	Rs.	14,25,000.00
Plant & Machinery	Rs.	6,70,000.00
Other Fixed Assets	Rs.	2,10,000.00
TOTAL	**Rs.**	**23,05,000.00**

TOTAL WORKING CAPITAL/MONTH

Raw Material	Rs.	9,00,000.00
Salary & Wages	Rs.	73,000.00
Utilities & Overheads	Rs.	53,500.00
TOTAL	**Rs.**	**10,26,500.00**

TOTAL CAPITAL INVESTMENT

Total Fixed Capital	Rs.	23,05,000.00
Total Working Capital for 3 Months	Rs.	30,79,500.00
TOTAL	**Rs.**	**53,84,500.00**

TURN OVER/ANNUM

By sale ot 1800000 sq.mts. of BOPP self adhesive tape at Rs.9/per sq.mt.

Rs. 1,62,00,000.00

PROFIT = RECEIPTS - COST OF PRODUCTION

= 1,62,00,000.00 - 1,37,52,187.00

= 24,47,813.00

PROFIT SALES RATIO = Profit/Sales x 100 = **15.11 %**

RATE OF RETURN = Operating Profit/T.C.I. x 100 = **45.21 %**

BREAK EVEN POINT (B.E.P.) = 45.15 %

7

CARBON PAPER

INTRODUCTION

Carbon paper is one of the first innovations in paper copying technology. In the modern office management system, every letter, every bill, every paper is required in more than one copy. Carbon paper is therefore used in every office, shop and in the small factories.

Simple paper is treated by the carnauba wax, paraffin wax, mineral oil, petroleum methyl violet, carbon black, iron blue and china clay to get the carbon paper.

As regards to its manufacturing and formulating process that formulating of the carbon dope was an art rather than a science. Although this maintained in the present day industry, science has been edging into the picture to control the quality, increase oputput, and to develope new manufacturing procedures, products and the raw materials. The chemists has gathered considerable information regarding many of the raw materials of the carbon paper industry but there still remains some facts about raw materials and the finished product that are not known therefore, it is an exception rather than rule that the technical man can make carbon dope and predict exactly its properties.

USES AND APPLICATIONS

Carbon papers are very common stationery items. These products are usually used for copying or duplicating of the original document for recording or communication purposes. Large quantities of these product are being used in Government institutions, banks, commercial establishments, business houses etc.

BIS SPECIFICATION

The following BIS specifications are available for carbon papers.

1. IS: 1551 - 1976 Carbon papers for type writers (with amendment 1 to 4)
2. IS: 3450 - 1976 Carbon paper hand writing (with amendment 1 to 3)
3. IS: 8279 - 1976 Hectographic carbon paper (Reaffirmed in 1983)
4. IS: 9055 - 1976 One time carbon paper (with amendment No. 1)

Above Specifications may be obtained from:

Bureau of Indian Standards,
9, B.S. Zafar Marg,
New Delhi - 110 002

NOTE :-

The use of the ISI Certification Mark is governed by the provisions of the Indian Standards Institution (Certification Marks) Act and the Rules and Regulations made thereunder. The ISI Mark on products covered by an Indian Standard conveys the assurance that they have been produced to comply with the requirements of that standard under a well-defined system of inspection, testing and quality control which is devised and supervised by ISI and operated by the producer.

ISI marked products are also continuously checked by ISI for conformity to that standard as a further safeguard.

Details of conditions under which a license for the use of the ISI Certification Mark may be granted to manufacturers or processors, may be obtained from the Indian Standards Institution.

FORMULATIONS OF DIFFERENT TYPES OF CARBON PAPERS

Application of the ink to the tissue demand skill and special equipment. The ink is applied in a molten state by machine which controls the thickness of the coating by careful adjustment of the tension on the paper web and at the same time controls the rate of cooling so as to ensure the formation of uniform, smooth and hard coating.

The ink formulas in themselves do not meet the demands of every manufacturer and should be considered as working bases for further experiment and improvement.

Since black one-time carbon paper are the most widely used they will be considered first. A typical carbon formula is as follows :

Carnauba Wax	12 Parts
Caddelial Wax	19 Parts
Paraffin Wax	17 Parts
Light Mineral Oil	32 Parts
Oleic Acid	4 Parts
Carbon Black	14 Parts
Methyl Violet Base	1 Parts
Victoria	1 Parts
Total	100 Parts

Typewriter Carbon Paper :

Carnauba	33 Parts
Ouricury Wax	5 Parts
Bees Wax	5 Parts
Light Mineral Oil	5 Parts
Amber Petroletuni	26 Parts
Good Grade Carbon Black	8 Parts
Crystal Violet Dye	13 Parts
Victoria Blue Base	2 Parts
Pigmented Purple Toner	1 Parts
Oleic Acid	3 Parts
Total	100 Parts

Typical of a black pencil carbon ink which is quite similar to the type writer ink is as follows :

MANUFACTURING PROCESS

Because of the nature of the waxes used in carbon inks, most of the equipment employed is heated, usually by steam or hot water and occasionally by electricity. All heated equipment should be maintained at approximately 200 °C. as this temperature is generally sufficient to maintain the waxes and finished carbon inks in a molten condition. In the cases where the finished carbon inks, particularly those that contain dye toners, are kept in a molten state for long periods of time, the temperature should not exceed 200°F. because excessive and prolonged heating has a tendency to destroy the dye toners. This not only eliminates the toning effect but usually causes the carbon ink to cecome thick and extremely difficult to apply. In many cases, the temperature of the ink-making equipment is maintained at about 220°F. for the purpose of releasing and removing any water which may be present in the raw materials. It has been found that when the water content of a finished carbon ink exceeds 1% , the ink is generally too thick for application and in many cases, it is very difficult to remelt the ink after it has once solidified.

In the manufacture of a carbon ink, all raw materials are metered in the predetermined proportions by weight and/or by volume into a heated, jacketted kettle. The wax is the first material added to the kettle and is allowed to melt while the remaining materials are mixed into the hot wax under constant agitation. After the crude ink has been thoroughly mixed, it is grounded in a pot mill, roller mill, or a ball mill. The ball mill is the most popular and the best means for grinding carbon inks. A comparison yields nearly the same results for the pot-mill method of grinding. Some analyses have shown that the pot mill has the highest cost of production and the ball mill the lowest cost, with the roller mill falling in between these two. After the ink has been properly prepared, it is ready for application to the carbonizing tissues.

A carbon-coating machine employs a breaking system on the mill roll of tissue as it is unwounded and threaded into the coater. This breaking action is used to produce considerable tension on the paper in order to obtain a uniform film of carbon ink and to change the speed of the mill roll as it becomes smaller. The paper coming form the mill roll passes through a system of idler rollers and bowed curved bars to remove any wrinkles that may occur in the paper and to straighten out the web as it passes over the inking roller. The heated ink roll which roates in the opposite direction to the paper web dips into a heated tray containing the melted carbon ink, picks up an excess of ink and deposits and excess on the tissue. The web containing an excess of ink then passes over an equalizer rod which removes the excess ink and at the same time meters a definite film thickness of ink on the paper. The equalizer rod rotates in an opposite direction to the paper web although most machines are consturcted so that the ink roller and the equalizer rod may be roated in either direction as may be desired.

The paper, with the film of hot carbon ink, passes over a series of chilled rollers that are cooled to the desired temperature by city water, ice water, or a mixture of cold and hot water, or a mixture of cold and hot water to obtain the desired chill temperature.

The chill rollers caused the hot ink to solidify and at the same time remove the heat from the entire web of paper before it is rewound into what is commonly called a jumbo roll. The temperature of the chill roll in a large part controls the crystal growth of the waxes present in the ink. The cooled web passes on through the coater over more idler rolls and bowed. Curved bars (dewrinkle bars) to the end where it is rewound into a jumbo roll.

The rewinding mechanism contains a clutch arrangement which permits the roll to wound as tight or loose as desired and at the same most desirable that the coated paper is cooled to room temperature before it is rewound into a roll as it is the usual tendency for the hot ink film to transfer itself or offset to the back of the paper which it contacts.

SUPPLIERS OF RAW MATERIALS

Mineral Oil:

Interchemie
246/3-B, Mangaldas Buildings,
Mangaldas Road,
Fort, Mumbai - 400 023

Carbon Black:

Bhagat ji Chemical,
31/2, Anand Parbat- Ind Area,
New Delhi - 110015
Ph : 5751097

Bees Wax:

Bajaj Chemical Inds
304, New Cloth Market
Ahmedabad.

Carnauba Wax:

Bhakti Petro Chem Inds.
20, Anand Bhuvan,
Dr. M.P. Vaidya Marg,
Ghotkopar(E), Mumbai - 400077

Paraffin Wax:

Bhakti Petro Chemicals Inds.
20, Anand Bhuvan,
Dr. M.P. Vaidya Marg,
Ghotkopar (E), Mumbai - 400077

PLANT AND MACHINERY SUPPLIERS

Reaction Kettle:

Sehgal Industrial Works,
T - 1698, Malkaganj Road,
Subji Mandi, Delhi - 110 007

Ball Mill:

Allied Groups Industries,
B-18, Sector - VII,
Noida Ind. Complex,
Noida - 201 301 (U.P.).

Pulverizers/Grinders:

Star Engg. Works,
B - 22, Ind. Estate Pratapnagar,
Udaipur - 1 (Rajsthan)
Ph: 24987

Baby Boiler:

S.P Engineering Corpn.,
79/7 Latovche Road,
Kanpur - 208 012

Packaging Machinery:

Wimco Ltd.,
Indian Marcantile Chambers,
Ramji Bhai Kamami Marg,
Mumbai

Coating Machines:

Cartonal Machines India Private Limited
62/3 Kapur Compd.,
Yestwantpur,
Post Box No. 2240
Banglore - 560 022

PLANT ECONOMICS OF CARBON PAPER

Rated Plant Capacity = 4,50,000.00 Boxes
100 Carbon papers in each box

COST OF LAND & BUILDING

(Total land area required 500 sq. mtr.) Rs. 9,90,000.00

LIST OF PLANT & MACHINERY

1. Plant mill, Size 30"x24" with all accessories
2. Baby boiler (Coal fired)
3. Tripple roll mill with complete accessories like motor, starter etc.
4. Steam jacketed vessel, made of Stainless steel
5. Carbon paper coating machine
6. Flexo graphic printing unit
7. One chilling unit with all accessories
8. Unwinding machine
9. Paper cutting machine
10. Miscellaneous charges like pipe, fittings etc.

LIST OF RAW MATERIALS

1. Carbonised tissue paper
2. Carnauba wax
3. Paraffin wax
4. Petrolatum
5. Mineral oil
6. Methyl violet dye
7. Carbon black
8. Card board boxes

FIXED CAPITAL

Land & Building	Rs.	9,90,000.00
Planmt & Machinery	Rs.	11,60,000.00
Other Fixed Assets	Rs.	1,90,000.00
TOTAL	**Rs.**	**23,40,000.00**

TOTAL WORKING CAPITAL/MONTH

Raw Material	Rs.	9,80,280.00
Salary & Wages	Rs.	59,997.00
Utilities & Overheads	Rs.	39,500.00
TOTAL	**Rs.**	**10,79,777.00**

TOTAL CAPITAL INVESTMENT

Total Fixed Capital	Rs.	23,40,000.00
Total Working Capital for 3 Months	Rs.	32,39,331.00
TOTAL	**Rs.**	**55,79,331.00**

TURNOVER/ANNUM

By sale of 4,50,000 Boxes of Carbon Paper of 100 papers in each boxes

Rs. 1,80,00,000.00

PROFIT = RECEIPTS - COST OF PRODUCTION
= 1,80,00,000.00 - 1,45,29,132.82
= 34,70,867.18

PROFIT SALES RATIO = Profit/Sales x 100 = **19.28 %**

RATE OF RETURN = Operating Profit/T.C.I. x 100 = **62.21 %**

BREAK EVEN POINT (B.E.P.) = 37.12 %

8

COMPUTER CONTINUOUS STATIONERY

INTRODUCTION

Information means paper on which to print it, and computer-processed information usually means high speed line printers and continuous forms business forms are usually printed on web off set presses of the unit in line design with a steel impression cylinder in each units, as the printing is done only one side of the paper.

Presses are equipped with a number of auxiliary functions such as punching numbering, slitting sheeting gluing or rewinding. Many business forms are printed for computer and punching of the hole is critical as these are used to position the sheet in the print out devices. Also many business. Forms are used in optical character reading (OCR) equipment. The paper used for this type of printing must meet stringent requirements especially in cleanliness.

The multiplication of computers has caused an unexpected proliferation of business-forms. The use of forms in computers has increased demands of the paper used for business forms.

Different raw materials are used for the manufacture of different grades of paper required for the use in computer stationary. The main criteria is low cost paper conforming side by side to the requisite properties with the advents of computers and its use in almost all walks of life it is expected that computers will use maximum production of paper.

USES AND APPLICATION

As the name suggest these papers are used in computer for data input as well as data output. Computer prints the data with the help of printer on it, to be output, on these papers which are very clean smooth and its mechanical strength is sufficient high to not tear during operation. It has high durability and reliability capacity to handle and undergoes high productivity.

Since computer operates at high speed it consumes much more stationary/ spurs than hundreds of clerks. We are listing the papers required by different computer units below:

Unit

1. Computer papers of various sheets size but of some hole diameter and Hard copy hole pitch perforated terminal
2. Computer papers of various sheet sizes but of same hole diameter Printer and hole pitch perforated.
3. Computer papers of same sizes 15" as for sheets also having same holes pitch and hole pitch and hole Printer diameter. These are also perforated.

MARKETSURVEY

To use computer for any task require first of all to communicate the data of the concerned problem to the computer and similarly to provide answers, computer requires to communicate results to the user. This to and fro communication is done through various media - one of which is stationery. Computer stationery is normally defined as the papers pre-printed or otherwise used to communicate data to computer or to user. Such communication normally is being done continuously by computer and so requires stationery in huge amount. Computer stationery many a times is known as Continuous Stationery.

Continuous Stationery is normally divided in two groups:

1. Single Ply Stationery.
2. Multi-Part Stationery.

Single Ply Stationery is used normally for simple tasks like preparing pay rolls or for training in computer programming, where computer at one point of time - performs only one duty.

As against this Multi-Part Stationery is used in computers having more than one terminals. When various jobs are handled by computer at a time and job is very complex, multi-part stationery is used. It facilitates to get different output at a time on different terminals and even to have more than one copies at a time from the same result. All large frame and medium computers use multi-part stationery.

PRESENT MANUFACTURERS OF COMPUTER STATIONERY

Continental Forms (P) Ltd.
B-9, G.T. Karnal Road Indl. Area,
Delhi - 110033
Phones : 7126464, 7123347, 7249503
Fax : 011-7249502

Glaxy Forms
G-13, Udyog Nagar,
Rohtak Road,
Delhi - 110041
Phone : 5473285

Nipoon Computer Aids (Pvt.) Ltd.
A-17, Shalimar Apartments,
Masjid Moth, N.D.S.E.-II,
New Delhi - 110019
Phones : 6212660, 6231208

Glaxy Forms Ltd.
1340 A, M.I.E.,
Bahadurgarh - 124 507
(Haryana)
Phones : 314019, 314029

Indus Forms Private Limited
31-B, Sector 31,
Faridabad - 121 003
(Haryana)
Phones : 8-212050

Arun Graphic Computer Forms (P) Ltd.
E-13, Sector-7,
Noida - 201 301
(U.P.)
Phone : 522584

MANUFACTURINGPROCESS

The sort of paper for printers you need depends on your printing device. Electrostatic and thermal types require special paper, but neither are suitable for business use. Dot matrix and daisy wheels allow you a wider choice. Continuous stationery, with pages linked together but perforated for repetitive work such as invoice is often used.

Printing:

Printing on computer papers will be done with the help of line printing press. Inks are applied to the press by which, the punching papers on surface dedicated with seven lines each in rows. The distance between two seven lines rows being concerned at about 1/5".

Even, the machine printed lines at a stack in continuous manner, lining should be complete upto both sides covering punching holes. Practically, the line printing are not forced for both sides of paper. Because there is no need of figure to be made in back side. Specially, the computer output dot matrix or line printers works only one side. Sometimes figures being drawn on the back side. But as a consideration of computer a paper printing only for one side.

There are today four major types of printing presses and printing systems for computer papers making lining letter press, offset. In letter press the image of lining to be reproduced is in relief. Ink is applied to the raised areas, and when a sheet of paper is pressed against then the film of ink is split, the image from the plate being left on the paper surface.

In offset lithography, a planographic process the image is in the same plane is the non-image areas. The printing of the image is from flat surface which is chemically treated so that ink is accepted in the image areas and repelled in the non-image areas.

Punching:

Computer papers are punched by five to eight tracks rows of dies striking against a steel matrix with a corresponding number of holes while the paper passes between the dies and matrix. The dies are activated by a mechanism under the control of computer output signals. Mechanisms used for the punching operation differ mainly in the movement of the dies and or the steel matrix. Although patents have been granted for poaches that have no moving parts because they are activated by Compression (air pressure waves) and operate at a speed of 1000 chps, no such devices are know to be on production.

The design of computer paper punches is complicated by the need. Punching was done on both sides of the paper. To examine the paper immediately after punching in small round shape. This means that the paper has to be punched in a horizontal plane, with the chads, or chips, from the punching being ejected upward.

Perforating:

is often done during a printing operation by a sharp steel rule just enough higher than the type of penetrate the paper. The perforated line is also inked, of course, unless the printer goes to the trouble and expense of cutting away a section of this ink rollers. On cylinder press a perforating can be attached to the cylinder.

Perforating is also handles as a separate operation on machines that punch or drill rows of tiny holes. This is considered as a finishing operating.

Mounting and Finishing:

Mounting is a fairly simple operation in which the mounting papers may be the major item in the total cost. Special mounting presses apply glue to the paper poster and to the cardboard backing and then squeeze both together in a short of winger.

The number and type of paper stacks can be varied to obtain a range of finishes (machine finish a stack of intermediates papers may be included before the last section of drying and depending on the finish required. An imitation art finish may be obtained on the paper machine by applying a thin film of water to the paper as it enters the nip of one or more of the paper unit.

Measuring Sizes:

The depth of 12 inches (304.8 mm) should be accepted in licenses of the depth of A4 in all cases where continuous forms are not reported. In other cases, the depth of 12 inches should be regarded as a untrimmed size which could, if so desired, be trimmed to the depth of A4. Of overall widths (including the sprocket holes), the following preferred sizes have been recommended, 180, 250, 340, 400 and 450 mm. For special applications wider forms any be required.

Removal of the edges of the paper containing the sprockets holes on the above sizes could lead to trimmed form widths identical to 'A' dimensions wider forms may be required. These width recommendations are not related to paper sizes of for on line data teleprinters and other machines with non-adjustables, pin feed platens.

In an article written for the publication about five. A sizes that may be used for business forms are:-

INCHES	MILLIMETERS	
A_3	11.69 * 16.54	297 * 220
A_4	8.27 * 11.69	210 * 297
A_5	5.83 * 8.27	148 * 210
A_6	4.13 * 5.83	105 * 148
A_7	2.97 * 4.13	74 * 105

Almost all the writing machines in the free world space in sixth of an inch and tenth of an inch horizontally.

SUPPLIERS OF MACHINERIES

Complete Plant & Machinery Supplier

Sud & Waren (P) Limited
72, Sector - 6, Indl. Estate,
Faridabad - 121 006 (Haryana)
Phones: 91-129-242342, 242402, 245027, 245028
Fax: 91-129-241243

Raj Trading Corporation
C-92, New Ashok Nagar,
New Delhi - 110092

Convertaid Engineers (P) Limited
Plot No - 1, Sanjay Memorial Indl. Estate,
Phase - II, Opp. YMCA, Faridabad - 121 006
(Haryana)
Phone: 0129-289607, 263160
Fax: 0129-283204

Continuous Printing Machines

Bandhu Systems Private Limited
56, Maruti Industrial Complex,
Sector-18, Gurgaon,
(Haryana)
Phone/fax: 8-340012

Sarvottam Appliances (P) Ltd.
98, Sector-25,
Ballabgarh. (Haryana)
Phone/fax: 8-232949

Printpack Machinery Limited
41-42, Link Road, Sector-28,
Faridabad - 121 003 (Haryana)
Phone/fax: 8-276849, 276289

PCM Engineering (P) Ltd.
B-170, D.D.A. Shed,
Okhla Indl. Area I,
New Delhi - 110020
Phone/fax: 6811993

Offset Printing Press Machines

Amit International
B-47, Cox House,
Naraina Indl. Area, Phase-II,
New Delhi - 110 028
Phones : 570 4301, 570 4201
Fax : 011-2249320

Diamond Engg. Works
6/12, DLF, Indl. Area,
Moti Nagar, New Delhi - 110 015
Phones : 541 4571, 541 8352

Aksis Engg. Works (P) Limited
139, Sector 25,
Ballabgarh, (Haryana)
Phone : 8-234942

Dominent Offset (P) Ltd.
Palam Road,
Gurgaon, (Haryana)
Phones: 340019, 341916, 341917, 341918, 340032
Fax: 0124-340131

Bharat Machine Tools
133-138, Sector 6,
Faridabad, (Haryana)
Phones : 8-241798, 241167

Fair Deal Engineers
89, Ramsaroop Colony,
Mujessar, Faridabad,
(Haryana)
Phones : 8-237143, 234314

Fair Deal Graphics
3 & 4, Dharam Kanta Road,
Mujessar, Faridabad.
(Haryana)

Venus Offset House
15A/1, Industrial Area, N.I.T.,
Faridabad, (Haryana)
Phones/fax : 8-236821

SUPPLIERS OF RAW MATERIALS

Papers:

Usha Paper & Board Industries
17, D.L.F. Industrial Area,
Mathura Road,
Faridabad, Haryana.

Sandeep Paper Mills (P) Limited
A-20, Sector-6, Noida Distt.
Ghaziabad. (U.P.)

Om Prakash Jitendra Kumar & Company
63, Darya Ganj,
New Delhi - 11 00 02.
Phone/fax : 326 96 80, 3271380

Narain Paper Mart
4034/3, Haryana Market,
Chawri Bazar,
Delhi - 11 00 06.
Phone/fax : 291 51 35.

Himgiri Paper Products
B-24, Indl. Area Lawrence Road,
New Delhi - 110035
Phone/fax : 718 9005

Ashok Kumar Mohinder Kumar
73, Swaran Park,
Mundka, New Delhi - 110 041
Phone/fax : 251 0037, 541 7011

Chetan Papers (P) Ltd.
A-6, Everest Building,
Tardeo Road, Mumbai - 400 034
Phone : 4943680
Fax: 91-022-4952546

Mahavir Traders
52, Dadiseth Agiary Lane,
Mumbai - 400 002
Phone : 201 6839, 208 8020
Fax: 91-022-2060459

Printing Ink:

Baluja Spectra
C-50 Okhla Indl. Area-II,
New Delhi - 110 020
Phone/fax : 6835715, 6835722

Ajanta Ink Company
Basai Road, Gurgaon (Haryana)
Phone/fax : 8-330028

Art Printing Inks Company
104 Site-4, Indl. Area,
Sahibabad, Ghaziabad.
Phone/fax : 767882

Inks India (Delhi)
C-49, Sector-8,
Noida-201 301 (U.P.)
Phone/fax : 523801, 011-8-557270

Van Inks & Chemicals (P) Ltd.
B-150, Phase-II,
Noida-201 305 (U.P.)
Phone/fax : 567141, 011-8-521507

Packing Materials:

Sonar Packaging,
Plot 48, T.D.L.F.
Industrial Area,
Faridabad, Haryana.

Printing Plates & Other Chemicals:

Alpha Graphic
19, Police Court Lane,
Fort, Mumbai - 400 001
Phone : 261 4441/42, 261 0603, 261 5191
Fax : 91-022-262 5534

PLANT ECONOMICS OF COMPUTER FORMS & SECURITY PRINTING PRESS

Rated Plant Capacity = 40 Boxes per Day Containing 1000 Sheets and Job Work for Railways, Banks etc.

COST OF LAND & BUILDING

(Total Land required 1000 sq. mtr.) Rs. 15,85,000.00

LIST OF PLANT & MACHINERY

1. Single Colour Offset Printing Machine
2. Slitter, Rewinder
3. Semi-Automatic Cutting Machine
4. Stitching Machine
5. Numbering Machine (Single phase)
6. Herdelberg Cylinder Letter Press
7. Chandler Machine (Single phase)
8. Lamination Machine
9. Pack to Pack Collector

LIST OF RAW MATERIALS

1. Plates for printing
2. Printing Inks
3. Graphic Films
4. Miscellaneous Stores & Consumables
5. Computer Stationery

FIXED CAPITAL

Land & Building	Rs.	15,85,000.00
Plant & Machinery	Rs.	22,60,000.00
Other Fixed Assets	Rs.	4,00,000.00
TOTAL	**Rs.**	**42,45,000.00**

TOTAL WORKING CAPITAL/MONTH

1.	Raw Material	Rs.	1,50,000.00
2.	Salary & Wages	Rs.	1,16,375.00
3.	Utilities & Overheads	Rs.	57,500.00
	TOTAL	**Rs.**	**3,23,875.00**

TOTAL CAPITAL INVESTMENT

Total Fixed Capital	Rs.	42,45,000.00
Total Working Capital for 3 Months	Rs.	9,71,625.00
TOTAL	**Rs.**	**52,16,625.00**

TURNOVER/ANNUM

1. By printing computer forms for Railway, Banks etc. on Job Work
2. Earnings from job-work of different printing works
3. By selling computer forms 12,000 Boxes (1 Box = 1000 forms)

Rs. 71,40,000.00

PROFIT = RECEIPTS - COST OF PRODUCTION
= 71,40,000.00 - 56,93,782.50
= 14,46,217.50

PROFIT SALES RATIO = Profit / Sales x 100 = **20.26 %**

RATE OF RETURN = Operating Profit/T.C.I. x 100 = **27.72 %**

BREAK EVEN POINT (B.E.P) = 64.62 %

9

COMPUTER RIBBONS

INTRODUCTION

Computer Ribbon is a narrow woven fabric (tape) of varying width, made of cotton, silk or nylon and has the highest thread count of any fabric in general use. The origin and growth of the typewriter ribbon industry have been closely interlinked with those of the type-writer industry.

The need for the ribbon did not arise until the invention of a prototype of modern typewriter in the later half of the 19th century. In the early stages long ribbons of cotton coated with carbon black were used in the typewriters to pass the improsesions of type face on the paper. Later ribbons of silk coated with colour pigments were introduced in the making of typewriter ribbons. Typewriter ribbons are of two types viz. single coloured and bicoloured. Single coloured ribbons are black, blue black red combinations. The edges of the ribbons are slitted for withstanding the striking blows of the typewriter type faces.

The fabric used for the production of ribbons should be closely woven and contain more thread counts than in ordinary cloth. This type of fabric is produced by several textile mills in the country.

PROCESS OF MANUFACTURE

Ribbons are made of narrow woven fabric tape of varying width, made of cotton, silk or nylon, having the highest thread count of any fabric in general use. Proportion of coating ink and coating of the base tape with the ink are the two important stages in the manufacture of computer ribbons.

For preparing the inks, ingredients such as igments, water soluble dye stuff etc. As per the formulation are the roughly ground in a 3 roller mill and mixed with the solvent and oils and heated in the steam jacketed kettle. Some computer ribbon inks are given below:

BLACKINK	1	2	3	
Carbon Black	17	18	6	Parts
Nigrosine Bass	5	3	9	Parts
Oleic Acid	2	5	-	
Ninerat Oil	5	3	-	
Petrolutum	-	73	-	
Trioresyl Phosphate	-	-	15	Parts
Diglyool Laurate	-	-	15	Parts

BLUEINK	1	2	
Blue Tuner	20	-	
Lard Oil	40	-	
Castor Oil	40	-	
Victorial Blue	-	26	Parts
Neatsfoot Oil	-	25	Parts
Oleion Acid	-	50	Parts

The base fabric is put on the roll of automatic slitting machine equipped with circular knives. The distance between them determines the width of the tape in which the cloth is to be slit. The roll of the cloth is out into tapes.

The edges of the tapes are sealed with suitable lacquers to prevent fraying. The ink is applied to the ribbon on a machine by a series of rollers. The ink is fed through a trough. The ribbon may be (a) impragented throughout (b) surface treated (c) Indeed one side only (d) Inked both sides simultaneouly. The ribbons are heavily inked, uniformly over the entire ribbon. Bicolour ribbons are inked in two stages and it required very careful alignment.

After inking ribbons are cut to standard lengths, and wound round spools on a spooling machine and wrapped in moisture proof tissues and further in aluminium foils or polythene film bags. These spools are then packed in printed plastic containers.

THE APPLICATION EQUIPMENTS

Because of the nature of waxes used in ribbons, most of the equipment employed is heated usually by steam or hot water and on occassionally by electricity. All heater equipment should be maintained at approximately 200°F, as this temperature is generally sufficient to maintain the waxes and finished carbon inks in a molten condition. In case where the finished carbon inks particularly thus that contain dye toners are kept in a molten state for long periods of time, the temperature should not exceed 200°F because excessive and prolonged heating has a tendency to destroy the dye tonners.

This not only eliminates the toning effect but causes the carbon ink to become thick and extremely difficult to apply. In many cases the temperature of the ink making equipment is maintained at about 220° for the purpose of removing and releasing any water which may be present in the raw materials. It has been found that when the water content of finished carbon ink exceeds the ink is generally to thick for application and in many cases it is very difficult to remelt the ink after it has been solidified. This is fully applicable to the ribbon ink.

In the manufacture of ribbon ink, all materials are metered in the predetermined proportions by weight and/or by volume into a heated jacketed kettle and is allowed to melt while the remaining materials are mixed into the hot wax. Under constant agitation. After the crude ink has been mixed, it is ground in a throughly pot mill, roller mill is the most popular and the best means for grinding carbon inks. The advantage of ball mill grinding are many and a may be summaries by the ability to produce the most uniform inks at the lowest cost.

The ball mill eliminates the human element in grinding by removing the manual adjustment required on other mill type and the major variable which determines the quality of the grind in million time. Inks ground in this manner are in many cases, transferred directly into the instead of premixing in a heated kettle. The mill which is jacketed and heated by steam or hot water, is then run for required number of hours after which the finished ink is discharged into trays and allowed to solidify.

After the ink has been properly prepared, it is ready for application to the ribbon tape. The application is performed on special machine which applied ink to only one side of the tape is called semi coater, whereas the machine that put in on both sides of the tape in one operation is known as a full coater.

The semi coater are usually of two types, one low speed coater that makes one time tape and the other low speed coater that makes one time tape and the other low speed coater is a slow machine which coats all type of tape inks producing ribbons and saddle coated ribbon In some cases the high speed coaters are precision built to the point that they can be used to coat any of the ribbons.

Ribbon Blenders:

Ribbon blenders provide end-to-end mixing and overall lifting of the blender contents by the pitch of the helical blades. Variations include closed vessel with a plo-shaped head on a horizontal rotor operating as relatively high speed to scrape the trough wall as well as to hurl the contents throughout the free space.

Similar applications also are handled in vertically mounted mixer equipped with a high speed blade. This blade scopes material from the bottom of the vessel, hurling it upward along the vessel walls, where baffles may be located to provide variation in turnover. Such mixer may be used for dispersion in thin slurries, or in wetting to coating of granular materials.

Cone-and-Screw Mixer:

A more gentle blender is the Nauta-type cone-and-screw mixer. this mixer uses an orbiting screw to provide bottom-to-top circulation. Reversing the screw aids discharge. Other variants are available that provide either an epicyclic orbit or two screw to provide greater volumetric coverage. The mixing action of cone-and-screw mixers is independent of the degree of fill.

Pan Muller:

A mixer similar to mortar and pestle is the pan muller, in which plows bring material into the path of the rolling mullers. Such mixers are used for applications where the final blend is neither very fluid nor very sticky, such as foundry sand, clay or chocolate.

Conmtinuous Mixers:

In most continuous mixers one or more screw or paddle rotors operate in an open or closed trough. Discharge may be restricted at the end of the trough to control holdup and degree of mixing. some ingredients may be added stagewise along the trough or barrel. the rotors may be cored to provide additional heat-transfer area. The rotors may have interrupted flights to permit interaction with pins or baffles protruding inward from the barrel wall.

Single-Screw Extruders:

Single-screw extruders incorporate ingredients, such as antioxidants, stabilizers, pigment, and other fillers into plastics and elastomers. In order to provide a uniform distribution of these additives, the polymer is brought to a fusion state primarily by the work energy imparted in the extruder, rather than by heat transfer through the barrel wall.

In additions to melting th epolymer, the extruder is used as a melt pump to generate pressure for extrusion through a die, shaping the molten product in a specific profile, strands, or pellets. the extruder screw drags the polymer through the barrel, generating shear between screw and barrel.

In addition, some axial mixing occurs in response to a back flow along the screw channel caused by the pressure required to get through the die. Mixing in a single-screw extruder can be enhanced by interrupting the flow pattern within the screw flight channel. This can be done by variations in the screw flight-channel width or depth, or by causing an interchange with spiral grooves in the barrel, or by interengaging teeth.

Twin-Screw Mixers:

Twin-screw continuous mixers provide more radial mixing by interchange of material between the screws, rather than just acting as screw conveyers.

SUPPLIERS OF RAW MATERIALS

Philips Carbon Black Ltd.,
31, Netaji Subhash Road,
Calcutta - 700 001

Shri Ram Rayons,
Akash Deep, 5th Floor,
Barakhamba Road,
New Delhi - 110 001

Shankar Chemical Industries,
26/4-II, Ramavarampura,
Nagarcoil, Tamil Nadu.

Oleic Acid:

Gandhi Parekh Investment Corp. Pvt. Ltd.,
Maker Bhavan, No. 2, 18,
New Marine Lane,
Mumbai - 400 020

Base Wax:

M.Mountoo and Co.,
26, Bonefield Lane,
Calcutta - 1

Paraffin ESC Wax:

Buma Shell Oil Storage and Distribution Co.,
Burma Shell House,
Ballard Estate,
Mumbai - 400 001

Carbon Wax:

Kirit Kumar Chandulal and Co.,
50, Izaji Street,
Mumbai - 400 003

China Clay:

English India Clay Ltd.,
Trivandrum - 7.

Carbon Black:

United Carbon India Ltd.,
Than Belapur Road,
Thana.

Mineral Oil:

Assam Oil Co. Ltd.,
Digboi,
Assam.

SUPPLIERS OF PLANT & MACHINERY

Acme Engineering Works,
60, Ferbes Street,
Mumbai - 400 001

Aggarwal Fabrication,
3, Wilson Gardens,
Poona - 3.

Anson Indl. Lining,
A - 17, Amrit Nagar,
Kandivli,
Mumbai - 400 061

COMPLETE PLANT & MACHINERY

Business Forms Ltd.,
6 A Middleton Street,
Calcutta - 71

Steam Boiler:

Nestler Boiler Pvt. Ltd.,
Love Lane,
Cross Lane,
Mumbai - 400 027

Mixer:

Anup Engg. Co. Ltd.,
Anil Starch Premises,
Anil Road,
Ahmedabad.

Coating Machine:

Bramoo Coating Machine,
361, Dr. D.N. Road,
Mumbai - 400 001

Ball Mills:

Atlas Engg. Works,
6 Dewan Hall,
Chandni Chowk,
Delhi - 110 006

Tripple Roll Mills:

Kripson And Co. Ltd.,
Mullund Check Naka,
Mumbai - 400 080

PLANT ECONOMICS OF COMPUTER RIBBON

Rated Plant Capacity = 500.00 Nos./Day

COST OF LAND & BUILDING

(Total land area required 1000 sq. mtr.) Rs. 7,05,000.00

LIST OF PLANT & MACHINERY

1. Ribbon fabric winding machine 15" size
2. Febric slitting machine 15" width
3. Ribbon Edging Machine 15" width
4. Triple roll paint grinding machine
5. Paint mixing machine
6. Ribbon Inking machine
7. Spooling machine
8. Vacuum sealing machine
9. Chilling plant
10. Boiler

LIST OF RAW MATERIALS

1. Fabric
2. Various chemical for repairing ink
3. Spool for packing

FIXED CAPITAL

Land & Building	Rs.	7,05,000.00
Plant & Machinery	Rs.	6,80,000.00
Other Fixed Assets	Rs.	1,80,000.00
TOTAL	**Rs.**	**15,65,000.00**

TOTAL WORKING CAPITAL/MONTH

Raw Material	Rs.	6,07,500.00
Salary & Wages	Rs.	41,311.00
Utilities & Overheads	Rs.	6,200.00
TOTAL	**Rs.**	**6,55,011.00**

TOTAL CAPITAL INVESTMENT

Total Fixed Capital	Rs.	15,65,000.00
Total Working Capital for 3 Months	Rs.	19,65,033.00
TOTAL	**Rs.**	**35,30,033.00**

TURN OVER/ANNUM

By sale of 1,50,000 Nos. Computer ribbons **Rs. 1,08,00,000.00**

PROFIT = RECEIPTS - COST OF PRODUCTION

= 1,08,00,000.00 - 85,86,781.44

= 22,13,218.56

PROFIT SALES RATIO = Profit/Sales x 100 = **20.37 %**

RATE OF RETURN = Operating Profit/T.C.I. x 100 = **62.20 %**

BREAK EVEN POINT (B.E.P.) = 31.55 %

10

CONFERENCE BAGS, FOLDERS, FILE COVERS, DIARY ETC.

INTRODUCTION

Generally the items such as conference bags, folders, gift bags, money purses, diary, file covers etc. are made from leathers, leather clothes, pvc leather cloths etc. Fancy leather goods and other novelty items include various articles of daily use viz. shopping bags, wallets, watch straps, key cases, book marks, comb cases, optical cases etc. These articles are considered in things and have special appeal to educated people and tourists.

The main export markets are U.S.A. Japan, Europe and Canada. These products may be given decorative designs with embossing with or without colourful paintings.

Among the gift items the file covers, diary covers, diary, etc. are being manufactured in our country, but those hardely create any essential appeal. Manufacturing technique of the existing variety of file covers, diary covers is not very sophisticated to make the products attractive and durable.

In developed countries file covers, diary covers with equisite look make of pvc foils are being manufactured by high frequency welding technique. Generally surface of the file covers is smooth, but it is possible to make designs on the surface by thermoforming process.

Since the introduction of plastic foil welding technology, it is the desire of the manufacturer to integrate supplementary equipments to high frequency welding plant in order to facilitate manual working steps e.g. to insert materials, cardboard, punched cardboard parts etc.

PROPERTIES AND USES

These products are used widely as they are water resistant, they potect the papers, notes from water.

They are used as gift items, as conference presentation items. Leather purses, bags, folders, pvc file covers, diary covers etc. are distributed in the new year to attract the customers.

File covers, diary covers made from fully automatic high frequency welding machine more durable and attractive than manually made one. The file covers and other multiform office requisites are manufactured completely off the blanks of the foil roll. In the process two layers of pvc with card board inserts between are welded by high frequency welding. The surface of the file can be incorporated by decorative raised surface design by the help of vacuum forming technique. In addition to the various types of file covers, diary covers, the manufacturing facility can also produce a host of other items like decorative pieces etc. For decorative pieces, pvc foil is thermoformed as per the required design and welded with pvc sheet.

B.I.S. SPECIFICATION

IS :	478-1971	for Chrome upper Leather.
IS :	3840-1966	for Lininer Leather.
IS :	1720	Thread Sewing
IS :	8002-1976	Reommended Procedure of Rewelding of Flexible P.V.C.

MANUFACTURING PROCESS

The production facility for office requisites (loose-leaf ring binder, files, covers, folders etc.) consists of a rotary-table system with 6 work trays capable of being lowered for welding by means of pneumatic cylinders. At station 1 bottom foil is inserted. Following a 60° rotation at station 2, automatic transfer of the complete card board is effected with a universal type cardboard inserting device. The cardboard is secured by pneumatic centering devices. At station 3 and 4 other parts can be applied manually. The high frequency welding process is carried out at station 5. At station 6 the finished part is removed automatically.

The blanks are produced by high powered longitudinal and cross cutting device. The foil is drawn off the roll, the side being slit simultaneously, cut across and deposited on a pile. The blanks are exactly rectangular and true to the size.

The PVC welded file covers with card board inserted between the two layers obtained from rotary table system with 6 work trays, are then subjected to further operations like punching for fitting eye lets, riveting for attaching ring mechanism etc.

For making file covers with design on its surface, outer layer of the file cover is thermoformed, as per the desired design. Machines are available in which vacuum forming, cardboard centering and high frequency welding all could be done in one cycle.

SUPPLIERS OF PLANT & MACHINERY

PVC Welder:

Bittoo Trading Corporation
9289, Gali Mata Wali, Tokriwalan,
Library Road, Azad Market, Delhi - 110 006
Ph. : 529896

SUPPLIERS OF RAW MATERIAL

PVC Leather Cloth:

Kalra Coated Fabrics Pvt. Ltd.
657, M.I.E., Bahadurgarh - 124 507 (Haryana)
Tel/Fax : 8-310818

Northern India Leather Manufacturing
16, Sector - 6, Faridabad (Haryana)
Tel/Fax : 8-241111, 241589

Thread:

Modi Thread,
Modi Nagar,
U.P.

Adhesive:

Dunlop India Ltd.,
4/3, Asaf Ali Road,
New Delhi - 110002

PLANT ECONOMICS OF CONFERENCE BAGS, FOLDERS, FILE, ETC.

Rated Plant Capacity = 400.00 Nos./Day

COST OF LAND & BUILDING

(Total land area required 250 sq. mtr.) Rs. 8,50,000.00

LIST OF PLANT & MACHINERY

1. Leather skiving machine
2. Flat bed industrial sewing machine
3. Cylinder bed sewing machine PAFAFF model 335 H3 17/01 BL
4. Stamping and embossing machine
5. Card board inserting machine
6. PVC welder
7. Printing machine
8. Eye let riveting machine

LIST OF RAW MATERIALS

1. PVC Leather cloth or leather for folder or bags
2. PVC Foil/sheet
3. Cardboard, rivet, eyelet, rivetedring mechanism, sewing thread.

FIXED CAPITAL

Land & Building	Rs.	8,50,000.00
Plant & Machinery	Rs.	2,54,200.00
Other Fixed Assets	Rs.	75,000.00
TOTAL	**Rs.**	**11,79,200.00**

TOTAL WORKING CAPITAL/MONTH

Raw Material	Rs.	1,10,000.00
Salary & Wages	Rs.	51,875.00
Utilities & Overheads	Rs.	29,700.00
TOTAL	**Rs.**	**1,91,575.00**

TOTAL CAPITAL INVESTMENT

Total Fixed Capital	Rs.	11,79,200.00
Total Working Capital for 3 Months	Rs.	5,74,725.00
TOTAL	**Rs.**	**17,53,925.00**

TURN OVER/ANNUM

1. By selling PVC leather bags, conference bags or folders
2. By selling file covers, diary cover diary covers

TOTAL Rs. 36,00,000.00

PROFIT = RECEIPTS - COST OF PRODUCTION

= 36,00,000.00 - 28,03,813.50

= 7,96,186.50

PROFIT SALES RATIO = Profit/Sales x 100 = **22.12 %**

RATE OF RETURN = Operating Profit/T.C.I. x 100 = **45.39 %**

BREAK EVEN POINT (B.E.P.) = 52.96 %

11

CORRUGATED SHEET BOARD AND BOXES

INTRODUCTION

Though no authentic record is available about when any thing like a paper box was first made, it is held that the ancient Egyptians made certain kinds of containers from an aquatic plant supplied fibers for paper sheets. There áre also records, though not clear of reaptacles made from rice paper in china during the Eleventh Century.

MANUFACTURINGPROCESS

Machine which usually takes container board from three rolls and combines it into a corrugated board consisting of two outer facings and an intermediate fluted members. The corrugator forms the intermediate sheet into a series of a riched trusses and attaches the facings to them with adhesive applied at the tips of flutes. The resulting sheet is called single wall corrugated fibre board by taking container board from five rolls, it also produce a corrugated board, commonly known as double well consisting of three facings and two corrugated mediums.

One essential components of corrugated board is a sheet known as 'Corrugating medium 0.009 thick (9 caliper) or 0.23 mm, has been given a wary shape by passing it through the rolls of a corrugating machine. Jute and kraft liner board, or any other board is attached to this sheet on one or both sides with starch and silicate of soda adhesive.

When only one liner is used the product is known as 'Single face'. This is flexible in one direction, when the corrugated element is combined on both side with other boards, it is known as 'Double face' corrugated board or corrugated shipping container board.

There are three standards sizes of corrugations, called 'A' flute 'B' and 'C' flute. In 'A' flute there are about 36 corrugations to the liners foot and the thickness of the combined board is about 0.205". In 'B' flute there are about 52 corrugations per liner foot with the board thickness being about 0.125". While in 'C' flute here are about 42 corrugations per liner foot with the board thickness being about 0.125", while in 'C' flute here are about 42 corrugations per liner foot with the board thickness being about 0.125". While in 'C' flute here are about 0.165". The usual basis weight of the corrugating medium is about 125 gms.

Corrugated board is fabricated on a machine known as corrugating machine which consists in its simplest form a set of corrugating rolls, glue applicator rolls and a shot plate section. Before entering the corrugation rolls, the corrugating medium is pre conditioned by steaming and is then further heated at the steam heated corrugated rolls.

Heat is very important in the corrugating operations. As mentioned, heat supplied by steaming is necessary to control the plastic properties of the corrugated medium at the time of corrugating.

The corrugated rolls are heated also using steam of about 30 to 175 psi to produce a surface temperature of about 320 to 341°F.

The treatment of the corrugating medium with moit heat make the paper soft and pleable so that also prevents a sticking of the paper of the corrugating rolls.

The number of corrugations per foot of board and the height of the corrugations are standarised as follows although there is a considerable variation from standard.

Type of Flute	Height of Flutes/in.	No. of flute/ft.
A		36
B	48	51
C	5132	41

'A' flute is used where high top to bottom compression and where maximum cushioning is desired e.g. for board used in the packaging of paper cartons and glass fars.

'B' flute is used where high end-to- end compression is desired. It is used for the packing of canned goods and where the box is stitched instead of being taped.

The flute contour is generally fairly sharp. Clearance between teeth must be allowed to so that the paper can flow into the nip to produce the flute without pinching. Uniform flute controns with no highs or lows is essential.

On leaving the corrugating rolls, the corrugating medium fluffs out to meet a glue applicator rolls which applied adhesive to one side of the paper. Long metal strips (gingers) are set to control the amount of this fluffing out, and setting of these fingers is ce of the most important parts of operation of corrugating machine.

The resulting board is known as single face. It double face board is to be made, the single faced moves up an elevator to a bridge where it collects in folds to provide a continuous feed for the double backer glue station. As the double back glue station adhesive is applied to the flutes on the other side of the corrugating medium and a second liner applied about 5-30 second later.

Adhesive consumption figures are generally reported in pounds/thousand sq.ft. or board. Because consumption depends upon the type of flute and number of sheet elements it is customary to use 'A' flute double face board as to the basis for reporting. Factors are used to convert other type of board to thia basis. One set fetor in use is:

A flute, double face	1.0
A flute, single face	0.3
B flute, double face	1.3
B flute, single face	0.4
A flute, double wall	2.6
A flute double wall	2.6

After leaving the double back glue station the combined board enters the hot plate section where the board is held against plates by means of heavy belts. Setting of the adhesive on the double back side takes places at this board. At the end of the machine the board is slit and flap scored. The blanks are then taken off the machine piled in such a way as to minimize wraping and sweating of the board.

There are many operating variables to watch at the single face stage to prevent defects in the final board. The importance of the proper setting of the figures has already been mentioned some corrugating media are very springy and it is extremely important that the fingers are adjusted close to the large corrugating rolls so that the paper will not spring out of the teeth before it reaches the relief or fluff out position. The setting of the transfer roll in relation to both the glue roll and the corrugating roll is very important.

The applicators roll has a slightly rough surface for picking up the glue. The speed of this roll in relation to speed of the paper is very important general practice is to run the glue rolls at a surface speed less than paper board speed.

The overall operating and mechanical feature of the corrugating machine which need checking included heating system, corrugating roll system, finger bar, machine live up from roll stands through hot plate section to keep paper centered, belting, and glue roll speed. The major sources of trouble are as listed below:-

1. Paper components too wet or too dry.
2. Improper heat balance on the machine.
3. This alingment, cross pull, or other mechanical stresses which prevent firm and continuous contact with the adhesive.
4. Moisture saturated or imprevious belts.
5. Dirty glue rolls.
6. Improperly prepared adhesive.

The wet glue bond must be fairly strong as the board comes off the machine to withstand and hand ling at this point. Later the adhesive sets to produce the final dry bond. This bond makes an important contribution to the overall strength of the finished board, affecting such properties a bending moment, compression tensile strength, puncture resistance, and water resistance. Improperly applied adhesive resulting in starved or flooded joints and poorly made corrugations, maked flutes and deep fingers lines reduce the strength of the board.

Dasmesh Mechanico,
14, Gali No. 8,
Anand Parbat Indl. Area,
New Delhi - 110 005
Tel/Fax: 5737112, 5754774

Perfect Paper Machines
34, D.S.I.D.C., Scheme-II,
Okhla Indl. Area - II,
New Delhi - 110 020
Tel.: 6844202, 6913500
Fax: 011-6849573

Nagpal Industries,
65, Sector - 6,
Faridabad.
Ph.: 8-2412289, 241589

J. K. Engg. Corporation
19-A, Rajendra Nagar,
Indl. Area, Mohan Nagar,
Ghaziabad.
Ph.: 720934

Corruga Machines
E-20, Sanjay Colony,
Sector - 23-24,
Faridabad.
Tel/Fax: 8-230132

Sapna Industries
40, SMIE, 20/2,
Mathura Road,
Faridabad.
Tel/Fax: 8-284436

LIST OF RAW MATERIALS SUPPLIERS

Kraft Paper:

Om Prakash Jitendra Kumar & Co.,
63, Darya Ganj,
New Delhi - 110 002
Ph. 326 96 80, 3271380

Narain Paper Mart,
4034/3, Haryana Market,
Chawri Bazar,
Delhi - 110 006
Ph. 291 5135.

Himgiri Paper Products
B-24, Indl. Area Lawrence Road,
New Delhi - 110 035
Phone : 718 9005

Adhesive:

Asistto Rubber & Adhesive Industries,
71, 10th Khetwadi,
Mumbai - 400 004

Surface Ltd.,
401/405, 4th Floor,
Jolly Bhawan No. 1,
10th New Marine Lanes,
Mumbai - 400 020

Stitch Wire:

J & K Wire Steel Industries Pvt. Ltd.,
9, Karan Nagar,
Jammu Tawi - 180 005

Hindustan Steel Wires Ltd.,
407, Akashdeep,
26 A, Barakhamba Road,
New Delhi - 110 001

Printing Inks:

Baluja Spectra
C-50 Okhla Indl. Area-II,
New Delhi - 110020
Phone/fax : 6835715, 6835722

Ajanta Ink Company
Basai Road, Gurgaon.
(Haryana),
Phone/fax : 8-330028

Art Printing Inks Company
104 Site-4, Indl. Area,
Sahibabad, Ghaziabad.
Phone/fax : 767882

Inks India (Delhi)
C-49, Sector-8,
Noida-201 301 (U.P.)
Phone : 523801
Fax : 011-8-557270

Van Inks & Chemicals (P) Ltd.
B-150, Phase-II,
Noida-201 305 (U.P.)
Phone : 567141
Fax : 011-8-521507

PLANT ECONOMICS OF
CORRUGATED SHEET BOARD AND BOXES

Rated Plant Capacity = 2650.00 Kgs./Day

COST OF LAND & BUILDING
(Total land area required 750 sq. mtr.) Rs. 16,80,000.00

LIST OF PLANT & MACHINERY

1. Corrugated sheet making unit single face paper corrugating machine 42" size
2. Two board cutters
   1. One 42"x 62" size
   2. One 52"x 62" size
3. One reel stand, light model
4. One sheet pasting machine 75" size
5. One sheet pressing machine 65"x 75" size
6. One eccentric slotter 75" size
7. One 4-bar rotary cutting & creasing machine 75" size
8. Two stitching machine
   1. One 36" arm, angular head
   2. One 30" arm, straight head
9. One partition slotter 42" size
10. One slotting machine
11. One vertical bending machine 62" size
12. Corner cutting machine
13. Two colour board printer
14. Laminating machine for lamination of printed corrugated board.
15. Miscellaneous charges as packing, forwarding, excise duty and all applicable taxes etc.

LIST OF RAW MATERIALS

1. Kraft paper in rolls
2. Glue (starch)
3. Stitching wire
4. Printing ink
5. Polyethylene film

FIXED CAPITAL

Land & Building	Rs.	16,80,000.00
Plant & Machinery	Rs.	8,65,000.00
Other Fixed Assets	Rs.	2,50,000.00
TOTAL	**Rs.**	**27,95,000.00**

TOTAL WORKING CAPITAL/MONTH

Raw Material	Rs.	18,57,370.00
Salary & Wages	Rs.	1,31,250.00
Utilities & Overheads	Rs.	66,500.00
TOTAL	**Rs.**	**20,55,120.00**

TOTAL CAPITAL INVESTMENT

Total Fixed Capital	Rs.	27,95,000.00
Total Working Capital for 3 Months	Rs.	61,65,360.00
TOTAL	**Rs.**	**89,60,360.00**

TURN OVER/ANNUM

Total receipt by sales of 7,95,000 Kgs. or the material from which boxes are manufactured	Rs.	3,18,00,000.00

PROFIT = RECEIPTS - COST OF PRODUCTION

= 3,18,00,000.00 - 2,69,36,735.20

= 48,63,264.80

PROFIT SALES RATIO = Profit/Sales x 100 = **15.29 %**

RATE OF RETURN = Operating Profit/T.C.I. x 100

BREAK EVEN POINT (B.E.P.) = 39.32%

12

DUPLICATING INK

INTRODUCTION

Duplicating ink is basically known as document reproduction ink. The duplicator sheet-fed machines require very press-stable, yet quick setting inks. They must also possess fine lithographic properties of high tolerance for water-fountain solution and of dense and sharp printing properties on a wide variety of papers. The inks contains drying oil alkyds or plain bodied oils, along with lithographic type(non-polar) resins and high boiling (280-370°C) hydrocarbon solvents. The rubber type inks are based on cyclized (depolymerized) synthetic rubber which exhibits exceptionally fast setting. This property results from rapid release of the solvent.

USES AND APPLICATION

Duplicating ink is also known as transferring ink or stencil ink.

It is used in printing on various items.

PROPERTIES

1. The material shall be in the form of a paste and shall be free from grit and objectionable matter, such as skins, lumps, and other separated materials.
2. It can manufactured in any colours.
3. The ink shall be emulsion based.
4. The consistency should be uniform. It shall neither run or drip off the cylinders nor it shall be stiff.
5. The ink shall be workable in all weather.
6. Impressions obtained with the ink shall not smudge after drying.
7. The material shall be in workable condition for at least two * years from the date of manufacture.

PRESENT MANUFACTURERS

Nylund Printing Inks Pvt. Ltd.
10-4-14, Humayun Nagar,
Masab Tank,
Hyderabad-500028
Tel-040-37939.

Shaleen Printing Ink's Formulary
11, Shanti Nagar,
Khajrana Road,
Indore-452001
Ph:0731-441916/411389.

FORMULATION

Duplicating Ink:

	Parts by weight.
Wax	55
Tallow	5
Soap	55
Shellac	25
Mastic	20
Spruce resin	5
Pine lamp black	15

MANUFACTURING PROCESS

Make a 30 % solution of glycoxal instead of glycoxal pyrulic aldehyde can be used. Make ammonium polyacrylate 25 % solution in water. In this ammonium polyacrylate solution disperse zinc oxide. Add ethylene glycol and wetting agent. Heat until all the ingredients are dissolved. Add water soluble dye instead of nigrosine lamp black or aquablack can be used. Stir to room temperature.

SUPPLIERS OF RAW MATERIALS

Bharat Organics
8/11, Samartha Nagar,
Chunabhatti Station (East),
Mumbai - 400 022
Ph: 5531335/5531670

Wetting Agent (Acid Slurry LABS)

Harsha Products
Unit No.-27, Bldg. No. 6,
Jogani Industrial Complex,
Ground Floor, Sion-Chunabatti Road,
Chunabatti,
Mumbai - 400 022
Ph: 5530211/5534321

Glycoxal:

Amzole India Pvt. Ltd.
41, Udyog Vihar,
Sukher, Udaipur-313001
Ph: (0294) 560947/560446
Fax: (0294) 560557

Ethylene Glycol:-

Rita Corporation
21, Chewool Wadi
(Kolbhat Lane)
Dr M.B. Velkar's Street
Kalbadevi Road
P.B. No.-2722
Mumbai - 400 002
Phone-2056895

PLANT & MACHINERY SUPPLIERS

Bhagsons Engineers & Consultants Pvt. Ltd.
9, Amar Park,
Rohtak Road,
New Delhi - 110035
Ph: 5412707/5410736

Engineers Syndicate
312 A Shiv Lok House,
2 Karampura,
New Delhi-110015
Ph: 5415628

PLANT ECONOMICS OF DUPLICATING INK

Rated Plant Capacity = 300.00 Kgs./Day
= 90000.00 Kgs./Annum

COST OF LAND & BUILDING

(Total land area required 350 sq. mtr.) Rs. 2,86,105.50

LIST OF PLANT & MACHINERY

1. Stainless steel vertical tank with stirrer
2. Stainless steel tank with motor stirrer
3. Heating furnace with blower
4. S.S. storage tank cap: 200 Lits.
5. Testing instruments & equipment
6. Pumps, valves and miscellaneous

LIST OF RAW MATERIALS

1. Nigrosine dye (water soluble)
2. Linear alkyl benzene sulfonate
3. Glycoxal (30 % solution)
4. Ethylene glycol
5. Ammonium polyacrylate (25 % water solution)
6. Zinc oxide
7. Container

TOTAL WORKING CAPITAL/MONTH

Raw Material	Rs.	2,86,105.50
Salary & Wages	Rs.	19,625.00
Utilities & Overheads	Rs.	75,500.00
TOTAL	**Rs.**	**3,81,230.50**

TOTAL CAPITAL INVESTMENT

Total Fixed Capital	Rs.	12,55,000.00
Total Working Capital for 3 Months	Rs.	11,43,691.50
TOTAL	**Rs.**	**23,98,691.50**

TURN OVER/ANNUM

By sale of duplicating ink 90000 Kgs.	**Rs. 67,50,000.00**

PROFIT = RECEIPTS - COST OF PRODUCTION

= 67,50,000.00 - 50,79,165.47

= 16,70,834.53

PROFIT SALES RATIO = Profit/Sales x 100 = **24.50 %**

RATE OF RETURN = Operating Profit/T.C.I. x 100 = **69.16 %**

BREAK EVEN POINT (B.E.P.) = 37.05 %

13

EXERCISE NOTE BOOK & REGISTER

INTRODUCTION

Exercise books are widely known & vastly used as day to day products. Note books are available in the market in various sizes, shapes & pages and having various types of covers paper bound, board and Rexine bound etc.

Exercise books are of different types and are used for many purpose. Their sizes very according to the requirement. Though mainly used by students whether school going or college going, yet not less important for a house wife who keeps her day expenses record & similarly for small business men for keeping their accounts and a labour who can write some songs for this recordation.

With the growth of education among the masses & industrialization with in the country, the demand of stationery note book for writing purposes has been increasing at a tremendous rate.

USES & APPLICATIONS

Exercise books are widely known & vastly used as day to day product . Note books are mainly used by students, teachers, house wives, business men, & office going people.

Student use it for noting down their class lessons, notes & important information. House wives keep their day to day expenses. Small business men keep their accounts & labour write some songs for their recreation.

MANUFACTURINGPROCESS

Exercise books are made in varying dimensions & pages, & having card board bound, paper bound, cover etc.

The paper is available in rim. The process follows the following steps:-

1. Cutting
2. Rulling
3. Pressing
4. Stitching
5. Binding
6. Finishing

Cutting:-

The paper size 16" x 26 which comes in rim is of bigger size already mentioned, which is cut in to the required size as paper cutting machine. It is shown that per each sheet of larger of size 16" x 26" given 16 Nos. larger or standard Exercise Book size. In one rim of size 16" x 26", contains generally 500 sheets and weight per rim is from 8.1 kg. to 8.9 kg per rim. The cost of one kg. of paper is 14.25/kg. It is very for time to time according to market demand.

Rulling:-

This paper is rulled in Automatic double set rulling machines because the note books are generally rulled.

Pressing:-

It is done so that the books may retain a required shape. This is done with the help of Dab press.

Perforating:-

It is the process of making holes in paper. It is done with the help of perforating machine.

Sticking:-

After cutting & rulling, the papers are sticked in a stitching machine. Each stitched book contain certain number of pages.

Binding:-

If the books is bound by ordinary paper or bard paper, usually such printed papers are doing stiching of paper stitched.

In case of hard board bound books, a ordinary printed paper is always pasted at the board. In case of hard paper & ordinary bound books no extra paper pasting is required & required printing is done on it from some printing unit.

Besides safe guarding the book from detoriation the cover also serves as a purpose of its identity, in that the title & the the name of owner & subject is also written on the cover.

The small scale unit generally get their coverprinted from other printers. The cover should have the following:-

1. No. of pages.
2. Name of the manufacturers.
3. Identity Chart, giving name of the owner, subject, name of school class, & Address etc.

Finishing:-

Finishing means to cut the edges of the book a little so that edges are smooth. If the book is bound by ordinary paper or hard paper this tep is done after stitching.

In case of card board bound books this step is done before the binding of the books.

SUPPLIERS OF RAW MATERIALS

Paper:-

Lakshmi Trader,
Chawri Bazer,
Delhi - 110 006

Ballarpur Paper &
Straw Board Mills Ltd,
Yamunanagar,
Haryana.

Straw Board:

Delhi Board Mills,
Chawri Bazer,
Delhi - 110 006

G.T. Industries,
202, Lotus House,
33A, New Merine Lines,
Mumbai

SUPPLIERS OF PLANT AND MACHINERY

Complete Plant can be Supplied by Following firms:-

Kay Iron Works Pvt. Ltd.,
Yamunagar P.O.,
Ambala Distt.

Printer House Pvt. Ltd.,
22/1, Mathura Road,
Ballabgarh.
(Haryana)

Industrial Paper Machinery (P) Ltd.,
A-32, Naraina Indl. Area,
Phase-1,
New Delhi - 110 026

Cutting and Creasing Machine:

Nagpal Industries,
1062, Bartan Market,
Sadar Bazer,
Delhi - 110 006.

Book Binding Machine:

Manjeet Industries,
8772, Shahidipura,
Near Filmistan Cinema,
New Delhi - 110 005

Stitching Machine:-

Yash Mechanical Works,
374, Azad Market,
Delhi - 110 006

PLANTECONOMICSOF EXCERCISENOTEBOOK&REGISTER

Rated Plant Capacity = 2520.00 Nos./Day

COSTOFLAND&BUILDING

(Total land area required 150 sq. mtr.) Rs. 2,95,000.00

LIST OF PLANT & MACHINERY

1. Automatic double set rulling machine
2. 2 Bar rotary cutting creasing, sorting and perforating machine with all access.
3. Paper cutting machine with rotary type fitted Heavy duty with motor starter
4. Shifting attachment with 2 setsof cutter
5. Extra set of blsades for machine
6. Wire swtitching machine complete\with. Iron stand wooden table, stiching.
7. Hand operated gumming machine
8. Dab press
9. Electrification and installation charges
10. Miscellaneous items tools and implements

LIST OF RAW MATERIALS

1. Paper white for excercise Notebook
2. Paper white for Register
3. Gray board, Card board, stitching wires
4. Stiching wires , ink, glue, thread, cloth etc.
5. Packing expenses
6. Miscellaneous items

FIXED CAPITAL

Land & Building	Rs.	2,95,000.00
Plant & Machinery	Rs.	5,26,000.00
Other Fixed Assets	Rs.	30,000.00
TOTAL	**Rs.**	**8,51,000.00**

TOTAL WORKING CAPITAL/MONTH

Raw Material	Rs.	2,18,710.00
Salary & Wages	Rs.	27,436.00
Utilities & Overheads	Rs.	12,800.00
TOTAL	**Rs.**	**2,58,946.00**

TOTAL CAPITAL INVESTMENT

Total Fixed Capital	Rs.	8,51,000.00
Total Working Capital for 3 Months	Rs.	7,76,838.00
TOTAL	**Rs.**	**16,27,838.00**

TURN OVER/ANNUM

1. By selling of 600000 excercise book 200 pages
2. Register 96 pages

Rs. 48,48,000.00

PROFIT = RECEIPTS - COST OF PRODUCTION
= 48,48,000.00 - 36,12,036.36
= 12,35,963.64

PROFIT SALES RATIO = Profit/Sales x 100 = **25.49 %**

RATE OF RETURN = Operating Profit/T.C.I. x 100 = **75.43 %**

BREAK EVEN POINT (B.E.P.) = 36.09 %

14

FLOPPY DISKS

INTRODUCTION

Disk for storing computer data magnetically come in two varities; floppy disks, & names for the flexible material they are made of and hard disk constructed from rigid metal platters. Floppy disks are less expensive variety. They are cut from huge sheets of polyester, a tough plastic, which have been coated in advance with a layer of magnetic material. All floppies the original ression (disks 8 inches in diameter), mini floppies (5 1/4 inch in diameters and micro floppies (3 1/2 inch in diameter) have a lower recording density than hard disks. However, they are rugged and can be easily removed from one computer's disk drive the combination recorder and player that spins the disk to store and recover computer data from its surface to that of another.

A 5¼ inch minifloppy

A protective jacket encloses a disk (inset) that has a magnetic coating on both sides of a polyster support. Inside the jacket, friction-reducing liner clean the surface of the disk as it spins. An index hole through both jacket and disk serves as a reference point for writing and reading data through a lozenge shaped access window. A floppy can always be read, but covering a notch in one side of the jacket with tape prevents data from being written or unintentially erased.

A 3½ inch micro floppy

In this smallest of floppies, a rigid plastic jacket protects the flexible magnetic disk. A spring-loaded door covers the jacket's access window. The door remains tightly closed until the floppy is inserted in to a disk drive, thus warding off dust and finger prints. A metal hub, bended to the underside of the disk, has one hole that serves to centre the disk and another for spinning it; indexing is by magnetic signal recorded on the disk. Protection against unintentional writing or erasure is achieved by sliding a tab to open a hole in the corner of the jacket.

Floppy Disk type	Data Exchange		Other Applications	
	Record length (bytes)	Sectors/ Tracks	Record length (bytes)	Sectors Tracks
One sided	128	26	256 512	15 8
Two sided	256	15 per side	--	--
Two-sided double Density	256	26 perside	1024	8 per side

Data Organization:

Data is stored on a diskette bit - serially in tracks. A track is the recording area on a single diskette recording surface that passes the read/write head while the disk makes a comlete revolution. The read/write head is mounted on carriage that can be moved to 77 distinct locations along a straight line from the centre of the disk. Therefore, each recording surface of the diskette has 77 concentric tracks on which data can be stored. The diskette drive for two-sided diskette has a read/write on each side.

Track Format:

Diskettes which are to be used for the exchange of information between two computers should be recorded in a standard format and such pre-formatted floppy disks can be obtained from the manufactors.

USES AND APPLICATIONS

It is used in computer key board development. More recently the floppy disk or diskette has been looked upon as the answer to the key board operator's escape from punched tape. These 7 1/2 inch dia. disks can have 2.7 megabit capacity. Although may have less and may not equal the capacity of one track of a 0.15 inch wide cassette tape. The currenttrend seems to be toward floppy disks or as a replacement for paper tape rather than magnetic tape cassettes or cartridges, this trends is likely to be accelerated by floppy disk stored text in word - processing system. The tenancity of paper tape as a key board - film setter interface can be seen from the varicomposer 1, which uses a floppy disk as a text store but a paper tape or magnetic tape cassette interface for the photocomposer.

Familarly, the ACE correction and editing equipment of monotype was designed with floppy disk text store but paper tape output's phototype setter can be driven by floppy disks. probably the most significant trend indicator is the AM international AM text 425 work processing system, which will now provide a floppy disk interface between word processing equipment and the AM COMP//set 4550 phototype setter.

WHY INFORMATION STORAGE IS NEEDED

Secondary storage media and devices.

The major purpose of secondary storage is to store:

i. Programs or parts of programs not being executed.
ii. Data needed for current or subsequent processing.

Disk technology is also being applied in other ways. Small floppy disks about the size of a 45 RPM records are being used for microprogramms or other purposes. Small single disks are being used to provide low cost and low capacity on line storage for small computer systems.

GENERAL PRINCIPLES INVOLVED

Magnetic Disk:

A magnetic disk consists of rotating metal disks on which data may be stored. The disk unit is re-frequently referred to as "random" access or direct access, storage because any storage position can be read or written directly without having to serially read other records. This direct access, although not strictly random, in access time, allows processing to be handled on unsequenced input date and without having to process any records not related to transactions.

A magnetize disk file is consists of a stack disks rotating on the common shape. There are from 5 to 100 disks measuring 1 1/2 to 3 ft. in diameter.

In appearance, the disk file suggests a stack of photograph records.

The disk units may be classified according to the no. of read write heads and the removability of the stack of disk as follows:-

i. Heads:

a. Moving head (single head serves more than one track)
b. Fixed

ii. Stack

a. Fixed
b. Removable (disk Pack)

The most common methods in terms of number of units installed is the moving head with one arm per disk and a removable disk pack.

The access arm for a disk contains two read and write heads. One for the top and one for the under side of the disk.

To read and writs a record, an access arm must be positioned on the disk over the location to be used.

The arm (if a moving head) moves in and out to locate itself in the epoper spot. The heads float on a cushion of air 35% in (micro inches) from the surface (about one fifth of the height of a smoke particle) thin closeness requires close alignment to avoid head alignment head crushes against the surface.

All the arms, in a moving head disk move in and out together, when one arm is positioned over a track on one disk, the to other arms are automatically position over and track on other disks. These disks are turned a cylinder.

Some disk units are available with a read and write head for each recording track, an arrangement that eliminates arm movements at together. Disks units can have fixed disks or portable replaceable packs, some system program and some frequently used files are required to be available virtually all the time. For this reason an installation may need to have some fixed disk storage and some removable disks.

The storage capacity of units varies, but a fixed disk may store several hundred million characters while each replaceable disk pack will store in 2 to 200 million character range.

Single disk pack does not have sufficient pack does not have sufficient capacity for large on line file processing. The trend is toward the use of multiple pack storage sub systems.

Disk technology is also being applied in other ways. Small floppy disk about the size of a 45 rpm record are being used for micro programs. Small single disks are being used to provide low cost and low capacity, on line, storage for small computer systems.

When comparing the performance of disks units, the following operating characteristics are important. These are considerable differences in performance, but some figures for commonly used medium and large capacity disk systems provide some idea of the disk performance.

Storage with a capacity of a hundred million characters is capable of holding the written position of 40 to 50 average text books, but due to the storage structures and technical requirements, not all available storage is actually used. The affective capacity is less than the heroritical capacity.

Data is stored in and retrieved from identificable locations on a disk file. The locations are uniquely identified by an address consisting of disk face track on the disk face and perhaps sectors of the track.

The block diagram gives the idea about track etc.

The block for disk reading and writing is typical either a sector, an entire track or a position of the track defined by a variable length record.

The time to access a record in a disk storage consists of the seek time and the rotational time.

a. Seek Time:

This is the time required to position a movable read write head over the recording track to be used. If the read write head is fixed. This time will be zero.

b. Rotational Time:

This is the rotational delay to move the storage location underneath the read write head.

The seek time is much more significant then the rotational time. Data on disk file is frequently organized to reduce the seek time.

A major system design and programming consideration with disk storage is the identification of the disk location of a record to be used in processing. In order to obtain a given record without searching a large no. of records, some methods of determining where a record is stored is needed. If for example, the main the inventory records are maintained on a disk file a withdrawal transaction will be used to up date the balance on hand for the item.

To process this transaction, the storage location on the disk on the master inventory record must be identified. The identification and location methods are explained in introduction to the various information storage systems, given earlier.

An evaluation of storage characteristics suggests that disk files have an advantage over magnetize tape in cases where direct access capabilities are needed or desirable. A disk file can be used exactly like a magnetize tape with records stored and processed is sequence. However, the advantage of having files on magnetize disk is that alternative processing modes may also be used which take advantage of direct access characteristic of the disk.

By comparison with magnetize tape, disk storage transfer is faster and access is direct. The major disadvantage of magnetize disk storage is that disk files are move expensive than magnetize tape. (about twenty times more for removable disk pack having a storage capacity anywhere from one fourth as great upto about the same as a red tape.

MANUFACTURING PROCESS & DESIGN FEATURES

The manufacturing process of floppy disks involves the various steps like.

1. Smoothening of plastic sheets of specific thickness. This involves removal of dust perticals from the surface of sheets and also the sheet un-evenness is removed.

2. Coating of Magnetic Material on the one of the one or both sides of the plastic sheet. Earlier the coating was done only on one side of the disk while very recently floppy disks are introduced which have magnetic material coating on both the sides.

And for the magnetic material painting the machines deployed must have fine accuracy because the unevenness in disk surface would given widetectable errors of just poor recording capabilities.

So the coating of magnetic material done be very very even the magnetic materials are nothing, but various iron oxides.

The magnetic material which consist of fine particles can be divided further into classes of oxides such as:

i. Fe_2O_3
ii. Fe_3O_4
iii. CrO_2

and metal particals of iron, cobalt and nickel, though the relation between the recording performance, in particular the reproduce out voltage, pulse width resoltution, noise and magnetize properties of given material are highly complex, where as the previously stated requirements for coercivity and remaince are in general vated. The effect of both factors appears to depend on the composition and thickness of the medium.

Typical oxide coatings are 100 to 500 each thick.

Further oxide coatings permit only small variation in coercivity (between 200 and 350 Oa)

Because of interaction of magnetic and mechanical parameters such as read and write head gap length, surface roughness head to medium separation, binder compostion in particulate media, write current medium thickness. practical problems arise in isolating the effects of magnetic parameters on the width and amplitude of the reproduce pulse.

PROPERTIES OF FINE PARTICLES

The classical theory of ferromagnetism, postulates that ferromagnetic substances are divided into domains weise zones which are spontaniously magnetized to saturation. Magnetization of the bulk material takes place by variation in the size of domains domain wall displacement and through change in direction of magnetization by rotation of magnetization by spontaneous magnetization. The magnitude of this spontatneous magnetization shows a temperature dependence, the general shape is that of a monotonous decrease with increasing temperature reaching zero at the curie point of the material. finally the interaction between the magnetization of a particle and mechanical stress acting on it determines a stress anisotropy.

The actual coercivity is obtained after mixing the gerromangnetic material with a non-magnetic binder. The ration normally in 1/3 oxide and 2/3 binder volume ration so that typical computer disks exhibit 250 to 300 Oa coerucivities.

Effect of particle Size :

It is always desirable for the recording material to exhibit a near rectangular hysterers loop, high saturation flux density, 100 temperature dependence and sufficiently for high coercivity to prevent self de magnetization other considerations made if desirable to choose single, domain particle sizes. The coericitivity was shown to be strongly dependent on particle shape.

The calculated value for acicular (needle-shaped) r Fe_2O_3 with 5 : 1 length width ratio gives 75° A°/150A° length/width dimensions, at which super paramagnetism will occur. For spherical r Fe_2O_3 the corresponding radius is 350 A° (16).

As the weight of sample of particulate material can be measured much more easily and to higher degree of accuracy than volume or crossectional area, it is customary to express the magnetize properties of material in terms of saturation moment per gram.

The most common process for making the particles uses hydrated ferric oxide (FeO OH) which exists in needle shaped crystalline form or can be made by a process described by M. cainaras. After dehydration red needle shaped crystals of hemmatit x Fe_2O_3 are obtained. The hematit crystals are reduced by heating in hydrogen at 300 - 400°C to black crystals of ferro so ferric oxide (Fe_3O_4 = FeO Fe_2O_3 = magnetitie).

Metal Particles:

Metal particles have higher saturation magnetization than oxide particles. This would allow the use of thinner recording layers without loss of output. The high density performance is helped by high coercivities obtained with metallix single domain particles. The materials which are of prime interest are iron cobalt nickel alloys.

Cutting and grooving of disks out of magnetic pointed plastic sheets the various size of disks are out with the help of automatic hydraulic and hydraulic cum pneumatic pressure, presses.

And before feeding the sheet to the press, the sheets are heated to specific temperature so that the sheet becomes soft and this softness is needed for disk cutting process. In the same press the concentric grooves are also imprinted and these concentric tracks are channels where the information is stored in the form of magnetic energy.

And as the surface, grooves of the disks have to be highly smooth and perfectly even, the whole of the process sequence is done under:-

DUST PROOF CONDITIONS

Packing of finished disks also involved special care. Design specifications for temperature and relative humidity are generally available and normally represent much wider limits than those given for each type of device.

DESIGN SPECIFICATIONS FOR DISKS

On large systems exchangeable disk units have design specifications of at least 15-32°C but there is some variation on RH conditions with 20-80% quite common

On filteration, the units generally are fitted with 0.3 micron two stage absolute filteration system, so that the main requirement is to prevent the disks from being contaminated during loading or storage disk packs have a builtin course filter at the base of the pack through which the air flows, when loaded or running.

If specifications not noted on pack, then operational specifications for temp. and humidity taken as:-

15 - 40°C, 8 - 80% RH.

and storage requirements for packs are typically

-40 to 65°C, 8 - 80% RH.

and no condesation for upto 5 years.

HEART DISSIPATION IN DISKS

One of the major problem in designing disk containing plant to give an even temp. through out the room is the volume and velocity of air being blown through computer equipment, this leads to higher than the normal ceiling heat.

Typical heat dissipations for mini computer and small main frame are as given below:-

Process	Small system	Mini system
Process	2.0-5.0	0.5-2.5
Disks	0.3-1.5	0.3-1.5
Magnetize tape units	0.6-1.8	0.2-1.3
Card readers	0.5-2.5	0.2-2.0
Paper type readers/ Punches	0.5-2.0	0.2-1.0

SCHEDULED MAINTENANCE TIME

Scheduled maintenance time is often specified for all electro- mechanical peripheral equipment for preventative maintenance, that is to change parts and carry out adjustments before operation of equipment is carried wrong by faults caused by wear and adjustment wandering.

Acceptance Trials:

When a computer system is delivered it will have undergone some form of pre-delivery factor testing, but in limited, not necessarily geared up to the requirements of the design and with drop shipped peripherals or new software, the ordered configuration may not have been tested as a system.

Peripheral Equipment Tests:

Functional engg test 1 programs are run on each peripheral sub-system in turn. transfer rate and other speed/capacity measurements are made, operational modes and formats, also error detection and correction are tested.

Compatibility test is run on disks and magnetic tape units to ensure that information written on one device of a type can be read on all others. An ideal compatibility test for example on disks would be to write a whole disk on each write and read it on all others. But practically it is not feasible.

PLANT & MACHINERY SUPPLIERS(GENERAL)

Brizes Plastic Machinery Corpn.,
55, Govt. Industrial Estate,
Kandivilli (West),
Mumbai - 400 067

Batlibol & Co. Ltd.,
P.B. No. 10011,
Porbes Street,
Fort, Mumbai.

Perfact Machine Tools Co.,
Sir P.H. Road,
Mumbai.

Peco Electronics & Electrical Ltd.,
68 - Shivaji Road,
New Delhi - 110 015

Associated Instruments Mfg.,
Asaf Ali Road,
New Delhi.

Gillanders Arbuthnot & Co. Ltd.,
4 - 1, Gillander Rouse,
Netaji Subhas Road,
Calcutta - 700 001

RAW MATERIAL SUPPLIERS

American Microsystems Ind.,
3900, Homestead Road,
Santa Clara,
CA 95051.

Hewleft Company
620, Page Mill Road,
Palao Aito,
CA 94304.

PLANT ECONOMICS OF FLOPPY DISKS

Rated Plant Capacity = 14000.00 Nos./Day

COST OF LAND & BUILDING

(Total land area required 500/- sq. mtr.) Rs. 1,10,00,000.00

LIST OF PLANT & MACHINERY

1. Complete plant comprising mylar sheet cutting,coating grooving and protective jacket making machines
2. Testing equipments
3. Misc. equipments & accessories

LIST OF RAW MATERIALS

1. Mylar sheets in roll form
2. Magnetic coating materials
3. Laminated flat jackets
4. Hub rings and tyres sleeves
5. Spring loaded door- covers
6. Boxes for packaging and other raw materials

FIXED CAPITAL

Land & Building	Rs. 1,10,00,000.00
Plant & Machinery	Rs. 3,20,00,000.00
Other Fixed Assets	Rs. 57,00,000.00
TOTAL	**Rs. 4,87,00,000.00**

TOTAL WORKING CAPITAL/MONTH

Raw Material	Rs.	65,00,000.00
Salary & Wages	Rs.	3,59,488.00
Utilities & Overheads	Rs.	4,02,000.00
TOTAL	**Rs.**	**72,61,488.00**

TOTAL CAPITAL INVESTMENT

Total Fixed Capital	Rs.	4,87,00,000.00
Total Working Capital for 3 Months	Rs.	2,17,84,464.00
TOTAL	**Rs.**	**7,04,84,464.00**

TURNOVER/ANNUM

1. By sale of 5.25"floppies 210000 packets
2. By sale of 3.50 inch floppies 210000 packets **Rs. 13,25,10,000.00**

PROFIT = RECEIPTS - COST OF PRODUCTION
= 13,25,10,000.00 - 10,83,25,387.52
= 2,41,84,612.48

PROFIT SALES RATIO = Profit/Sales x 100 = **18.00 %**

RATE OF RETURN = Operating Profit/T.C.I. x 100 = **34.06 %**

BREAK EVEN POINT (B.E.P.) = 50.14 %

15

FOUNTAIN PENS

INTRODUCTION

Fountain pens are very well known for writing on papers, exercise books etc. Fountain pens use inks of desired colour and gloss and other properties for writing ink is filled into the pen tank through the open end. This end, in turn, is fitted with nib and lip assembly that regulates the flow of ink from the tank to the nib-tip which from nib-tip comes into the contact with paper surface being used for writing by hand.

Several ink verieties are in use mfd. under different brand names. Black and royal blue ink colours are commonly used in pens followed by red and green w.r.t. quantity being consumed at arge.

Earlier the sheet formed metallic nibs with welded irridium tip were used but the pen designs has undergone a vast change. Today, micro tip pens, ceramic/ metallic ball pens etc., have become quite popular; however the demand for fountain pens is always at rise. Education persons feel fountain pens as their essential weapon to carry with wherever they are. It is so because, use of pens can be necessiated at any point of time besides its scheduled use at the reading/writing table at home, in the office, etc.

USES & APPLICATIONS

Fountain pens are very commonly known stationery items which need not explanation regarding their uses. Literate people know the best use of fountain pens.

PROPERTIES

Fountain pens, and for that matter, all other pens are the stationery items of, mass consumption. Pen industry is a composite plant in which assembly of complete pen requires a number of ancillary components.

Fountain pen body can be made of plastics material solely by injection moulding or of some iron-corrosive metal. Metallic body is normally made by deep drawing of sheet metal or by forming & welding the seam. In either case, the body has an open side with internal threading for fixing the nib assembly holder and outer threading for securing the pen cover when it is not in use.

This pen body serves as the reservoir/tank for liquid ink for regular writing. Ink in a conventional nib type fountain is directly filled into this tank and the same ink passes through the passage between tongue & nib of the pen till the ink stock exists.

The body can be one single piece or may be fitted with some auxiliary items like rubber ink tank inside the pen body which is compressed or expanded by pressing a lever by hand in order to fill ink into the rubber tube for maling the pen operative.

Similarly, the pen cover is normally fitted with a clip that helps keeping it stuck-up with the pocket carrying safely.

All the components of a fountain pen need to be mfd. in proper designs, suitable materials and by matching processes followed by suitable finishing treatments prior to their adequate assembly.

RAW MATERIAL & PROCESSES

A wide variety of industrial raw materials are used for mfg. different components of a fountain pen.

1. **Nib-Feeder :-**

This part is made by compression moulding of thermosetting plastic materials. Backelite powder (moulding grade) is most commonly used for the purpose. After shaping the tongue (nib-feeder), it is buffed. This is an intricate part and needs to be mfd. with every clearity of details. To achieve the highest order of finish on every detail & dimension of this part, good dies, good m/c, and good working condition is necessary besides tested good quality raw material used.

2. **Pen Body (Ink Tank) :-**

Normally high density poly ethylene (HDPE), low density polyethylene (LDPE) or high impact polystyrene (HIP) are the main types of plastics used for mfg. the fountain pen body in transparent, translucent or opaque sections. The body is normally tapered cylinder, perfect cylinder or streamline shapes.

3. **Pen Cap :-**

The cap is made of LDPE or HDPE with attractive colour pattern to match the body colour. Quite often, the caps are made of metal sheets/strips. Generally brass or stainless steel sheets are used for mfg. pen caps. If CR-MS-sheet is used, it must be nickel/chromium coated for corrosion-resistance. Hard chrome plate is a guarantee against scratch and it can also be mildly coloured for attractive look. The pen body and its caps are mfd. by injection moulding if these components are to be made in thermoplastics materials.

4. **Pen Clip or Handle :-**

On the tail end of the pen cap, a metallic or plastic handle is provided which is linged centrally on the cap end. For this fitting, an internally threaded hole is provided in the cap. This hole has its axis (centre line) coinciding with the pen axis. A backelite screw or metallic screw can be used to assemble the chip with the pen cap.

5. **Other Components :-**

If the fountain is of tank type, then, its internal space in the body serves as ink tank which can be directly re-filled when the ink exhausts in the course of writing. But, if it is of pump type, then, a rubber tube is fitted with the nib-holder which actuates by a lever action by hand.

6. **Finishing Operation :-**

The metallic components are subjected to mechanical & chemical cleaning followed by surface coating. Mechanical cleaning may include fine grinding, sanding, buffing & polishing. Chemical cleansing includes etching, degreasing, pickling/neutralizing & process drying etc.

7. **Assembly :-**

At the completion of all the parts-mfg. processes, the individual components are tested and test results are systematically recorded for reference in future. Components are manufactured in lots. Test-pieces are selected at random from a lot in conformity with the relevant B.I.S.-guidelines and tested as per the method specified.

PROCESS FLOW DIAGRAM

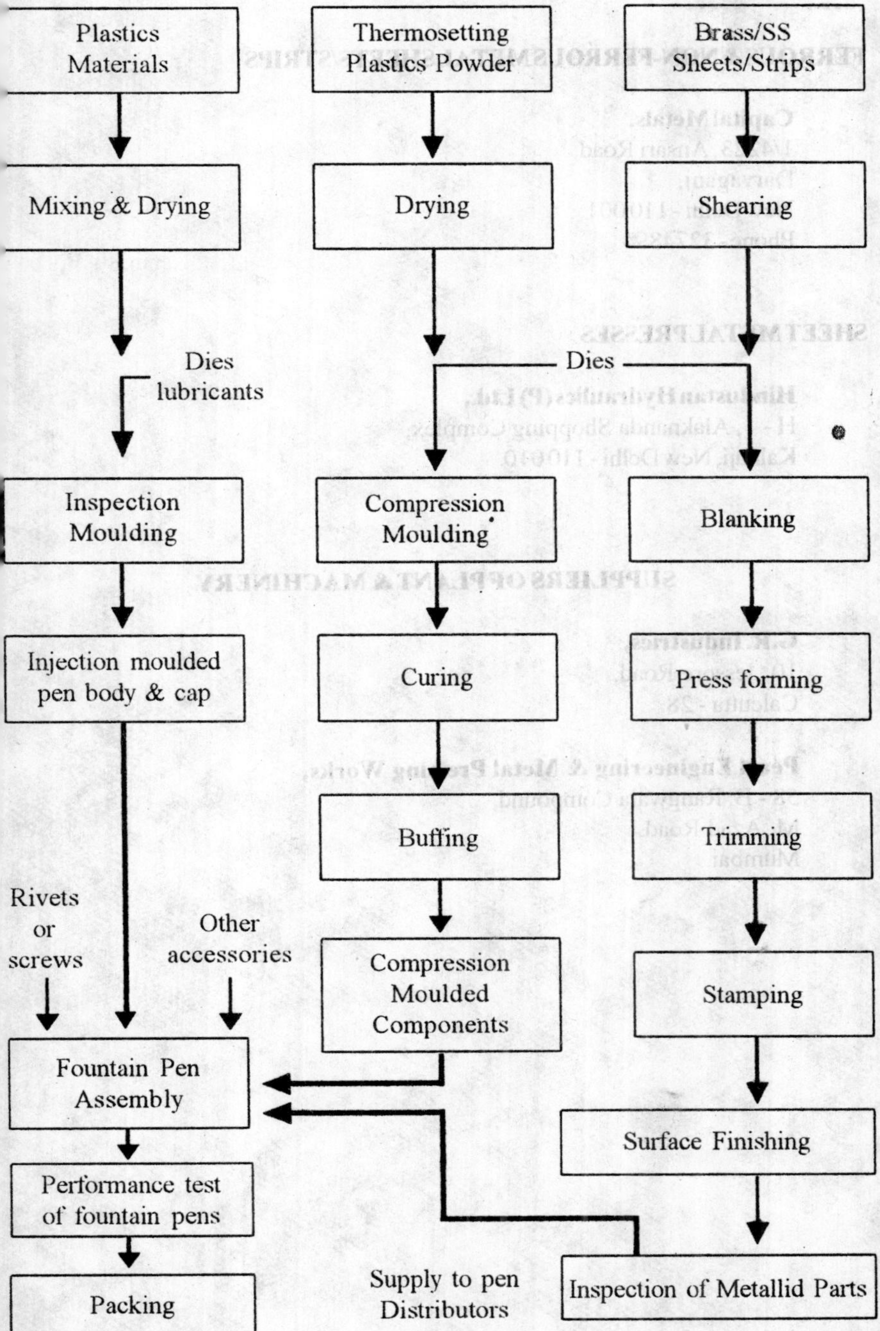

SUPPLIERS OF RAW MATERIALS

FERROUS & NON-FERROUS METAL SHEETS/STRIPS

Capital Metals,
1/4223, Ansari Road,
Daryaganj,
New Delhi - 110001
Phone - 3274894

SHEET METAL PRESSES

Hindustan Hydraulics (P) Ltd.,
H - 1, Alaknanda Shopping Complex,
Kalkaji, New Delhi - 110010

SUPPLIERS OF PLANT & MACHINERY

G.R. Industries,
10, Jessore Road,
Calcutta - 28.

Pearl Engineering & Metal Pressing Works,
58 - B, Rangwala Compound,
M. Azad Road,
Mumbai.

PLANT ECONOMICS OF FOUNTAIN PENS

Rated Plant Capacity = 3,00,000.00 Nos./Annum

COST OF LAND & BUILDING

(Total land area required 400 sq. mtr.) Rs. 12,00,000.00

LIST OF PLANT & MACHINERY

1. Injection moulding machines (automatic)
2. Manually operated compression moulding machines
3. Barrel type Buffing machines with 1/2 H.P. motor & Acessories
4. Bench type power press
5. Hand Fly presses, motorised shearing machines and press tools
6. Nib-point press welding, point grinding & point polishing machines
7. Point slitting machines
8. Automatic Nib - fitting & Cap-Clip fitting machines
9. High speed mixing & colouring machine
10. Zinc/Copper/Chromium/Nickel electroplating plant
11. Automatic Gold plating plant
12. Material handling/Testing equipment
13. Pollution Treatment system
14. Miscellaneous

LIST OF RAW MATERIALS

1. HDPE/LDPE compounds for Injection moulding
2. Thermo setting plastic powder - compounds
3. CR - MS. Sheet
4. Cold rolled brass sheets
5. Stainless steel sheet (Imported)
6. Irridium balls for nib - tips
7. Cleaning, electroplating chemicals buffing compounds & polishing formulations.
8. Packaging materials
9. Miscellaneous consumables

FIXED CAPITAL

Land & Building	Rs.	12,00,000.00
Plant & Machinery	Rs.	20,00,000.00
Other Fixed Assets	Rs.	12,00,000.00
TOTAL	**Rs.**	**44,00,000.00**

TOTAL WORKING CAPITAL/MONTH

Raw Material	Rs.	3,00,000.00
Salary & Wages	Rs.	1,16,619.00
Utilities & Overheads	Rs.	45,000.00
TOTAL	**Rs.**	**4,61,619.00**

TOTAL CAPITAL INVESTMENT

Total Fixed Capital	Rs.	44,00,000.00
Total Working Capital for 3 Months	Rs.	13,84,857.00
TOTAL	**Rs.**	**57,84,857.00**

TURNOVER/ANNUM

1. By sales of Chrome/Nickel plated Nibs
2. Gold Plated Fountain pen Nibs
3. Fountain pen Feeders 6 lakh Nos.
4. Fountain pens complete 3 lakh Nos.

TOTAL **Rs. 93,00,000.00**

PROFIT = RECEIPTS - COST OF PRODUCTION
= 93,00,000.00 - 74,98,735.40
= 18,01,264.60

PROFIT SALES RATIO = Profit/Sales x 100 = **19.37 %**

RATE OF RETURN = Operating Profit/T.C.I. x 100 = **31.14 %**

BREAK EVEN POINT (B.E.P.) = 60.06 %

16

FOUNTAIN PEN NIB

INTRODUCTION

Fountain pen nibs form an integral part of a fountain that uses writing ink for writing on paper of various qualities. Nibs are produced separetly and in their finished form, nibs are fitted into the writing end of the fountain pen. Nibs are classified as (i) fine (ii) medium & (iii) coarse writing types. This classification is based on the width of the nib-tip. Nib body is formed from brass or stainless steel strips of 32 swg thickness and tipped with a ball or a suitable non-corrosive hard metal block. Normally, iridium alloy or USMO or Tingstencobalt-chromium alloy tips are used. Nibs are available in Gold & Planium coated finish. As the-education is rising in the country, the demand for all stationery items, including foutain pen, ball-pen & other special purpose pens, is bound to increase at a fast pace. If so, the future of nib industry is bright.

The fountain pen nibs which was developed in Japan made its debut at the stationery sample fair in 1961 bringing about the present book. The manufacture of fountain pen nibs may be said to have been achieved to the present level through Japan's superior technique.

As for the structure of the fountain, pen nibs, the fibrous matter which constitues the wick is made a bundle of synthetic fibres. The hydrate ink solution is cmposed in such a way the ink does not run even when written on thin paper. Moreover, the ink dries instantly.

The fibrous ink reservoir is also a manufactured protected by a mouth piece, the writting end is instabilised.

The wick utilizes anti-wear and chemical resistance properties which are the features of synthetic fibres. Accordingly, there is not need for reshaving due to wear. Nor is any damage likely to occur due to corrosion.

Ink is fully stored in the fibrous wick set assembly which automatically and smoothly causes ink to flow out via the wick by a capilliary action. Fibrous products such as wick, ink resevoir and fibrous wick set assembly which automatically and smmothly causes ink to flow out via the wick by a capillary action.

MANUFACTURING PROCESS

The manufacture of fountain pen nibs includes the following operations :-

1. Metal sheets shearing into narrow strips.
2. Multi cavity blanking die sets making
3. Nib blanks separation from sheared narrow strips
4. Multi-cavity drawing/cold forming die sets
5. Nib body forming under the two die-halves fitted to the suitable press's ram & bolster.
6. Ink passage slit making at the writing-end of the nib.
7. Centre hole puching in the body
8. Stamping the brand name & other details on the nib surface under press.
9. Attaching irridium tips to the writing-end of the nib by welding.

   At the end of all these mechanical processes, the nibs are washed, degreased and pickled followed by drying.

10. The nib slit central run from the tip end down to the central hole of the nib.

11. Finally the buffing & polishing operations are used for surface finishing of the nibs. These nibs may or may not be electroplated with gold or nickel or platinium before packaging & supply.

MACHINERY SUPPLIERS OF

G.R. Industries,
10, Jessore Road,
Calcutta - 28.

Pearl Engineering & Metal Pressing Works,
58 - B, Rangwala Compound,
M. Azad Road,
Mumbai.

SUPPLIERS OF FERROUS & NON-FERROUS METAL SHEETS/STRIPS

Capital Metals,
1/4223, Ansari Road,
Daryaganj,
New Delhi - 110 002
Phone - 3274894

Chopra Brothers,
297, Inside Ajmerigate,
Delhi - 110 006
Phone - 732396

SHEET METAL PRESSES

Hindustan Hydraulics (P) Ltd.,
H - 1, Alaknanda Shopping Complex,
Kalkaji, New Delhi - 110019

PLANT ECONOMICS OF FOUNTAIN PEN NIB

Rated Plant Capacity = 30,00000 Nibs/Annum

COST OF LAND & BUILDING

(Total land area required 500 sq. mtr.) Rs. 13,00,000.00

LIST OF PLANT & MACHINERY

1. Sheet shearing machine (48") treadle type with feed table & sheared straps collection pan,racks, etc.
2. Bench type power presses with 3 H.P. and 2 H. P motor drive & accessories
3. Hand fly presses
4. Automatic nib tip welding machine
5. Point slitting machine
6. Point grinding machine
7. Buffing & polishing machine
8. A compact gold plating plant
9. Ready press tools
10. Material handling/testing eqpts.
11. Miscellaneous

LIST OF RAW MATERIALS

1. Cold rolled Brass Sheets
2. Stainless Steel/sheets
3. Osmo Irridium Ball for nib tips
4. Gold plating salt (Cyanited) and other plating bath chemicals
5. Packaging materials & miscellaneous stores

FIXED CAPITAL

Land & Building	Rs.	13,00,000.00
Plant & Machinery	Rs.	11,00,000.00
Other Fixed Assets	Rs.	4,00,000.00
TOTAL	**Rs.**	**28,00,000.00**

TOTAL WORKING CAPITAL/MONTH

Raw Material	Rs.	2,00,000.00
Salary & Wages	Rs.	54,872.00
Utilities & Overheads	Rs.	45,000.00
TOTAL	**Rs.**	**2,99,872.00**

TOTAL CAPITAL INVESTMENT

Total Fixed Capital	Rs.	28,00,000.00
Total Working Capital for 3 Months	Rs.	8,99,616.00
TOTAL	**Rs.**	**36,99,616.00**

TURN OVER/ANNUM

1. By sales of Fountain Pen Nibs of the following qualities:
   Nickel plated stainless steel Nibs
2. Plain/Chrome plated Brass Nibs
3. Gold/Platinum Coated Nibs **Rs. 72,50,000.00**

PROFIT = RECEIPTS - COST OF PRODUCTION

= 72,50,000.01 - 46,36,075.20

= 26,13,924.81

PROFIT SALES RATIO = Profit/Sales x 100 = **36.05 %**

RATE OF RETURN = Operating Profit/T.C.I. x 100 = **70.15 %**

BREAK EVEN POINT (B.E.P.) = 37.19 %

17

GEOMETRY BOX (Mathematical Instruments)

INTRODUCTION

Geometry Box is a new approach of its inventor Sri Chacko Varghese from Ernakulam, kerala to the basic calculations and measuring device of scientific and industrial importance. Till now, various means of drawing, drafting, measuring, checking are invented depending on various systems like electronic, magnetic, electro-magnetic or mechanical etc. Almost all these device are based on two dimensional systems.

Geometry Box has been invented with the view of doing all two dimensional measures and also is capable of handling three dimensional problems. It can be diversified as manual or electronically operated device. The idea is to commercialize the manually operated "Geodrafters" first and then developing electronic/automatic Geocom (uter's) for various institutions/industries/trades.

INDUSTRIAL PROSPECTS

Geometry Box is the device to be used by artist/draftsmen, workmen, engineers, students and teachers, surveyors etc. It is used to measure high accuracy angle - aiming, high - frequency sky - scrapper - skeletoning apart from the jobs done by almost all the existing major instruments like angle-gauges, varnier caplipers, sextants, drawing and drafting board machines etc.

India is a fast developing country and major break-through achieved during last decade is the field of science and technology besides basic educations.

The number of technocrats and artisans are increasing very rapidly and so the progress of work. This requires a lot of improved devices to measure, check, calculations and trigometric is problems handling. The answer for all these requirements is Geometry Box is in the process of patent-instruments. These instruments cover scientific. These instruments cover scientific, surveying, optical instruments, laboratory analytical instruments and mathematical instruments.

RAW MATERIAL SUPPLIERS

Printing Inks :

Baluja Spectra
C-50 Okhla Indl. Area-II, New Delhi - 110 020
Phone/fax: 6835715, 6835722

Ajanta Ink Company
Basai Road, Gurgaon (Haryana)
Phone/fax: 8-330028

Van Inks & Chemicals (P) Ltd.
B-150, Phase-II, Noida-201 305 (U.P.)
Phone/fax: 567141, 011-8-521507

Paints & Varnishes:

Associated Paints & Chemicals
Near U.C. College,
Alwaye, Kerala.

New Paints & Rubber Industries
Industrial Estate,
Ollur.

Plastic Dies :

Unique (India) Dies
13, Sainath Industrial Estate No. 2
Goregaon East, Mumbai - 400 063

Fibreglass/Fibreglass Products :

Airwell Engg. Corporation
Safaid Pool, Vassanji Road,
Mumbai - 400 072

PLANT AND MACHINERY SUPPLIERS

Cutting Tools and Other Machines:

Wud Tools,
G.P.O. Box - 90 A, Dada Manzil,
67-69, Mohmedaly Road,
Mumbai - 400 003

Power Presses:

Surjit Industries
4/6, Industrial Area,
Kirti Nagar,
New Delhi - 110 015
Phone : 531 070

Shearing Machines:

J.K. Industries
41, Shivaji Marg,
Industrial Area,
New Delhi - 110 015
Phone : 534 788, 531 244

Lathe Machineries:

Jay Jay Cee Engg. Corpn.,
308/1, Shahzada Bagh,
Old Rohtak Road,
Delhi - 110 035

18

GREETING CARDS BY OFFSET PRINTING

INTRODUCTION

Greeting is the expression of ones feeling towards kindlness, of other person. Greeting becomes the usual practice of human beings. These days we usually greets other person with the expression of good morning with a smile. Others ways of greeting the other person is with the shower of flower of glanding the person to be greeted, sometime we greet with presentation like toys, bunch of flower (boyquet) interesting books, pens etc.,

Besides above , we express our feeling with the greeting card. The invention of greeting card was from greek..

These greeting cards are the symbol of the expression of printed on the good quality paper with the picture of colourful flowers, scenery of gardens, parks, Mills tation, Historical buildings, Artistic view, and many other things like " *good Wishes*" "*Happy New Years*" "*Happy Christmas Day*" , & *Happy Birthday*" etc.,

These greetings cards are produced by two types of printing. some greeting cards are produced with Intoglio or Gravu printing process and most of Greeting cards today are produced on planographic or lithographcy process which these days known as offset printing process.

COMPARISON OF THE PRINTING PROCESSES

Lithographing is an idieal process for text and pretorial reproduction for short and medium runs that are sheet fed or web fed upto 10^6 impressions letter press printing is good for text matter, flexibility, broad, lettring, solid backgrounds and large expanse of colour from short to long runs. Gravuze printing is best for long run pictorial reproduction such as magazine , mail order catalogues and packaging. Research in these and other processes e.g. flexography and waterless lithography, could result in improvements that could change these use catagories radically. Other printing processes , e.g. ink-jet and electronic printing could be completive with lithography, letterpress, flexography or gravure printings.

CHARACTERISTICS OF OFFSET PRESS

The offset press is characterised by the following important advantages over other printing methods:

1. The rubber printing surface conform to irregularities in the paper surface. Less printing pressure is needed, and print quality is improved. Half tons of high quality can be printed on rough papers.

2. Paper does not come into contact with the metal printing plate. Therefore, the plate is les subjected to abrasive wear and can run much longer editions.

3: Speed of printing is increase. The offset of press improvements on printing speeds in shwon by the following statisties for offset presses:-

Press	Printing Speed, Impressions/Hour
Litho Hand - Proving Press	10-20
Litho Power-Proving Press	1200
Direct Rotary Press (Hand fed)	2000
Rotary Offset Press (Stream fed)	upto 15000
Web Offset Press (Roll-fed)	upto 60000

4. The image on an offset printing plate roads right instead of in reverse or wrong reading. This facilitates both and and chemical photomechancial preparation.

5. Less ink required for equal coverege. This reduces trapping problems and decrease the tendancy of the printed sheet to smudge and set off, ie. produce mirror image on the back, in the delivery pile. Also, drying is quicker.

PROCESSOFMANUFACTURE

The steps involves in the offset printing of greeting cards are as follows:-

Design and Layout
Image Generation
Copy Preparation of the Camera
Photography
Colour Scanning
Slripping and Platemaking
Offset Press Operation
Finishing

DESIGN&LAYOUT

All designers follow certain basic ideas in planning and laying out a printed piece. These ideas serve as a starting point and as guides rather than hard and fast rules. The five basic elements of design are balance , rhythm, contrast, proportion and unity. Two other factors, colours, and type style, also affect the design of the printed piece.

Balance Basically , there are two methods of achieving balance. formal balance has elements of equal weight placed on both sides of an imaginory vertical centre line on the page. Informal balance gives an illusion of equal weights on both sides of an imaginary vetical centre line. a design is balanced by use of colour or different wieght of type, by placement of the elements or by using ohter design principles. Different kinds of balance create different feelings.

Formal balance, for example, for example. Can give a feeling of performance, dignity, tradition, strength, security, or oder,. In formal balance on the other emphasize the novelty and originality.

Rythem:-

Rhythem is that element of design that directs the reader's eye in a certain direction over a printed pice. Placing the elements vertically leads the eye in a vertical direction, horizontal positioning directs the eye in a horizontal direction. When used property, rhythem relates the messages forcefully and directly. Improperly used, rhythem may move.

The readers too quickly to next message.

Contrast :-

Contrast creates interest in the printed piece by providing veriety in the design. The designer adds contrast by changing colours, shapes, weights, sizes and similar facter in by out. Contrast may also be achieved by varying the type style. Under-scoring, changing the type weight size or face, using capital or small letter , adding colour , reversing the type, using tints or bracketing the words are some of the variations possibles.

Proportions:-

How the parts of a page relates to one another and to the whole is called proportion. All our lifes we have been exposed to materials printed in good proportion. Since the time of the ancient greeks, the 3 to 5 ratio, sometimes called the " Golden Rectangle" has been used in design throughout the world because of its pleasing proportions, Generally printing pages are longer in one dimension than the other. Greeting cards, for example come in standard size of 3x5, 4x6, 5x7, in dus. a square shape (equal in height and width) is seldom used for printed materials because it is static and uninteresting.

Unity:-

Unity hold the design together through the use of similar shapes , similar type styles, or similar colours. All elements should look as if they belog together.

Colour:-

Colour usually adds interest to a printed price and makes a design more attractive. It also presents some new problems for the designer. Some colour look good together; others appear to clash or greate a disturbing feeling. Colours can also create moods. For example red orange, and yellow seems to be warm and exciting, while green and blue are considered cool and calm. A good designr will use there principles to advantage.

Type:-

The printed word is the heart of the message you want to communicate. The type style or the design of the teller choosen, helps communicate the message. Type can be classified in siz main styles, roman, sqare seriff, sans serif, seript, text, and occasional or speciality types.

LAYOUTPRINCIPLES

A layout is to the printer what a blue print is to be contractor. It describes in detail what is to be done to complete the printed job. There are there type of layouts. Thumbail rough, and comprehensive.

Thumbanail layout is the first step in designing a printed price. It is a rough , quick sketch generally not drawn to scale. It presents designers first ideas. The rough layout is the next step in design. The design is there more carefully refined and drawn to scale to be right for the job. After rough layout, comprehensive layout is done. It is done by using drafting instruments to prepare drafting istruments to prepare a comprehensive layout as close as possible to the final printed product or the same paper that will be used for the final printing or white cardboard.

Image Generations:-

Image generation or type setting type characteritics to make up words, sentence and paragraphs for the printed prices.

The two basics methods of producing type are hot type composition, using cast metal, and cold type decomposition, which includes direct impression and photosetting. Hot types includes direct impression and photosetting.

Hot types includes all cast metal type whether set by hand or malchine cold type reffers to all other methods of setting type by a direct impression such as typewriter type, hand assembled alphabets, and phtoprocessors. In recent years, typesetting has probably changed more than any other aspects of offset lithography. At present, a large number of offset units gets their phto-type done from service units.

COPYPREPARATION

Once the printed price is designed, the illustrations choosen, and the type set, all the elements can be put together in to a single composite, called a mechanical this process is called paste-up. After pasteup, it is hand over to proof reader. The make certain corrections and then it is again reset. The tools and materials required for paste up is the browing board, or T-square, clear plastic triagnles, 45^0 and 30^0 - 60^0 - 90^0, ruler or scalem, marked in both under and mm. Cutting tools, scissors, light blue non- reproducing pencils for marking guidelies, writting and drawing pencils, black pens with various sizes of points, grease penuts, clean, white or hard gum creasens marking tapes and transparent tape, conpass, french curves, opaque brushes, opague fluid and any special materials needed for a particular Machancial or paste up.

Photography:

Photography is a way of recording an image. This recorded image used to make a printing plate. Some plate making methods require negatives and other require positives.

Some are reverse reading on the emulsion side and some are straight on the reading, depending on the pointing process. the photographic materials can be continus tone, line , or half tone. Many of the materials and techniques used in process photography are similar to those in photography.

Colour Scanning:

To print a full colour price as the eye sees it, each colour must be filtrered out, Additive primery filters are used, the break white light into primary colours, red and blue. When added together, those three colours have the potential of creating any colour visible to the eye.

For example, when a red filter over a camera lense is place, a negative record of all the red light reflected from original. The result is a red filter separation negative in which the clear area are a true record of the other two additive colour (blue and green). When blue and green light are mixed, a colour called cyan results.

In the same way, a green filter will yeild a printer that records the additive primary colours red and blue. When red and blue lights are mixed, magneta results.

The blue filter works in the same way to produce a negative record of all the blue in the subject. The clar areas left, record the red and green colours, which when mixed, from yellow. This negative then become the yellow printer.

The three colours cyan, magnets and yellow are called the substractive primary colours because each represents the two additive primaries left afte one primary has beeb substracted from the white light. Cyan, magneto and yellow are the colours of process inks and used for process color reproduction .

Stripping and Plate Making:

When the photo conversion is produced, the assembeled negatives into a unit flat for stipping anmd then plate is made offset printing works.

Stripping:

Different techniques may be used for stripping. The important thing to remember is that the end results depend on the negatives being sassembled on the gold enrold sheet in the proper oposition., Many lithographers use the following method:

1. Place a gold sheet on the light table with the head of the sheet within at the top or towards the left.

2. Line up the making sheet with the T-sqare some masking sheets, particularly for small press come gridded with guidelines already drawn on them. Larger presses require the stipper to mark gripper margins centre lines, and other necessary guidelines. The follwing information is based on the use of gridded goldenrold sheets.

3. The tape is goldenrod sheet down along the top endge only ,

4. Locate the paper are to be printed on the masking sheet and mark the exact position of the image. The iamge area must not extend into the gripper matrgin or the making sheet because this area will nto print when the plate is burned.

5. Carefully side the negative, emulsion side down, under the masking sheet. Emulsion side down means that type copy will appear correctly: it will be right reading. On halftones you can determine the emulsion side of the negative by observing the texture of the surface. On most negatives the emulsion side will have slightly flat or dull finsih.On some halftones, however, this is not true. If scaratched on the emulsion side, a mark will show. You will have to scratch the negative in a non image non -printing are to determine the emusion side.

6. Place the negative in the proper position in the area marked on the goldenrod sheet. Align the negative with a T-square and triangle or follow the gridded lines on the goldenrod sheet.

7. Once the negative is aligned, hold the negative and goldenrod sheet down with onehand , and iwth the other hand cut foodball whapped holes in non image area,. Be careful not to cut through the negative. Apply red lighographer's tape over the holes, to hole the negative and goldenrod together.

Plate Making:

After the flat has been prepared, an offset plate is made from it for the press. Many different types of presentizd plates can be used for this operation. Most shops use a negative acting additive plate, which will be discussed here. Most of these plates are either metal or foil types.

The negative -acting additive plate is exposed in a plate maker. This platemaker is usually a vaccum frame to hold negative and plate in very tight contact and a source of high-intensity light. Because the light on a platemaker is so strong, it can damage eyes.

OFFSET PRESS OPERATION

Offset presses are rotary in nature and use the principle that gressts and water do not misc to deliver the desired impressions on paper.

The printing section of the press includes a plate cylinder, an impression cylinder a blanket cylinder, inking rollers, a moisture system and a plate adjustment (Registration) devices. In addition of course, it has a feeder system to move the paper into the press and a delivery system for the finished work.

That all material to be printed is on one thinflat, and pliable plate is one of the virtues of the offset proces. Make ready is no problem, and the plate is easily apped around, the plate cylinde much in the fashion that amimeggraph stencil is applied.

Once the plate is on the press the operator must apply, the moisture (water plus an additive) to the surface of the plate. The water adheres to the nonimage area of the plate and is repelled in the image areas. When ink a grease, is applied it adheres only to the image area and is repelled by the water wat portions. Because of the water grease action and its photographic nature, offset printing is considered a chemical process.

It is called an indirect process because impression are not made directly from the plate.the plate never touches the paper, instead it deposits the inked image on the blanket cylinder with each revolution.

The paper receives the image from the blenket cylender as the sheet or web goes through the press between the blanket and impression cylinders. The impression cylinders is simply the surface backing up the paper as the blanket squezes against it serving the same function as the platen in a typewriter or the bed of a traditional flat bed press.

Each revolution of an offset press therefore consists of:-

1. Application of greasy ink to the image areas of the plate.
2. Application of greasy ink to the image areas of the plate.
3. Trasfer of the ink image to a rubber, blanketted cylinder.
4. Pickup of the paper by the feeding system of the press which inserts the paper between the blanket and impression cylinders.
5. Deposit of the image from the blanket to the paper.
6. Delivery of the sheets or web of paper.

Although is may seem to be a lengthy series of a lengthy series of details. It is accomplished instantenously. Because offset presses operates on the rotary principle, they are capable of extremely high speed. In general their speed, are basically determined by the efficiency of their feeding and deliver system the cylinders can rotate as fast as an electric motor can turn a drive a shaft.

The most frequent problem in connection with offset press operation is the maintenance of a proper balance of moisture and ink change in humidity sometimes, give pressure a change in humidity sometimes give pressure a great deal of difficult in this regard.

A cross section of an offset press indicating the various system.

Finishing:

As printed cards come from the press, they usually require further operations to prepare them for use. These operations may be cutting, folding, collating, binding packaging. etc.

Paper Weights and Sizes:

Paper is sold by the Kgs hundered kgs, or by tones (1000kgs). Some company sells the paper sell the paper by number of varying size.

The price of paper depends on the kind of paper, quality and economic conditions. They are purchased the market in dimension of 28" x 22" size, 26" x 16" size with varying in the weight by 75,80,85,90,95,100, 110,120,130,140 etc, gram per square meter other paper characteristics:-

In addition to size and weight , other characteristics mus tbe considered in the selection of paper. They include colour, strength, strench, and opacity. Colours even mill to mill, vary in whitners. so, it is better to order to company that produced the original.

Papers also vary in strength depending on how the fibers are interminglesd. This important for web fed offset. All pape rwill stretch a cetain amount. This is more important in finer printing. Paper capacity is related to the thickness of the sheet and the fillers that have been added when the paper was made. a lithanium compound is often added to increase the opacity. If the stock is to be printed a both sides, high opacity is important.

PLANT & MACHINERY SUPPLIERS

Offset Printing Machines:

Victor Engg. Works
C-1/357, GIDC Estate,
ODHAV Road, ODHAV,
Ahmedabad-382415 (Gujrat)

Amit International
B-47, Cox House, Naraina Indl. Area,
Phase - II, New Delhi - 110 028
Phone/fax : 570 4301, 570 4201/011-224 9320

Diamond Engg. Works
6/12, DLF, Indl. Area,
Moti Nagar, New Delhi - 110 015
Phones : 541 4571, 541 8352

Dominent Offset (P) Ltd.
Palam Road, Gurgaon.
Phone/fax : 340019, 341916, 341917, 341918, 340032/0124-340131

Bharat Machine Tools
133-138, Sector 6,
Faridabad.
Phones : 8-241798, 241167

Paper Cutter:

MSL Graphics
15, J.N. Heredia Marg,
Ballard Estate,
Mumbai - 400038
Telex:-262711-13

RAW MATERIAL SUPPLIERS ADDRESS

Offset Printing Ink Suppliers:

Baluja Spectra
C-50 Okhla Indl. Area-II,
New Delhi - 110020
Phone/fax : 6835715, 6835722

Ajanta Ink Company
Basai Road, Gurgaon.
(Haryana) Phone/fax : 8-330028

Art Printing Inks Company
104 Site-4, Indl. Area,
Sahibabad, Ghaziabad.
Phone/fax : 767882

Inks India (Delhi)
C-49, Sector-8,
Noida-201 301 (U.P.)
Phone/fax : 523801, 011-8-557270

Van Inks & Chemicals (P) Ltd.
B-150, Phase-II,
Noida-201 305 (U.P.)
Phone/fax : 567141, 011-8-521507

Art Paper Suppliers:

Om Prakash Jitendra Kumar & Company
63, Darya Ganj,
New Delhi - 11 00 02.
Phones : 326 96 80, 3271380

Narain Paper Mart
4034/3, Haryana Market,
Chawri Bazar, Delhi - 11 00 06
Phone : 291 51 35

Himgiri Paper Products
B-24, Indl. Area Lawrence Road,
New Delhi - 110035
Phone : 718 9005

PLANT ECONOMICS OF GREETING CARDS BY OFFSET PRINTING

Rated Plant Capacity = 20,000:00 Nos./Day

COST OF LAND & BUILDING

(Total land area required 500 sq. mtr)	Rs.	3,41,000.00

LIST OF PLANT & MACHINERY

1. Plate process 24x28 vaccum printer complete with all accessores
2. Single colour sheet bed offset press size 22x31 (560x790)complete with all accessories.
3. Miscellaneous equipments, light table, drawing board, T square, metal trianges, plastic clear trangles scissors.
4. Paper cutting machine(semi-automatic) Size 32" complete with all standard equipments.
5. Miscellaneous tools and jigs weihig balance etc. laboratory equipment

LIST OF RAW MATERIALS

1. Arts paper of dimension (26x22) 2250 kg.
2. Offset ink 200 kg.
3. Fount, 18 litre
4. De sensitisor, 18 litre
5. Blanket cleaning, 18 litre
6. Metal Plate (anodised aluninium) size 22x31 av. Life /plate 10000/- coppies
7. Paper, paper plates, sheets, for stripping, designing layout, typing etc.
8. Rubber Blanket
9. Miscellaneous like gum, tape pins etc.

FIXED CAPITAL

Land & Building	Rs.	3,41,000.00
Plant & Machinery	Rs.	9,00,000.00
Other Fixed Assets	Rs.	1,14,000.00
TOTAL	**Rs.**	**13,55,000.00**

TOTAL WORKING CAPITAL/MONTH

Raw Material	Rs.	2,45,343.00
Salary & Wages	Rs.	14,924.00
Utilities & Overheads	Rs.	35,000.00
TOTAL	**Rs.**	**2,95,267.00**

TOTAL CAPITAL INVESTMENT

Total Fixed Capital	Rs.	13,55,000.00
Total Working Capital for 3 Months	Rs.	8,85,801.00
TOTAL	**Rs.**	**22,40,801.00**

TURNOVER/ANNUM

By sale of Greeting Cards 3"x5" with one fold 500000 doz.

Rs. 60,00,000.00

PROFIT = RECEIPTS - COST OF PRODUCTION

= 60,00,000.00 - 42,79,597.22

= 17,20,402.78

PROFIT SALES RATIO = Profit / Sales x 100 = **28.67 %**

RATE OF RETURN = Operating Profit / T.C.I. x 100 = **76.28 %**

BREAK EVEN POINT (B.E.P.) = 36.18 %

19

GUMMED TAPE

INTRODUCTION

Gummed paper and cloth tapes are used for the sealing or closing of corrugated or solid fiberboard boxes, paper cartons and small packages. These tapes are also used for reinforcing joints and corners of paperboard boxes. These tapes offer security against pilferage and tampering as they cannot be peeled off without tearing the tape or the material on which they are applied. These tapes are easy to stick and they can be printed or decorated to give excellent advertising value, identification and individuality.

Types:

The standard type of gummed tape consists of a kraft paper backing with an adhesive which can be activated by water. However, some tapes require water and solvent for activation.

The kraft paper used is generally of 60 gm per sq. m. (gsm) but heavier kraft paper of 90 gsm or 140 gsm may also be used for heavier packages. Reinforced tape is made from reinforced kraft which consists of glass, nylon, rayon or sisal fibers embedded in asphalt or rubber-base layer between two layers of kraft. Cloth impregnated with clay or laminated to kraft may also be used as backing material.

Gummer bi-directionally reinforced tap can be applied in the 'two-strip' method of closure for corrugated boxes. This method required only one strip of tape on top and bottom compared to three strips of tape on top and bottom in the conventional 'six-strip' method of sealing. A strippable version of reinforced gummed tape is also available. This allows quick opening of boxes.

Adhesives:

The adhesives commonly used on gummed tapes are animal and fish glues, dextrins, water soluble natural gums and some synthetic resins or combinations of these. Animal glues are the most important for this purpose; they are made from either hide flashing or animal bones. Hide glues of about 150 gm gel strength and bone glues of about 70 gm gel strength re used; their average viscosities are 70 and 40 cps respectively. the quantity of glue required depends on gel strength; the higher the strength the lesser will be the quantity required. Special adhesive formulations are employed for water resistance, extra strength and application to cold surface.

Dry animal glue is quite and for this reason plasticizers such as glycerin, glucose etc. are used in the adhesives mix in about 2 to 4 per cent on the dry weight of the animal glue. Fish glue imparts the quick tack needed for tapes used on high speed automatic machines, preservatives such as zinc sulfate and chlorinated phenols are added to prevent spoilage. Dextrins are added at about 10% in animal glue to reduce cost and to increase its ability to be wetted. Scents may be used to mark the odour of animal glue.

Preparation of Gumming Mix:

For the preparation of the gumming mix a jacketted kettle with agitator is used. Cold water is run into the kettle, the weight of cold water being the same as the weight of glue to be dissolved. the agitator is started. the glue is added slowly to the water so that lump formation does not take place. Agitation is continued for 10 to 15 minutes and then stopped. The glue is soaked for about 1 hour. The water is bated to 60°C and the mixture agitated till the glue is completely dissolved. Other ingredients such as fish glue, plasticizers, preservatives and scents etc. are also added.

The mixture is strained and is ready for use. Care should be taken to ensure that during this mixing and use later on too, the temperature does not exceed 60°C, otherwise the quality of the glue will deteriorate.

For dissolving dextrins for flat gumming and as extenders for glue mines, similar equipment is used with the similar procedure. About 90 per cent of the water to be used is poured in the kettle and agitated, dextrin is then slowly shifted into it so that no lump formation takes place. After the addition of all the dextrin the remaining water is also added. After agitating further for a period of 15 minutes heating is started and the temperature is raised to 85 to 90°C. It is allowed to stand for 1/2 to 1 hour. If any modifiers are to be added , they should be added before this stand by period. If this mix is to be added to the glue solution, it should be cooled before-hand to 60° C. If it is to be used for fiat gumming, it should be strained and allowed to stand for 1-2 days before use.

MANUFACTURING PROCESS

Gummed tapes are manufactured by coating kraft paper roll on side with a water soluble adhesive composition on a gum coating machine. the roll is then dried and wound. The roll is then slit and printed if required.

The gum-coating machine may be of kiss coating tyupe or pressure coating as shown in figure. Kiss coating is easier to apply than the pressure coating.

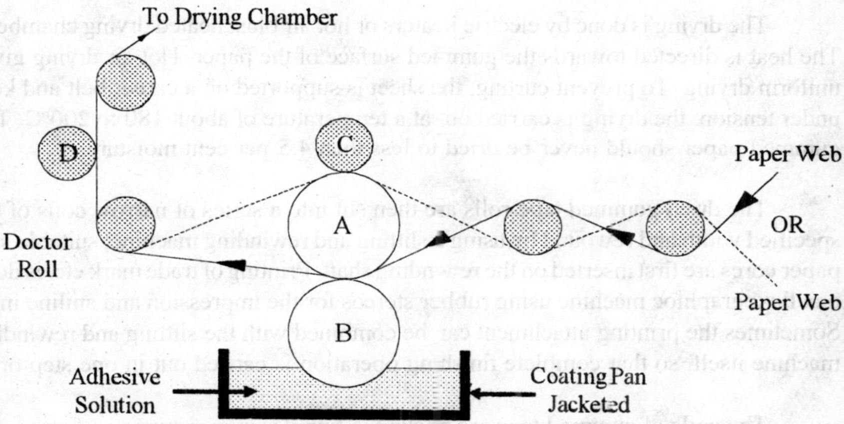

Process for the Manufacture of Gummed Tape

The paper web may follow any of the two paths indicated by full line and dotted line. If the web follows the dotted path, Kiss-coating is produced. However in this case a small, light rubber-covered roll (C) is used to press the paper against the gum applying roll (B) to prevent air from lifting the paper from the face of the surface. This producer gives more uniform coating, because the coating splits as it leaves the nip of rolls A and B and it splits a second line at the nip where the paper leaves the surface of roll A. If the paper web follows the path of the full line, pressure coating is produced. If the rolls A and B are ground true and made of chilled iron, the coating will vary as the paper varies in thickness. If roller A is rubber covered, it will generally produce a more uniform coating. The paper tensioning rolls are driven at a 1 per cent lower speed than the gumming rolls. After the gun is applied to the paper web by the upper gumming rolls, two small brass doctor rolls, driven in opposite directions to the travel of the paper and at one-tenth its speed, help distribute more uniformaly the applied gum. The small diameter rolls reduce the coarse ribs in the coating to finer rins. The coating pan in this machine is a jacketted type with electrical heater and thermo-regulator. The glue temperature is never allowed to exceed 60°C. The glue from the glue tank is constantly fed into this pan and a steady level is maintained, the inner pan is made of copper and the jacket is made of iron.

Pressure coating has the disadvantage of not gumming the paper web uniformly if the paper varies in caliper. the reverse roll coater is prefered for applying gum on the web because it needs no doctor roll and it applioes uniform coating regardless of the variation in the caliper of the web; slack edges are no problem either.

The amount of adhesive used (dry basis) is about 12 to 15 lb/ream for light weight tapes, 15 to 18 lb for medium weight tapes and 17 to 20 lb for heavy weight tapes. Gumming speeds are restricted by rate of drying, usually 50-200 metre/min speed is employed.

The drying is done by electric heaters or hot air blast heated drying chambers. The heat is directed towards the gummed surface of the paper. Hot air drying gives uniform drying. To prevent curling, the sheet is supported on a career belt and kept under tension. the drying is carried out at a temperature of about 180 to 200°C. The gummed paper should never be dried to less than 4.5 per cent moisture.

The dried gummed tape rolls are then slit into a series of narrow coils of the specified width and rewound by using a slitting and rewinding machine; suitable size paper cores are first inserted on the rewinding shaft. Printing of trade mark etc. is done ona flexographioc machine using rubber stereos for the impression and aniline inks. Sometimes the printing attachment can be combined with the slitting and rewinding machine itself, so that complete finishing operation is carried out in one step only.

The coils of gummed tape are packed in bundles in moisture proof strapping such as polythylene film of bituminised kraft paper. the normal trade packing is a bale of 30 reels of 2.5 cm x 27 meters size tape. the bale of 1.25 cm width tapes will contain 60 reals and a bale of 5 cm. width tapes will contain 15 reels, and so on.

20

LAMINATIONS

INTRODUCTION

Laminations are combinations of two or more plies of paper, foil film and fabrics which are combined with the help of an adhesive or laminating agent or by applying heat or pressure. A variety of combinations are possible e.g. paper/foil, paper/PE, paper/paper, foil/film, film/film, paper/fabric, film/fabrics, paper/film/foil.

There are five main laminating processes (a) wet lamination (b) dry lamination (c) heat lamination (d) hot-melt lamination (e) extrusion lamination. These processes may be used either singly or in combination to produce multi-layer laminates.

MANUFACTURINGPROCESS

Wet Lamination:

Wet lamination or wet bonding process consists of applying a water or solvent based adhesive to one of the substrate and then combining it with another substrate or ply before drying the adhesive. This method is only applicable when one or more of the plies are permeable to water or other solvent used in the adhesive formulation so as to allow escape of water or solvent before the plies are joined together. For this reason this method is generally used to laminate paper to other materials e.g. foil or film.

Adhesives commonly used in wet bonding are water based e.g. sodium silicate, starch, casin, polyvinyl acetate emulsion, animal glue, rubber latex etc. Resin emulsions and latex-type adhesives provide a thought and flexible bond plus water resistance and fast drying. Solvent solutions of resins, gums, rubbers etc. may also be used as adhesives. Solvent solutions or lacquer type adhesives are used for laminating substrates which are impervious to water and cannot be laminated with aqueous or emulsion type adhesives. They are suitably for moisture-proof cellophane and varnished or lacquered papers.

The most common example of wet bonding is the ordinary paper-backed foil used in cigarette packaging. It is bonded with sodium silicate. Foil laminated paper is also used for bottle labels, gift wraps, packaging of confectionery etc. Usually foils of 0.00625 mm. to 0.00875 mm. gauges are used for making foil laminated paper. The base paper is usually of 20 to 30 lb. per 3000 sq.ft. or 30 to 45 gms. basis weight.

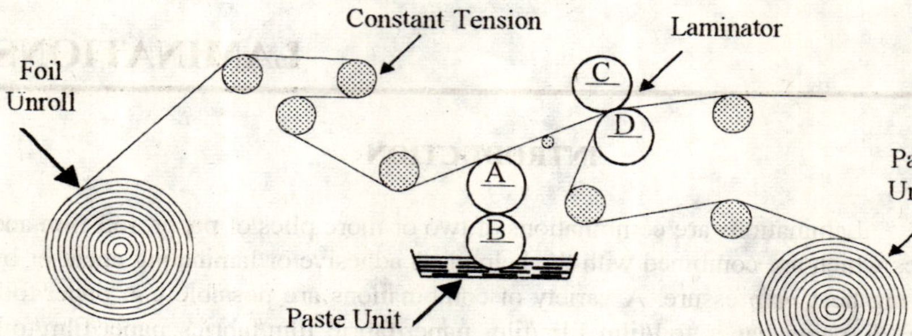

Wet Lamination of foil with Paper

Lamination of foil on paper is done on a laminator consisting of rubber covered and metal rolls. the adhesive is applied by either gravure-roll applicator, three roll nip applicator or kiss roll applicator with post smoothening rolls. The adhesive is generally applied to paper and then foil is laminated with paper by pressing between a set of rubber and metal rolls. The rubber roll is preumatically loaded and the metal roll is usually fixed. The combined web is then passed through a air heated dryer or turnel or by passing it over steam heated cylinders or drums. Drying must be accomplished through paper side to alloy the moisture to escape. Moisture control is very important otherwise curling or blistering may take place. When paper or board is to be bonded with paper or board drying is not generally necessary for the solvent is a absorbed in the substrate. Wet lamination of foil with paper is shown in figure.

Dry Lamination:

In dry lamination or bonding process the adhesive is applied to a ply and dried before bonding it with the second ply by the application of heat or pressure or both. Heat lamination, hot-melt lamination and extrusion lamination are also included in dry bonding but these are discussed separately. Here we will discuss only solvent dry bonding process.

Dry bonding process used acqueous or solvent based adhesives such as resin lacquers, rubber and various solvent cements. The adhesive is applied generally with direct gravure or reverse-kiss roll applicator. The adhesive is properly dried to remove the solvent. The two plies are then joined together in a pressure nip formed by a preumatically loaded rubber roll and a fixed steel roll. The metal roll may be heated in some cases to give a pressure-temperature nip.

Dry bonding process is used for bonding foil to paper or cellophane or other films to paper and paperboard. This method is particularly suitable for combining materials to coarse or rough surface because the adhesive is applied and set before combining and thus the irregularities of the surface may be covered up by using excess adhesive.

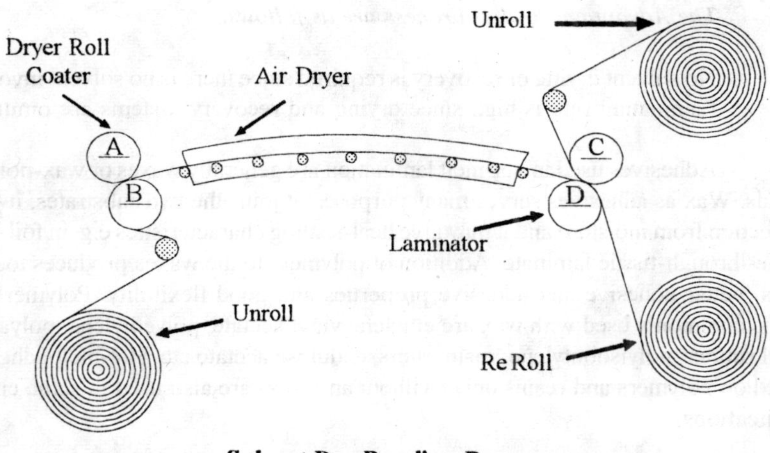

Solvent Dry Bonding Process

Figure shows a typical laminator used for combining cellophane with paper or board. In this laminator the reverse roll application of the adhesive provides a uniform distribution across the web. The arch between the adhesive applying unit and the laminating section prevents wrinkling of the cellophane and the length of travel permits the solvent to evaporate.

Heat Lamination:

Polymer-coated paper, cellophane or foil are frequently combined with other substrate by preheating the coated web and then pressing the two webs between rubber and metal rolls. Heat may also be applied during pressing by heating the metal roll on the laminator. Thus this method is a variation of dry lamination process. In this case application of adhesive is not necessary as one of the substrate is already coated with a heat sealable polymer coating. This method is widely used for laminating polymer (Saran etc.) coated cellophane to cellophane. This technique is usually employed after the polymer coated web has been printed.

Hot Melt Lamination:

Hot-melt lamination process consists of melting a solid or semi-solid adhesive in a heated reservoir and applying it to one of the web, after and a fixed steel roll. After lamination the web is run over a chill roll to solidify and set the adhesive. The hot adhesive coating layer is usually applied by a reverse kiss, dip, curtain or fountain type coater.

The Advantages of this process are as follows:

1. No solvent drying or recovery is required since there is no solvent involved.
2. Laminating rate is high since drying and recovery systems are omitted.

Adhesives used in hot-melt lamination are generally waxes or wax-polymer blends. Wax as adhesives serves many purposes: it joins the two substrates, it gives protection from moisture and it may give heat-sealing characteristics e.g. in foil-wax-strike-through-tissue laminate. Addition of polymers to the waxes produces tougher films, better cohesive and adhesive properties and good flexibility. Polymers and resins commonly used with wax are ethylene vinyl acetate, polyethylene, polyamide butyl rubber, polyisobutylene, rosin esters, cellulose acetate etc. Hot-melt adhesives based on polymers and resins only (without any wax) are also used in some critical applications.

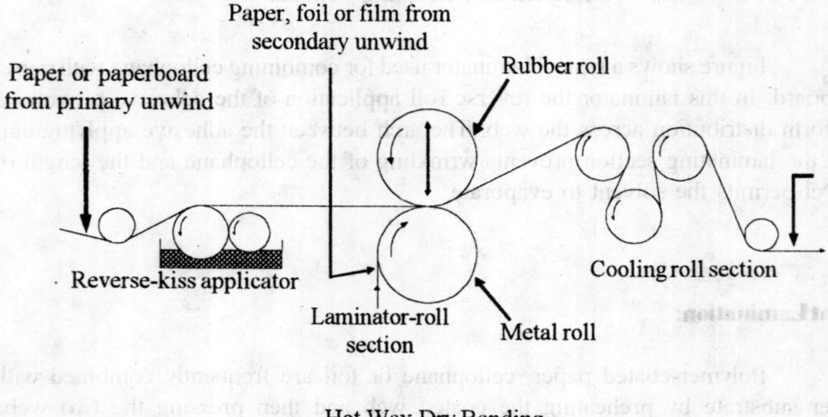

Hot Wax Dry Bonding

Hot Melt Lamination Process

The most common example of wax lamination is glassine-wax-glassine laminate used for packaging of cereals, cake mix, cookie product and gelatin. Another example is foil-wax-tissue laminate used for packaging of candy, soaps, detergents, pharmaceuticals and as carton overwrap.

Asphalt or bitumen is another common hot-melt adhesive Bitumen also gives water-vapour barrier properties. It has high ductility, tackiness and viscosity but it has black colour and bad odour. Blown asphalt has reduced odour and it gives tougher and more flexible films. About 40 to 80 kg. bitumen is used per 1000 m^2 of the laminated area. Bitumen is applied at about 70 to 100° C. It is sometimes used in combination with other hot-melt materials add tough ness and tack to the asphalt and sometimes improve flexibility and water-vapour resistance.

Asphalt lamination is used for combining kraft paper to kraft paper or to laminatew kraft paper to jute or other fabrics. It is also used to join polyethylene film to paper or to jute fabric. combinations of paper asphalt and foil are also possible.

Bitumenized or Asphalt Paper:

Bitumenized paper are generally made from kraft paper although other papers may also be bitumenized. The paper may be saturated with asphalt or bitumen or it may be coated on one side only. However, since bitume is a tacky material with black colour, the bitumen is usually sandwitched between two sheets of paper to produce a laminated sheet. Non-tacky asphalt may be used to coat a single sheet of paper.

The base paper is generally of 25 lb. to 90 lb. basis weight although other weights may also be used. Asphalt used for laminating purpose usually has softening point of 60° C to 90°C. The amount of asphalt applied may vary from 25 to 90 lb per 3000 sq. ft. The most commonly used combination is 30 lb. kraft. 30 lb. asphalt and 30 lb. of kraft represented as 30-30-30 AL or 90 AL. Apart from kraft paper and asphalt other reinforcing materials may also be used such as glass fibres, sisal, jute, hemp, cotton, and rayon, nylon or polypropylene yarns.

The equipments used for manufacturing asphalt papers is similar to the equipment used in the waxing and hot melt coating operations with the exception that frequently the construction is much heavier and built to handle much wider sheets. the roll coater used to coat the paer with asphalt consist of 2 to 3 chilled iron rolls. the lower roll revolves in a pan of asphalt and applied the asphalt to the underside of the paper web. The upper roll merely acts as a backing roll. When operating at high speed, a third roll is used; it rotates in opposite direction to the bottom roll and feeds asphalt to the lower coating roll.

The three rolls are hollow so that they can be heated and the asphalt is applied at 60 to 75°C. The asphalt pan is also fitted with coils to maintain the asphalt at the proper application temperature. Air cylinders with gauges and micrometer controlled stops govern the opening in the nip of the rollw and thus ensure that the correct amount of asphalt is applied. After applying the asphalt on one of the webs, the two webs of paper enter a pair or a series of combining rolls or press rolls which are often covered with oil resistant rubber and are hydraulic, weight or spring loaded to achieve the required combining pressure. the web then passes over cooling cylinders or drums prior wound into rolls.

It can be used for laminating paper to paper, paper to board, paper to hessian, hessian to polyethylene etc. This equipment can also be adopted for kraft paper situation or impregnation.

Asphalt laminated papers are used as water vapour barriers in the construction of multiwall sacks and fibre drums. They are also used as overwraps on coils of tinplate, small machinery and equipment etc. They can be used as liners in the manufacture of fibreboard boxes. Fertilizer bags may be made from asphalt laminated papers.

21

LEAD PENCILS

INTRODUCTION

The manufacture of lead pencils on a commercial scale originated in England in the reign of Queen Elizabeth. At that time (1564) the Borrowsale graphite deposits in cumberland was discovered much of the graphite of this deposit was such purity that it could be taken out in the large blocks and cut into pencil rods and it was not necessary to subject the material to any refining process. The graphite that was too impure (as a result of the admixture of other materials) to be suitable for pencils, was used for crucible making.

The first pencils consisted of rods of pure graphite cut from the massive mine material. Later these rods were inserted between picies of grooved wood forming pencils of the same type as those of the present day although they were probably larger and contained thicker lead.

To obtained the harder lead, the graphite rods were heated in molten sulfur before being placed between the wood strips. Pencils continued to be made in this manner until 1795 when another method was invented.

This consisted of powdering the graphite and mixing it with a finely ground clay so that a thick paste was made. The lead was then moulded or shaped in some other manner and afterwards baked. This made a much more uniform product. Changes of the properties of clay and graphite in the mixture allowed the production of varying degrees of hardness.

Pencil making employes a soft amorphous graphite which may be more readily ground to a powder of uniform particle size. Flake graphite no matter how finely ground, still preserves its flake form. Clay is the binding element and the proportion of clay determines the hardness of the lead. Much attention is devoted by manufacturers to produce pencils adopted to different classes of sketching and drafting work. The mixing of graphite and clay is done the closest supervision.

USES AND APPLICATION

Pencil proposed for manufacture in this project is known as lead pencil in the market. This is an item of use almost in every household, office, school, college etc. for writing on paper, making sketches, drawing and such other purposes. Depending on the type of carbon used in them, pencils are categorized as soft medium and hard. Due to smooth and easy handling of pencils it has got a wide application in various field like copying, sketching, writing etc. Coloured pencils are much popular in drawing and paintings. Important factors for the popularity of the pencils are :-

1. Considerable life
2. Can be erased
3. Smooth in copying
4. Less wear and tear
5. Availability in almost all the colours.

B.I.S. SPECIFICATIONS

The following Indian Standards are available for pencils.

I.S. : 1375-1981 - Black Lead Pencil *(first revision)*

I.S. : 2079-1982 Graphite for pencil slips *(first revision)*

I.S. : 3084-1975 - Pencil slats *(first revision)*
with amendments No. 1 and No. 2.

I.S. : 3214- Engineer's drawing Instruments, pencil point *(Reaffirmed 1977)*.

Specifications of the pencils to be manufactured

Now-a-days due to a wide variety of this product many types of pencils are manufactured. Hence it is quite difficult to give the specifications of all types of product. Generally the following varieties are most popular.

1. H Hard type
2. F-HB medium type
3. B-6B soft type
4. Eraser fitted HB pencil
5. Coloured pencils for business use in vermilion blue, stenography perussion blue and red blue colour.

Inspection of Quality Control :-

Inspection of hardness of the lead slip should be assured and it is too be seen that marketing on the pencil is done properly according to the degree of hardness of lead. Proper gluing and setting of the same is to be assured so that the pencil does not split while in use. Finishing of the painting and embossing also is to be checked to assure good outlook of the product. For all the above mostly usual inspection is done with simple testing devices.

PROCESS OF MANUFACTURE

The proposed project is to manufacture wood pencils. It comprises of one lead core sheathed into wood lead core of pencil is for writing purpose and wooden sheathing is for convenience of holding the same and to prevent it from breaking. The main raw materials for making pencils are the lead and the wooden slats. These wooden slats are normally manufactured by a number of units located in the area where the good quality pencil, timbers are available. Wooden slats are available in length slightly more than that of finished pencil with thickness half of that of a pencil, and width suitable for making 6 pencils out of it. Name and addresses of some units where from slats may be available and also those who manufacture pencil lead are given at the end of this profile. It is possible to purchase both slats and lead and * make pencils. But it is more advantageous and economical if the lead can be manufactured in the unit itself. This project profile has got provision for making lead in the unit itself. The lead and slat are procured separately.

A. Process of manufacture of lead slip

High grade graphite powder is mixed with ball clay in proportion and charged into ball mill with sufficient quantity of water for wet grinding. After grinding the material from 18 hrs. to 22 hrs. the mixed material is discharged in a suitable tank where it is pumped out and fed into filter press for removal of excess water content. After filter pressing the material is in the state of clot which is again fed into baking oven for elimination of moisture. Dried material is then allowed to press through kneeding machine for further homogeneous mixing, kneaded material is now processed in the form of billet and billet is fed in extrusion machine for extrusion of leads slip of desired diameter.

Extruded lead slip is then kept over wooden pallet and slightly rolled for straghening and kept in the rack in room temperature for about 24 hrs. Prepared lead slip is now packed into refractory box (sagger) with packing of carbon material for obtaining reducing atmosphere.

B. Process of manufacture of pencils from slats

The slats are fed to the automatic shaping and grooving machine when grooves of required dimensions are made. Then in the gluing machine glue is spread on the slats and leads which are provided in the grooves. Two slats with lead slips in between secured in the grooves are put under pressure and allowed to set. Thereafter they are fed to the automatic shaping machine where from pencils of required shape come out. Before painting sending the surface and end cutting is necessary and these are done with the help of polishing and end cutting machine. Thereafter the pencils are passed through painting machines where drying of paints also takes place simultaneously. Then trade mark and degree of hardness etc. embossed in the embossing machine. The finished pencils are packed in card board boxes each having 10 pencils and marked.

PENCILMANUFACTURINGPLANT

Pencil manufacturing plant may be classified into three major categories, Pencil lead plant, Saw mill and pencil making.

Pencil Lead Plant :-

This should be equipped with a furnace for the baking of lead.

Saw mill :-

The saw mill must necessarily be large in scale of operation. It there is a saw mill on the spot or near by the matter is simplified because the mill then can be utilize to advantage.

Pencil Manufacturing :-

All that is left to be installed is a plant for the manufacture of pencil slats and subsequent processes namely shaping, grooving, cutting and finishing.

PENCILS WITH ERASERS

In making the pencils with an eraser, on end of the pencil is cut in the process of end cutting while the other end is left as such. After the stamping and finishing lacquering is performed, an eraser is attached to each pencil using a tipping machine. Generally in normal practices the eraser attaching process is not performed.

ADDRESSES OF SUPPLIERS OF MACHINERY

Oriented Machinery Supplying Agency (P) Ltd.,
12, Mission Row, Extension,
Calcutta - 700 001

Industrial Engineers,
3, Mamgpe Lane,
Calcutta.

SUPPLIERS OF RAW MATERIALS

Slats:

Bhatia Saw Mills,
Rishikul Brhamcharya Ashram,
Jwalapur Road,
Haridwar.

Pencil Leads:

Sajatha Pencil Industries,
Nallur, P.O. Feroke,
Kozhikode, (Kerala)

Graphite:

Barum International (M),
28/163, Naval Niwas Gumanapura,
Kota-7, Rajasthan

Glue:

Glue Products Ltd. (M),
Nagra Road, Com.,
Kaira Gujarat.

22

METAL CLIPS AND HOOKS

INTRODUCTION

Hooks of wall fitted hangers, Brackets, Clips, hinges, removable hangers Roofing nails, Door & window fittings, curtain rods with end fittings etc, are the metallic hardwares used for interior decoration, in Offices as Stationery, space s ng, and shelving systems, in all residential houses, show rooms, commercial b ildings, hotel rooms, restaurants, offices & exihibitions. Both mild steels & stainless steels are used in mfg. iron & steel based varieties of these items. Aluminium & brass metal fittings & hardwares are also very much popular. These fittings are mfg. ina wide range of surface finishes. Anodized aluminium hangers, hooks & curtain rods are well-known among all category of users.

This project does not require sensitive & sophisticated line- up of machiner-ies. Even the special purpose m/c, installed for specific operation in the field,are quite simple in design & easy to operate & maintain.

MANUFACTURINGPROCESS

The manufacture of wire & sheet products, in general involve,

i. Mechanical works (i.e. bending, drawing, etc.)
ii. Cutting & Shearing for either blanking before press work or to separate the wire-product, formed during a work-cycle, from the feeding wire coil.
iii. Cleaning, degreasing & pickling.
iv. Drying & Stress - relieving.
v. Surface coating for wear/corrosion resistance, after proper finishing operations.
vi. Testing/sampling & Inspection,

vii. Packaging
viii. Tool room activities to feed the press-shop with adequate press tools.
ix. Effluent treatment & disposal of treated liquid/gases or recycling.

This is a simple engineering project which uses M.S. wire & cold rolled sheets or strip coils to convert into a variety of household items, like Hooks, clips, hangers & brackets, etc. The mechanical processes include cold working of steel in a press shop. Special purpose hooks making m/c is fed with the wire blanks, party shaped under a suitable mechanical bender. This machine makes the joint by forming hooks at the blank ends and interconnecting the two end-hooks. Hooks can be made in a range of designs. Similarely the sheet metal pressing operations include, (a) Shearing into narrow strips (b) Feeding these narrow, straps into a blanking press, (c) drawing deep drawing followed by edge/fringe trimming.

Where, required the stamping/embossing operation can also, be carried on the sheet metal parts, inorder to specify the information about the company &the product (i.e. date of manufacture, Trade mark, product's name, etc.).

SUPPLIERS OF PLANT & MACHINERY

Weighing Machine:

Atlas Weighing Eqpts.,
735, Dr. Mukerjee Nagar,
Opp. Batra Theatre,
Delhi - 110 009
Phone - 7258437

Wire straightening Eqpts. & Galvanising Plants Suppliers:

Assomac Machines (P) Ltd.,
546, Bisrakh Road, Chapraula,
Ghaziabad (U.P) - 9,
Phone - 8714529.

Cold Header and End Threading or Thread Rolling Machine:

S.S. Sabharwal & Sons,
664, Military Road, Anand Parbat,
New Delhi - 110 005
Phone - 5781414

Power Presses Suppliers:

Bharat Machine Tools,
118, MS Block, Harinagar,
Mayapuri Road,
Delhi - 110064
Phone - 5401771

Precision Instruments Suppliers:

Fair Deal Engineers,
A/16 -5, DLF Indl. Area,
Faridabad - 3,
Phone - 6468086

Precision Jigs/Fixtures/Tools Suppliers:

Brecko Precision Engg. Pvt. Ltd.,
19, Rajindra Park,
Delhi - 110060
Phone - 5710658

Cable Terminals, Lugs, Sockets Suppliers:

Allied Traders & Exporters,
3626, Parkash Bhawan,
Daryaganj,
New Delhi - 110002
Phone - 3270653

Electroplating Chemicals Suppliers:

Amit Distributors (P) Ltd.,
W H - 38, Mayapuri Indl. Area,
New Delhi - 110064
Phone - 594243.

Suppliers of Steel Wires:

Accurate Wire Industries,
3666, Chawri Bazar,
Delhi - 110006
Phone - 3260314

Welding Electrodes & Welding Fluxes:

Asian Industries Corporation,
Patel Road,
Near DTC Colony,
New Delhi - 110 008
Phone - 5700834

Welding Machinery & Accessories:

Arora Brothers,
T - 940, Arya Nagar,
Bagh Raoji,
Delhi - 110 006
Phone - 7519011

HR/CR - Steel Sheet Suppliers:

Advance Strips (P) Ltd.,
21/4719, Daryaganj,
New Delhi - 110 002
Phone - 3273051

PLANT ECONOMICS OF METAL CLIPS AND HOOKS

Rated Plant Capacity = 0.50 Ton/Day

COST OF LAND & BUILDING

(Total land area required 600 sq. mtr.) Rs. 12,00,000.00

LIST OF PLANT & MACHINERY

1. Automatic hooks making machine
2. Sheet metal clips making machine
3. Cold heading machine
4. Thread rolling machine with 5 kw connected load
5. Power Presses
   (a) 20 Ton. capacity with 5 kw motor
   (b) 10 tonne capacity with 3 kw motor
   (c) 5 Ton capacity with 1.5 kw motor
6. Hand Presses welding facilities & Buffing machine
7. Tool room machinery
8. Surface grinder & Tool grinder
9. Electroplating plant for Cu/Ni/Cr-plating with all accessories
10. Weighing/Testing/Material Handling Eqpts. & Semi-automatic injection moulding machine

LIST OF RAW MATERIALS

1. M.S. wire
2. CR -strips coils
3. Electroplating salts/solvents/catalysts metallic coating powder/solvent/ flux etc.
4. Hardwares, dies/moulds making steel lubricants, cutting oil, greases, etc.
5. PVC-compounded for covering Iron & steel surfaces and additives
6. B.O. items for bracket assembly, packaging materials & miscellaneous stores.

FIXED CAPITAL

Land & Building	Rs.	12,00,000.00
Plant & Machinery	Rs.	20,00,000.00
Other Fixed Assets	Rs.	5,00,000.00
TOTAL	**Rs.**	**37,00,000.00**

TOTAL WORKING CAPITAL/MONTH

Raw Material	Rs.	3,00,000.00
Salary & Wages	Rs.	95,000.00
Utilities & Overheads	Rs.	55,000.00
TOTAL	**Rs.**	**4,50,000.00**

TOTAL CAPITAL INVESTMENT

Total Fixed Capital	Rs.	37,00,000.00
Total Working Capital for 3 Months	Rs.	9,00,000.00
TOTAL	**Rs.**	**46,00,000.00**

TURN OVER/ANNUM

1. By sales of ready hooks
2. By sale of coat hangers
3. By sale of Brackets
4. By sale of sheet metal clips
5. Recovery from sale of steel scraps

Rs. 93,60,000.00

PROFIT = RECEIPTS - COST OF PRODUCTION

= 93,60,000.00 - 66,82,600.01

= 26,77,399.99

PROFIT SALES RATIO = Profit/Sales x 100 = **28.60 %**

RATE OF RETURN = Operating Profit/T.C.I. x 100 = **58.20 %**

BREAK EVEN POINT (B.E.P.) = 42.49 %

23

OFFICE PASTE (STARCH BASED)

INTRODUCTION

Office paste is a common item known by everyone, it is made by utilizing number of raw materials such as dextrine, starch, gum and sodium silicate etc. Here in this report starch based on office paste has been considered and more emphasis has been given for quality.

The office paste is available in the market by several trade names of the manufacturer. Office paste is an adhesive which is used for adhesing paper and paper boards together.

USES & APPLICATIONS

Office paste is used in every office for bonding paper together by adhesion. Apart from this paste it is also used for making paper boxes. Almost in all the offices, this paste is used, it is very much needed for pasting papers, stamps, envelopes etc. It is a consumable product. There are various manufacturers of office paste.

It is not possible to manufacture all the raw materials in the one plant as they are manufactured by medium scale or large scale manufacturers. For instance, starch is being manufacturerd in India by number of large scale units.

The most widely used materials for office paste is starch in the foregoing scheme is based on the same. Apart from the starch, the paste can be starched with sodium silicate also.

Office paste is an essential commodity for daily use in every office, industrial establishment and homes.

B. I. S. SPECIFICATION

IS: No. 2257 - 1970

Paper adhesives liquid gum and office paste type.

Prescribes requirements and method of sampling and test for adhesives for joining paper to paper or other surfaces lke paper board, wood, cloth and metal in general office use. Covers two types of adhesves, viz, type I liquid gum, basd on gum arabic and type 2 office paste based on starch . Does not cover adhesives used for making costoms and quick setting adhesive used for labelling with high speed mechinery.

MANUFACTURINGPROCESS

The process for making office paste is very simple, and involve only mixing of the starch and other chemicals in water and filling these ar in bottles.

There are various fomulations for office paste, which are described separately inthe report. The most common andcheap method has been taken inthis report. The main raw materials for starch based office paste is starch (corn or patota) and calcium chloride. Mostly potato starch is taken which is much cheaper than corn starch.

First of all the calcium chlorides is dissolve in water and when the homogeneous mixture has been prepared. The starch is added slowly with contenuous stirring. In order to get the uniform product, a slight heatingby jacket in the maxing tank is provided. The following is the formula for starch based after paste.

Starch	28 lbs.
Water	14 gallon
Calcium chloride	23.8 lbs.

After about one hour, the paste is ready and discharged in the paste storage tank. From this storage tank the bottles are filled and sealed. The product is now marketed with the manufacturers trade mark.

SUPPLIERS OF RAW MATERIALS

Starch:

Thakorial Dhagatlal & Co.
Eranad Hall, Dapasianazar,
Ahmedabad - 2.

Biping Chemicals,
1st Floor, Knuga Mansion,
660, Kapasia Bazar,
Ahmedabad - 2.

Calcium Chloride:

Transworld Trading Corpn.,
41, Popatwadi,
Kalbadevi Road,
Mumbai - 400 002

SUPPLIERS OF PLANT & MACHINERY

Mixing Tank:

Bhasker Enterprises
70/1/1, Mangolpur Kalan
Delhi - 110 083

Manoj Consulting Engineers
D - 20, Sector - 6,
Noida - 201 301 (U.P.)

Goyal Engineering Works
40/10, Bawana Road,
Samaipur,
Delhi - 110 042
Phone : 729 3145

Mech-fab-Engineers
E - 8, Greater Kailash - II,
New Delhi - 48
Phone : 641 5548 (Factory at Noida, Ghaziabad)

Boilers:

Vikram Equipment Company
E-63, Sector - IX,
Industrial Complex,
Noida, District Ghaziabad,
(U.P.)
Phone : 89-236 43

Urjex Industries,
S- 26, Indl. Estate,
Pratapur, Meerut - 250 102
(U.P.)

Indcon Boilers
D - 170. Okhala Indl. Area,
Phase - I,
New Delhi - 110 020

Bottle Filling & Sealing Machine:

Sarabhai Machinery,
P.B. No. 72,
Baroda - 7.

Indian Metal Industries,
108, Tilak Bazar
Delhi - 110 006

PLANT ECONOMICS OF BOTTLES OF OFFICE PASTE

Rated Plant Capacity = 1000.00 Nos /Day

COST OF LAND & BUILDING

(Total land area required 100 sq. mtr.)	Rs.	2,00,000.00

LIST OF PLANT & MACHINERY

1. Mixing tank M.S. construction jacketed
2. Paste storage tank M.S. construction
3. Baby boiler
4. Screw Coveyour
5. Bottle filling and sealing machine
6. Water tank
7. Water pump and rotary pump for paste transfer
8. Other ancillaries

LIST OF RAW MATERIALS

1. Starch
2. Calcium chloride
3. Bottles
4. Water

FIXED CAPITAL

Land & Building	Rs.	2,00,000.00
Plant & Machinery	Rs.	2,51,000.00
Other Fixed Assets	Rs.	70,000.00
TOTAL	**Rs.**	**5,21,000.00**

TOTAL WORKING CAPITAL/MONTH

Raw Material	Rs.	1,39,540.00
Salary & Wages	Rs.	30,561.00
Utilities & Overheads	Rs.	11,300.00
TOTAL	**Rs.**	**1,81,401.00**

TOTAL CAPITAL INVESTMENT

Total Fixed Capital	Rs.	5,21,000.00
Total Working Capital for 3 Months	Rs.	5,44,203.00
TOTAL	**Rs.**	**10,65,203.00**

TURN OVER/ANNUM

By sale of 300000 office paste bottle **Rs. 30,00,000.00**

PROFIT = RECEIPTS - COST OF PRODUCTION

= 30,00,000.00 - 24,88,648.66

= 5,11,351.34

PROFIT SALES RATIO = Profit/Sales x 100 = **17.05 %**

RATE OF RETURN = Operating Profit/T.C.I. x 100 = **48.00 %**

BREAK EVEN POINT (B.E.P.) = 50.00 %

24

OFFSET PRINTING INKS (COLOURED)

INTRODUCTION

Printing ink is essentially on intimate mixture of pigments, oils, varnish, dryers, and frequently, wax or greasy compounds. The ink must posses suitable physical characteristics such a viscosity length and stock on which it is to be used. Each type of press and each kind of grade of stock require an ink of different physical characteristics to ensure that it will distribute properly and transfer correctly from the type to the paper. It must print sharply and give lightly prints of the desired colour. The ink must dry sufficiently fast to enable the printed sheets to be handled within a reasonable time, without off setting or smudging. Besides these general properties it is usually important that the ink print a sufficient number of impressions per pound.

Printing ink are divided into three main classes corresponding to the three major divisions of printing.

1. Typographic inks
2. Planographic inks
3. Intaglic inks

PRODUCT INTRODUCTION OF COLOUR PRINTING INK

Printing-ink pigments may be defined as substances or mixtures of substances which import color and opacity to inks also, pigments serve to some degree in increasing the body of the ink.

Printing inks may be divided into three general classes, Planographic, intaglio and typographic inks. For lithographic inks, pigments must be completely free from acids and insoluble in water. Pigments containing acidic substances would cause continued etching of the stone or plate during the printing operation with consequent blurring of the printed impression. Further, lithographic and offset printing are effected by utilization of the principle that oil and water do not mix. For this reason it is necessary that the pigments be in soluble in water.

Otherwise bleeding of the pigment into non - printing areas would occurs, causing a blurred impression on the final printing surface. Also pigments employed for planographic printing must have great color strength. This is particularly true in offset printing, where a thin film of ink is transferred from the plate to a rubber blanket and them to the final printing surface.

Pigments employed in offset printing plates. Thus, sulphur containing pigments generally are avoided when Zinc is employed in the printing plates.

PROPERTIES AND CHARACTERISTICS

The general characteristics of offset printing inks are similar to compositions used on stone lithographic press. However, since it is transferred from plate to blanket and then to the paper, the ink must have properties that will permit this operation without loss of any printing characteristics. The type of paper to be printed also determines the properties of the ink. The terms "heavy" "soft" "short" and "long" are employed in describing the characteristics of offset compositions.

A long ink is one which is stringy or of molasses - like consistency. Short ink has the consistency of hard. The ink stays in spot, without creeping. Offset inks are not prepared in standard grades. As a result, it is common practice for the lithographer to buy a heavily bodies ink and to regulate the consistency to fit this particular requirements.

Linseed varnish apparently is the most satisfactory lithographic vehicle. It should be free of acid to minimize chemical action on the plate. A vehicle having the consistency of No. 1 lithographic varnish is used for the majority of offset inks. The viscosity of the resulting ink will vary with the particular pigment to be ground into the varnish.

The behaviour of the ink during offsetting is the main criterion for the inks composition. With each revolution of the press, a thin layer of ink is laid on the paper. The ink must adhere to but must not raise fuzz from the surface of the paper.

As a general rule, soft surfaced papers take lithographic inks better than hard ones. With soft bond or cheap sulphate paper, a medium bodies ink employed. If the ink has a heavy body, it should be thinned with number 0 0 lithographic varnish of there is a fuzzy surface on the paper, as on newspapers, Kerosene may be included in the ink to prevent lifting of too much lint. However, an excess of kerosene, machine oil or hydrocarbon oil in the ink permits too much penetration ink the paper. This results in plate, lifters work with proper offset paper and ink, the printing is characterised by a softness which is difficult to obtain by direct letterpress printing.

PRINCIPLES OF INK FORMULATION

The first important consideration is the type of ink to be made and the particular printing process for which it is to be used. The ink to be formulated may be letterpress or gravure, quick set or aniline, silk screen or litho - offset, copper - plate engraving or a metallic ink. These, and many other types of inks, are in daily use on different machines.

However, a number of fundamental tests are applied when formulating an ink : they are colour matching, grind, consistency and drying tank. It is also important that the flow and general printing qualities of the ink should be good.

1. Colour Matching:-

The ink being formulated must be matched for colour and shade with the print supplied. The general rules of colour matching apply. A cautious method is to make a small quantity of ink in the laboratory as near as possible to that requirement, and then pull prints on a hand press or vendor cork on a similar type of paper as that supplied with the print.

When the prints are dry, these are composed with the original print. If there is any difference in colour, the ink is adjusted.

During the early stages of the colour matching, a 'scrape' of the ink on paper can be compared with the given print.

2. Grinding:-

Inks are made by grinding, on a three roll mill; The pigments should be ground at higher shear into paint of the varnish. The paste should be tested on a grinding gauge and the milling continued down to a Hegman number of about ten. Some cheap inks may not have to be ground so well.

The thinner + ink constituents can then be ground in by thinning on the mill, and normally paste and liquid dryers are added on the last passage. Dryers, however, one normally, only used for dry oil and certain synthetic resin types inks.

3. **Consistency:-**

Inks should be tested for viscosity on a rotational type of viscosity. It is most important that inks should be used at a definite consistency, and very little margin should be allowed in this matter. A minor difference in the viscosity of the ink can lead to quite a different printing result and appearance. The Empirical Flow Test is useful but less important; it is usually omitted if it is known that the flow and general properties of the inks are satisfactory.

4. **Drying Times:-**

The drying time on paper is determined by the P.A. T.R.A offset method, and the drying time on the machine is measured by rolling up an ink film on glass. These drying times should be very near the standard time required.

DRYING OF SYNTHETIC INKS BY AIR CURING

Offset inks can be made from drying oil alkyd resins thinned with solvent (240°/ 260°C, printing ink oil), and containing no free drying oil. The solvent evaporates when the print is exposed to air, leaving a thin viscous film which dries by absorbing oxygen. Metal dryers catalyses cross-linking, between drying oil carbon chains. Inter molecular and interim molecular oxidation and polymerization occur; the result is a large macromolecular in three dimensions.

The films are not so hard as those produced by storing but in favourable cases are sufficiently firm, adhesive, and flexible for ink-making uses. With such media, the solvent evaporation leaves a highly viscous film, which dries by air curing due to poly concleusation, and molecular cross-linking.

OFFSET RED FOR INKS:

	Parts
Lithographic varnish	13.0
Lithographic Varnish	20.5
Lithographic Varnish	06.15
Glass white dry	13.50
Barium red for lacks, dry	42.0
Paste drier	02.5
Offset ink compound	00.5
Lithographic varnish Abs. viscosity for no.3 and 515	34.0 and 120.0

OFFSETMILO5IBLUE:

00 Lithographic Varnish	04.5
1 Lithographic Varnish	32.0
Aluminium hydrali, dry	04.0
Blue Fixe, dry	04.0
Milori blue, dry	49.0
Refined wool grease	04.25
Offset-ink compound	02.25

INTAGLIOINKS:

(a). Red Plate Ink:

Helio red	20
Titanium dioxide	8
Whiting	33
Magnesium carbonate	4
53% asbortol III (in refined linseed oil)	34.5
Cobalt linsoleate (6% metal content)	0.5
Total	**100.0**

(b). Blue Plate Inks:

Ultramarine blue	15
Titanium dioxide	5
Whiting	30
Varnish	49
Drier	1
Total	**100**

MANUFACTURE OF OFFSET PRINTING INKS

There are three general methods for the manufacturing of printing inks.

1. Grinding of pigment in a vehicle using a mill
2. Heating a dye in a vehicle with stirring
3. Replacing water in the wet pigment pulp by an ink vehicle

The last is known as the "flushing" process and is conducted in a mixer.

MILL GRINDING

They are many types of mills used for the grinding of inks, three roll, fine roll, two roll, colloid, ball mill etc.

Three Roll Mill:

The popular mill for the manufacture of offset ink is the horizontal three roll ink mill. It consists of three hard rolls made from an iron alloy. The rolls are manufactured in several sizes, such as 9 * 24 in, 12 * 30 in, and 16 * 40 in.

The first number indicates the diameter and the second number indicates the operating length of the roll. On any one mill, the three rolls are exactly the same in size. Although the rolls are generally placed in a plane, they can also be placed in other positions.

MIXING AND GRINDING

There are three steps needed when making an offset ink on the roll mill: careful weighing, through mixing, and the actual milling. If the milling operation done, then many properties of the offset printing ink are affected, especially the color strength, printing qualities, and smoothness of the resultant print poor texture of ink due to improper grinding,can be cause of screens filling and general specking. It can also yield a pilling and caking on the printing plate or even on the litho graphic blanket.

There are other variables that contribute to these failures such as paper fibers, and the nature of the pigments used.

The weighing of the pigments and vehicles is generally conducted in large tubs placed on portable scales. It is not wise to weigh small amounts of ingredients such as dryers, anti-skinning agents, ink compounds, etc. on large scales; these should be weighed on smaller scales that are more sensitive.

The mixing operation is designed to wet the surface of the pigment portion by the vehicle. It the mixing is thorough, the grinding effort is reduced.

The average pigment that has been manufactured in water solution and subsequent filtered contains particles of very small size, most of which are less than 1/10 of a micron.

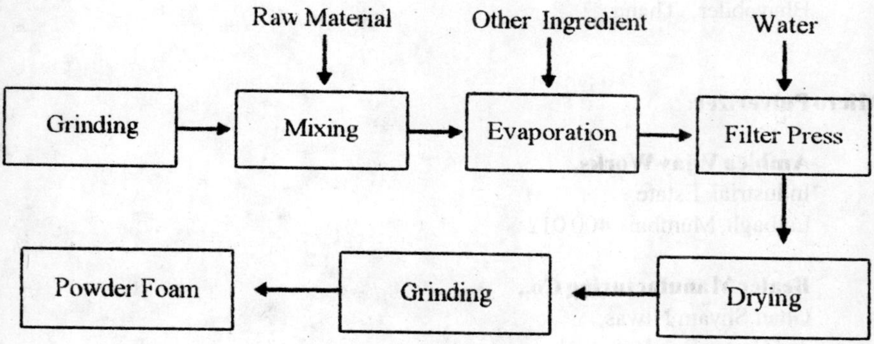

SUPPLIERS OF PLANT & MACHINERY

Three Roll Mill:

Atlas Engg. Works,
8, Dewan Hall, Chandni Chowk,
Delhi - 110 006

Alpha Chemical Engg. Ltd.,
25, Aradhna Indl. Estate, Jav Ghar Road,
Bhayabder, Thana.

Micro Pulverizer:

Ambica Vijay Works,
Industrial Estate,
Lalbagh, Mumbai - 400 012

Bealer Manufacturing Co.,
Ghan Shyam Niwas,
3rd Carter Road,
Borivli, Mumbai - 400 092

Boiler:

Amin Chand Payare Lal
Thana Road,
Jullundur City - 144 004

Annupurna Metal Works,
2, Ashu Biswas Road,
Calcutta - 700 025

D.R. Kumar Brothers
A-3/15, Asaf Ali Road,
New Delhi - 110 002

Dryer:

Control Instruments Unit,
No. G-25, Shalimar Indl Estate,
Mumbai - 400 019

Filling Machine:

Amar Engg. Works,
Deepramjan Indl Estate,
Pokaran Road, No.-1,
Thana - 6 (M.S.)

Auto Fill Engg.
D/95, Chittaranjan Nagar,
Ghatkopar, Mumbai - 400 077

Fil - Mag Industries
S.N. 35A/1, Erandwana,
Pune - 4. (Maharashtra)

SUPPLIERS OF RAW MATERIALS

Resins:

Asian Paints (India) P. Ltd.,
25, Data Street, Fort,
Mumbai - 400 001

Atul Paint & Varnish,
Roakhedi, P.O. Mangalia,
Distt. Indore, M.P.

Solvent:

Ashok Brothers,
11-A, Karim Chambers,
Hamam Street, Mumbai - 400 001

Organic Pigments:

Calour Chemicals Ltd.,
22, Dadabhoy Naroji Road,
Mumbai - 400 001

Sudarshan Chemicals Industries (P) Ltd.,
162, Wellesby Road,
Poona - 1 (Maharashtra)

Inorganic Pigments:

Olpherts (P) Ltd.,
1/2, Moti Sil Street,
Calcutta - 13

Stand and Traders,
14-A, Govindpuri,
Modinagar,
Meerut (U.P.)

Oils and Driers:

Jagnath Bhagwandas
319/21, Modi Chambers,
3rd Floor, Kharek Bazar,
Narsi Nath Street,
Mumbai.

Driers:

National Chemical & Dyes Ltd.,
P.B. No 70, D-43/22,
Sadanand Bazar,
Varanashi (U.P.)

Ashok & Sons (Agencies)
27/3, Shakti Nagar,
Delhi - 110 007

PLANT ECONOMICS OF OFFSET PRINTING INK (COLOURED)

Rated Plant Capacity = 200.00 Kgs./Day

COST OF LAND & BUILDING

(Total land area required 1000 sq. mtr.) Rs. 18,22,500.00

LIST OF PLANT & MACHINERY

1. Three rool mill
2. Micro pulverizer
3. Filling machine
4. Boiler
5. Dryer
6. Weighing machine
7. Pumps & Misc. items
8. M.S. storage tanks for solvents oil etc.
9. Dough mixer
10. M.S. dutch filler
11. M.S. slurry jacketed
12. Capping closing machine
13. Erection & installation

LIST OF RAW MATERIALS

1. Wood resin
2. Resin oil
3. Black mineral oil
4. Methyl violet
5. Channel black

FIXED CAPITAL

Land & Building	Rs.	18,22,500.00
Plant & Machinery	Rs.	5,47,000.00
Other Fixed Assets	Rs.	95,000.00
TOTAL	**Rs.**	**24,64,500.00**

TOTAL WORKING CAPITAL/MONTH

Raw Material	Rs.	54,780.00
Salary & Wages	Rs.	63,497.00
Utilities & Overheads	Rs.	47,000.00
TOTAL	**Rs.**	**1,65,277.00**

TOTAL CAPITAL INVESTMENT

Total Fixed Capital	Rs.	24,64,500.00
Total working Capital for 3 Months	Rs.	4,95,831.00
TOTAL	**Rs.**	**29,60,331.00**

TURNOVER/ANNUM

By selling of 60,000 Kg of Colour Offset Printing Inks

Rs. 36,00,000.00

PROFIT = RECEIPTS - COST OF PRODUCTION

= 36,00,000.00 - 28,59,768.82

= 7,40,231.18

PROFIT SALES RATIO = Profit/Sales x 100 = **20.56 %**

RATE OF RETURN = Operating Profit/T.C.I. x 100 = **25.00 %**

BREAK EVEN POINT (B.E.P.) = 65.28 %

25

ONE TIME CARBON

INTRODUCTION

Carbon paper essentially provides a medium for making duplicate copi of printed, typed or hand written documents, vouchers, invoices and the lik One of the earliest methods of making duplicate copies involved the utilization copy-writing ink. Because the copy ink had exceptional colour strength, it w possible to produce additicnal copies by placing a thin sheet of dampened tiss against the original. Carbon papers of commerce today are obtained by coatir a base paper, usually a carbononizing tissue, with a suitable ink formulation. variety of ink formulations are available for producing different types of carbc papers for several specific purpose. A vast variety of carbon papers are no produced depending upon the base paper, ink formation and the coating methc used.

The extensive demand for carbon papers essentially emerges out c the constantly increasing volume of written documents required in modern busi ness procedures. In addition, more copies of each original are required to provid the necessary line of communication between departments. Despite the fac that many new methods of producing copies have been developed, carbon pape still remains unmatched for its ability to provide inexpensive multiple copie under a wide range of operating conditions and the sales of carbon paper continue to grow.

In addition to economy, carbon paper provides extreme versatility. Carbon perform in tropical heat and arctic cold as well carbon images are usually optically and magnetically read, and in addition to the varied conventional uses, carbon has even designed for data recording in orbiting satellites.

It has to meet varied specifications and requirements depending upon the end-uses. Hence, literally hundreds of different varieties of carbon papers are produced and sold today to satisfy these requirements. However, all these varieties can be broadly classified into the two main categories, namely, single-use carbon and multiple-use carbon. Since each category covers a wide variety of products, they can be further sub-divided into two small class each, as the following.

1. **Single-Use Carbon**

   (a) One Time Carbon
   (b) Book Carbon

2. **Multiple-Use Carbon**

   (a) Typewriter Carbon
   (b) Pencil Carbon

USES AND APPLICATION

One-time carbon is usually custom-coated to match the form in which it is used. The ink formulation is also matched to the conditions of use. The choice of formula depends upon the number of copies in the manifold, the thickness and type of the manifold paper, the method of imaging, the temperature of use, and the desired intensity to copy.

INTRODUCTION OF RAW MATERIAL

Most one-time carbonizing tissues are unbleached kraft, and are produced on high-speed fourdrinier paper machines in widths upto 210 in. and speeds as high as 3000 ft. min. This combination of wide width and high speed yields a low cost paper. An ideal carbonizing tissue has a uniform thickness, is free from pinholes and mechanical defects, and has a surface designed to provide the proper clinch for the carbon dope.

The basis weight for carbonizing paper is generally stated in pounds per reem of 500 sheet (20 x 30 in.). On this basis, one time tissues are produced in the weight range of 5 to 12lbs. The 8 to 10 lbs weights account for a large share of the total production because they provide good performance at minimum cost. The thinner papers are generally used in forms that require a large number of copies, and the heavier tissues in applications were greater mechanical strength is desired.

NAME OF THE IMPORTS COUNTRY

1. Burma
2. Egypt
3. Ethopia
4. Hongkong
5. Kuwait

INK FORMULATIONS FOR ONE TIME CARBONS

One time inks consists primarily of a pigment dispersed in a suitable vehicle The vehicle for one-time ink usually consists of a small amount of hard wax, minera oil, plasticizers and paraffin wax. Carbon black is the common pigment for black ink whereas iron blue provides the colour for blue inks. Small amounts of dyes are ofter used for additional colour strength and improved ink flow. The following formula: illustrate the materials commonly used in one time carbon inks.

Black One Time Carbon:

Ingredients	Parts
Carnauba Wax	6
Montan Wax	8
Paraffin Wax	33
Mineral Oil	25
Carbon Black	15
Methyl Violet	1
China Clay	12
Total	100

MANUFACTURINGPROCESS

Most one time coating are produced on either Mayer or Flexographic coating machines. The Mayer method is the older one, and employees and equalizer rod to control the ink film. The equalizer rod can be a plain steel drill rod, or a similar rod basically wound with piano wire. Wore-wound rods are generally numbered to indicate the fineness of the wire used in their windings. They are made with wire diameters as fine as 3/1000 and as heavy as 60/1000 in. Since the heavier wires apply thicker ink films, only the thinner wires are used for one time carbon coating.

The equalizer rod allows only a metered amount of ink to remain on the web. As the coating is applied in ridges, one must rely upon the levelling qualities of the ink to yield a smooth coating of uniform thickness. Ink formulations for Mayer coating must therefore provide excellent flow.

The dope roll carries a thick layer of ink from the heated pan to the bottom of the paper web. The paper then passes over an equalizer rod, which removes the excess ink. The coated web then contacts a chilling roll to solidify the ink and passes on to the rewind roll. Uncoated strips and clean edges are provided by placing strips of thin metal across the dope roll to prevent the transfer of dope to the paper in the strip area.

The newer one time coaters utilizes the Flexographic principle. These coaters are similar to the flexographic printing process that have been used for many years by the printing industry. Because Carbon inks are solid at room temperature, the ink pan and transfer rolls must be heated to maintain the dopes in a fluid state. Figure provides a schematic representation of the flexographic coating method for one time carbon.

The dope roll picks up a relatively thick layer of ink from the heated ink pan and carries it to the metering roll. The squeezing action between the metering and dope rolls rejects most of the ink pan, but allows a thin film to pass through the nip between the two rolls. This ink film is then transferred to the print roll which in turn transfers the ink to the paper as the passes over the impression roll. The coated web of paper then passes over a chilling rolls and into the rewind roll.

PLANT AND MACHINERY SUPPLIERS

Jessop and Company Ltd.,
63, Netaji Subhash Road,
Calcutta - 700 001
Telephone - 255041
Telex 021-7564

Boiler:

Indcon Project Equipments Pvt. Ltd.,
D-170, Okhla Industrial Area,
Phase - I,
New Delhi - 110 020

Mixers:

Jayems Engineering Co. Ltd.,
139, M. Connaught Circus,
2nd Floor,
New Delhi - 110 001
Phone : 332 4146, 332 3680

Coating Machine:

Brimco Coating Machine
361, Dr. D.N. Road,
Mumbai - 400 001

Ball Mill:

Allied Groups Industries,
B-18, Sector - VII,
Noida Ind. Complex,
Noida - 201 301 (U.P.)

Triple Roll Mill:

Atlas Engineering works,
Diwan Hall,
Chandani Chowk,
Delhi - 110 006

RAW MATERIAL SUPPLIERS

Tissue Paper Manufacturers:

Tribeni Tissue Ltd.,
3,Netaji Subhash Road,
Calcutta.

Ajanta paper and General Production Ltd.,
Vodavali Road,
Kalyan, Mumbai.

Bees Wax:

M. Muntoo & Company,
26, Bonefield Lane,
Calcutta - 1.

Paraffin Wax:

Burma Shell Oil strorage & Distributing Co.,
Burma Shell House,
Bellard Estate,
Mumbai.

Carnauba Wax:

Kanti Lal Sanghvi & Co.,
Union Co-Operative Insurance Society Building,
Fort, Mumbai - 400 001

China Clay:

English India Clay Ltd.,
Trivendrum - 7,
Kerala.

Carbon Black:

Phillips Carbon Black Ltd.,
31, Netaji Subhash Road,
Calcutta.

PLANT ECONOMICS OF ONE TIME CARBON

Rated Plant Capacity = 165000 Kgs./Annum

COST OF LAND & BUILDING

(Total land area required 500 sq. mtr.)	Rs.	2,000.00

LIST OF PLANT & MACHINERY

1. Mixing Machine
2. Ball Mills
3. Storage Tanks
4. Carbonizing Section
5. Boiler
6. Chilled Water Plant

LIST OF RAW MATERIALS

1. Tissue Paper
2. Ink Required
3. Misc. Chemicals

FIXED CAPITAL

Land & Building	Rs.	2,000.00
Plant & Machinery	Rs.	5,70,000.00
Other Fixed Assets	Rs.	1,92,000.00
TOTAL	**Rs.**	**7,64,000.00**

TOTAL WORKING CAPITAL/MONTH

Raw Material	Rs.	7,65,500.00
Salary & Wages	Rs.	36,000.00
Utilities & Overheads	Rs.	36,950.00
TOTAL	**Rs.**	**8,38,450.00**

TOTAL CAPITAL INVESTMENT

Total Fixed Capital	Rs.	7,64,000.00
Total Working Capital for 3 Months	Rs.	25,15,350.00
TOTAL	**Rs.**	**32,79,350.00**

TURN OVER/ANNUM

By sale of 165000 kgs of one carbon **Rs. 1,32,00,000.00**

PROFIT = RECEIPTS - COST OF PRODUCTION
= 1,32,00,000.00 - 1,08,61,197.00
= 23,38,803.00

PROFIT SALES RATIO = Profit/Sales x 100 = **17.59 %**

RATE OF RETURN = Operating Profit/T.C.I. x 100 = **71.32 %**

BREAK EVEN POINT (B.E.P.) = 34.20 %

26

PAPER BAGS FOR GENERAL USE

INTRODUCTION

Paper bags are the oldest types of packaging material and are very much prevalent in the modern days in various fields. Infect, paper bag is one of the most common and popular form of packaging. The hand made bags of paper have been a commodity of common use. However, for the manufacture of bags, the introduction of machines is of recent origin about the middle of 19th century. Since then the manufacture of paper bags has become an important industry in itself. Paper bag is the cheapest form of packaging. Such paper bags have the speciality that they are light weight, free from any contaminants like dust, and are, as well, free from shifting or 'puffing' which results in loss of contents.

Paper bags are made from a variety of papers both bleached and unbleached. However for making of the paper bags for general use, kraft paper and imitation kraft paper are the most common papers used. Papers most common by used for commercial and office envelopes include manila, brown wrapping paper or white papers. The type of paper used for bags depends upon the requirements of the product to be packed. Kraft paper used for bag making is usually of 20 to 40 'lb. basis weight.

SIZE OF PAPER BAGS

`Paper bags are made in wide variety of sizes. However the most common sizes are 15 cm x 7 cm, x 42 cm to 22 cm x 8 cm x 53 cm in case of gusseted bags and 12 cm x 18 cm, 22 cm x 38 cm, 26 cm x 38 cm. an 36 cm x 50 cm. in case of flat or satchel bags. Most popular sizes including in 10 cm x 5 cm. , 15 cm. x 9 cm., 18 cm. x 13 cm., 23 cm. x 10 cm., 26 cm. x 12 cm., 25 cm.x 20 cm., and 30 cm. x 23cm..

Bags and envelopes are also custom made in varying sizes according to the customers requirements and satisfaction. Pouches are made in various sizes depending upon the quality or the product to be filled in them.

USES AND APPLICATION

Paper bags are common packaging material being used by bakers and confectioneries, grocers, textile and cloth merchants, dry cleaners, sweet meat dealers, general merchants, etc.

Due to some distinct advantages, particularly lower prices over the other conventional packaging medium, paper bags are even used by the hawkers and vendors on the footpath for packing fruits, vegetables candies, etc.

PRODUCTION DETAILS AND MANUFACTURE

The whole process involved n the manufacture of paper bags is stacking up of finished bags. The paper rolls may be initially cut into proper with and they are fed into the machine where the roll goes into the bag making section, where it is folded, pasted, sheared an stacked. The bag making medium also has automatic mechanisms for gluing.

In order to manufacture paper bags, we make use of Rotary Upright Sheet Fed Machine. A feed table is provided at the foot of the machine to take the cut sheets in a huge pile. A suction feed takes there under most sheets, so that the pipe can be replenished without affecting the run of the machine, and passes it upwards through a series of rulers which in twin paste, fold and secure the side seams until the finished bag emerges from the top of the machine on the a delivery table.

Of this particular machine, the main advantage is that the bags are delivered in an open condition ready for filling and their appearance is somewhat improved by not having been previously crossed or folded. As great pressure is applied to the bottom end of the bag, it can be used for packing of fine powders.

While working on the sheet fed machines, it is necessary for the paper to be cut prior to being fed into the machine. This is achieved by using either a aniline or a punching out fresh. It is customary to use the guillotine for this process when lither a straight edge or one with a slight projection is required or for a center or side seam bag. When a required shape is needed, as for bags with closer flaps, it is preferable to use a shaped center and punching out press.

PLANT & MACHINERY SUPPLIERS

Automatic Paper Bags Making Machine:

Industrial Paper Machinery (P) Ltd.,
A 32, Phase I, Naraina Industrial Area,
New Delhi-110015

Aprotech Engineers Pvt. Ltd.,
1573, Sector 7E, Faridabad - 121 006
(Haryana)
Ph. : 0129-242140, 244726 Fax : 0129-243452

Sandhu Mechanical Engg. Works,
Industrial Area, 'A' Plot No. 32,
Ludhiana .

Indo Europa Trading Co.,
1980, Chandni Chowk,
Delhi - 110 006

Fabricators:

Larsen of Taubro Ltd.,
L & T House, Ballard Estate,
Mumbai - 400 038

Alfa Laval (India) Ltd.,
Mustafa Building,
7 A, Sir Phirozeshah Mehta Road,
Mumbai - 400 001

Guillotine Shearing Machines:

Akay Engg. Company
8, Swati Building, Ram Nagar,
Narghar Road, Bhayander East,
Distt. Thane - 401 105 (M.S.)

Allied Engg. Works,
143, Upher Dumcan Road,
Mumbai - 400 008

Presses: *(Punching out Press)*

Adarsh Engg. Company
8, Swati Building, Ramnagar,
Marghar Road, Bhayander East,
Distt. Thane - 401 105 (M.S.)

Slitting Saws and Slotting Cutters:

Addison & Co. Pvt. Ltd.,
158, Mount Road,
Chennai (T.N.)

Basal Tools Co.,
23, Factory Area,
Patiala (Punjab)

Hindustan Small Tools Ltd.,
4, Mandevelli Garden,
Ballygunge, Calcutta.

Paper Bag Machines:

Print & Paper (Sales) Pvt. Ltd.,
Post Box No. 394, 4/7 A,
Watelov Street,
Calcutta - 700 069

Paper Rolls Slitter/Rewinder:

J.D. Enterprises
16, Syed Amir Ali Avenue,
P.Box No. 16005,
Calcutta - 700 017

Slotting/Cutting/Rewinding Machines:

J.& K. Industries,
Udhava Udyog Nagar,
Jawahar Road, Udhava Distt.,
Surat

SUPPLIERS OF RAW MATERIAL

Kraft Paper:

Om Prakash Jitendra Kumar & Co.,
63, Darya Ganj,
New Delhi - 110 002
Ph. : 326 9680, 327 1380

Narain Paper Mart,
4034/3, Haryana Market,
Chawri Bazar, Delhi - 110 006.
Ph. 291 5135

Glue:

Debha Glue Products,
P.Box. NO. 12,
Falna 306116,
Rajasthan.

Gums:

Bbor Industries (P) Ltd.,
392, Veer Savarkar, Marg,
Mumbai - 400 025

PLANT ECONOMICS OF PAPER BAGS FOR GENERAL USE

Rated Plant Capacity = 150000.00 Nos./Day

COST OF LAND & BUILDING

(Total land area required 840 sq. mtr.) Rs. 11,12,000.00

LIST OF PLANT & MACHINERY

1. Automatic paper bags making machine
2. Rolls slitter motorised with 2 HP
3. Working tools, instruments scales etc.

LIST OF RAW MATERIALS

1. Kraft paper
2. Glue

FIXED CAPITAL

Land & Building	Rs.	11,12,000.00
Plant & Machinery	Rs.	1,22,000.00
Other Fixed Assets	Rs.	45,000.00
TOTAL	**Rs.**	**12,79,000.00**

TOTAL WORKING CAPITAL/MONTH

Raw Material	Rs.	3,19,180.00
Salary & Wages	Rs.	57,500.00
Utilities & Overheads	Rs.	16,400.00
TOTAL	**Rs.**	**3,93,080.00**

TOTAL CAPITAL INVESTMENT

Total Fixed Capital	Rs.	12,79,000.00
Total Working Capital for 3 Months	Rs.	11,79,240.00
TOTAL	**Rs.**	**24,58,240.00**

TURN OVER/ANNUM

1. 18000000 Nos paper bags(Cap. 1/2kg) 19 x 14 cm)
2. 13500000 Nos. paper bags(Cap. 1 kg) (21 cm 16 cm)
3. 9000000 Nos. paper bags (Cap. 2 Kg.) (22.5 x 21.5 cm)
4. 4500000 Nos. paper bags(Cap. 5 kg) (31.5 x 26.5 cm)

Rs. 58,59,375.00

PROFIT = RECEIPTS - COST OF PRODUCTION

= 58,59,375.00 - 53,47,172.80

= 5,12,202.20

PROFIT SALES RATIO = Profit/Sales x 100 = **8.74 %**

RATE OF RETURN = Operating Profit/T.C.I. x 100 = **20.84 %**

BREAK EVEN POINT (B.E.P.) = 65.79 %

27

PAPER CONES AND TUBES

INTRODUCTION

Amongst the various industries in India, the textile industry plays a very prominent role and supports many other ancillary industries. Paper cone and tube making is one of such ancillary industries. Paper cones and tubes are used for thread winding purposes in textile industry. Cotton, nylon, rayon, woolen and other synthetic threads are wound on paper cones and tubes on winding machines and then used for spinning, weaving, warpping etc.

Paper tubes are required by the manufacturers of sewing and embroidery thread. The thread is wound on the tubes in measured lengths or in weight and the tube of thread is sold in the market. Paper tubes are also used for packaging agarbatties gum tapes, spices etc.

Paper cones are made of number of layer or plies of chips or mill board. Sometimes an outer-ply or kraft paper is pasted on the cone to provide smoother surface. Coated or laminated paper or board may be used for special purposes.

Paper tubes for winding sewing and embroidery thread are generally made of paper including kraft paper and other papers. Paper tubes for packaging and other purposes are generally made of chip or mill board. Paper tubes for textile applications may have impregnated, coated or laminated plies for special purposes e.g. to improve steam or water resistance.

Paper cones and tubes can be produced on small and cottage scale with semi-automatic and hand-operated machinery. All the equipment and machinery and raw material for the manufacture of paper cones and tubes are available indigenously. Small scale and cottage scale sector contributes more than 50% of the production of paper cones and tubes in India.

SIZES AND SPECIFICATIONS

Paper cones are manufactured in a variety of sizes depending on end-use requirements. Specifications for paper cones include.

1. Length of the cone
2. Internal diameter of the cone base or apex(top)
3. Apex angle or taper
4. Thickness of cone wall
5. Weight of the cone which depends on the basis weight of the board and thickness of the wall.

ISI has issued one standard on Paper cones for Winding Yarns, namely IS : 4888 - 1975. This specification covers open top cones with 3°30' or 4°20' apex angle (taper) and rolled in-top cones with 3°30' or 9°15' apex angle.

The most common paper cones has an apex angle of 9°15' with length of about 15 cm. to 18 cm. The surface of the cone may be smooth or it may have small regular projections or patterns embossed on the surface so that the thread or yarn does not slip from the surface. The surface of the cone may be impregnated, Bakelised, steam-proofed or water-proofed for special requirements.

Paper tubes are also available in various sizes. The specifications for paper tube include:

1. Length of the tube
2. Internal diameter of the tube
3. Wall thickness
4. Weight of the tube.

The length of paper tube may very from 6 cm. to 40 cm. and the diameter of the tube may be as high as 15 cm. or more. The thickness of the wall may very from 2.25 mm. to 6 mm. Paper tubes may be spiral winded or straight winded. The outer surface of the tube may be smooth or have projection, patterns etc. embossed or engraved on it.

MANUFACTURING PROCESS

Paper cones and tubes are formed out of chipboard or mill board and kraft paper on a specially designed cone forming or tube winding machine which forms a cone or a tube out of the paper or board fed to the machine.

Paper cones are formed by straight or convolute winding of several layers of board on top of each other upto the required thickness with adhesive applied between the layers and at each end to join the various layers. The paper board is fed to the machine and embossed between two rollers. The required shape is cut by two pairs of knives and one end of the piece is automatically sucked on to the winding spindle by vacuum. Now paste is applied to the piece and it is wound in the shape of a cone by the rotating spindle. The base and apex is trimmed by circular knives. The wet cones are dried in drier or in the sun. Finally the apex part is turned smooth and the cones are packed.

Paper tubes can be spiral wound or convolute-wound as described in the chapter on Fibre Cans and Drums. In convolute winding the various layers are carried over glue rollers and then fed into the revolving mandrel and the layer are coiled on top of each other. In spiral winding several layers of board or paper are joined with angled overlapping joints. Tubes may be inpregnated with resin and then cured. Finally they are cut to the required sizes.

Cone forming or tube winding machines may be either automatic or semi-automatic type. In completely automatic machines the paperboard or paper is fed from rolls and the tubes or cones are cut and trimmed automatically. In semi-automatic machines the board or paper is fed in the form of sheets of strips and the tube may have to be cut to size in a separate operation.

Completely automatic machines may have to be imported. However, less sophisticated machines are available in India also. Semi-automatic machines are used by small manufacturers in India. Hand-operated machines are used by cottage scale units.

28

PAPER ENVELOPES

INTRODUCTION

Paper envelopes is well known to all persons as it is a routine article of use, with the growth of education, industrialization and commercial activities, the demand for office stationery and allied items is increasing rapidly. Paper envelopes paly an important role as a stationery material in any type of correspondence.

Now-a-days the envelopes are used in the publicity-advertisement very frequently. There are varrious tpes and sizes of envelopes and also of various quality. The size and type of envelopes depend upon the quality of lgkpaper which is used in envelope making, demand of lusers and market. Various types and sizes of envelopes are now used quite extensively. Some envelopes are self adhesive type,due to already pasted gum on their brims. These self adhesive type envelopes are very convenient to use and have very important applications in post & telegraph department, offices and in many commercial departments.

Some other special type of envelopes are used in special fiels as pocket envelopes. Some varieties of pocket envelopes are pparticularly suitable for substances such as seeds, powders, hairnets, postage stamps, wedges wireless parts, gramophone needles and their small articles. Some important sizes of the envelopes are given here under:

1. 15 x 9 cm.
2. 18 x 13 cm.
3. 23 x 16 cm.
4. 26 x 12 cm.

The above sizes of evnelopes are most important and well known sizes. These sizes are mostly used in offices and P & T Departments.

USES & APPLICATIONS

- The main uses of envelopes are as follows :-

1. In post and telegraph department
2. In Offices
3. In commercial centres
4. In publicity-Advertisement
5. In sampling (for putting seeds, powders hair nets etc.)
6. In Industrial for official corespondence.

FORMULA FOR SELF SEAL ENVELOPES ADHESIVE

Parts:

1.	Natural Rubber Latex (Ammonial Preserved - 60%)	10
2.	Potassium hydroxide (10%)	0.2
3.	Aquous Dispersion of Zinc Diethyl-Dithiocarbonate (50%)	0.5
4.	Water as required	

MANUFACTURING PROCESS

The process of making paper envelopes is quite simple and involves the following steps :-

1. Envelope making
2. Flap gumming
3. Packing

The most common and popular machine for paper envelope is Rotary Sheet Fed Type envelope making machine. In this type of machine, blanks are put on the feeding table in high stack and the flap paint downwards.

While the envelope making machine is running, additional blanks can be put on the table. A sucking device takes the blanks from below and carried them to the receiving cylinder. The printing attachments are slewable and can be stopped individually. After this the flap gumming follows. Now the blank is conveyed through turning cylinder and then brought rapidly to the format pit where it is aligned. The folding of the blanks is achieved by folding rules, thereafter the finished envelope falls into the drying chain.

When drying process is finished, the envelope is coneyed by means of sucking dies to the receiving table where the finished envelopes are stacked up and counted by 25 0 50 envelopes.

The brown, wrapper or white paper, white coloured or brown wrapper and also manila is usually employed for various types of envelopes. The Gums (Gum arabic or local) are generally used as the common adhesives. The paste made from tapioca flour are also used to a lesser extent.

Now the envelopes are allowed to affix the stamps and the different kinds of Advertisement are stamped on the back of the envelpes. Now these envelopes are allowed for use. They are bounded or packed in hundred or thousand bundle.

SUPPLIERS OF RAW MATERIAL

Standard Type Foundry,
Barshah Bala,
Chawri Bazar,
Delhi.

SUPPLIERS OF PLANT & MACHINERY

Harish Engineering Works,
Opp. Mayur Soap Factory,
Tavadipura,
Ahmedabad - 380 004

Super Standard Industries
Pratap Estate Hard Water Works,
G.T. Road, Ram Talai,
Amritsar - 39

PLANT ECONOMICS OF PAPER ENVELOPES

Rated Plant Capacity = 60000.00 Nos/Day

COST OF LAND & BUILDING

(Total land area required 150 sq. mtr.)	Rs.	4,90,000.00

LIST OF PLANT & MACHINERY

1. Paper cutting machine
2. Envelope making machine continuous reet fed type
3. Flap gumming machine
4. Drying chains
5. Receiving tables
6. Sucking desk
7. Other miscellaneous equipments such as testing equipments etc.

LIST OF RAW MATERIALS

1. Paper
2. Gums/Adhesives
3. Packing boxes

FIXED CAPITAL

Land & Building	Rs.	4,90,000.00
Plant & Machinery	Rs.	1,06,000.00
Other Fixed Assets	Rs.	85,000.00
TOTAL	**Rs.**	**6,81,000.00**

TOTAL WORKING CAPITAL/MONTH

Raw Material	Rs.	40,875.00
Salary & Wages	Rs.	44,061.00
Utilities & Overheads	Rs.	11,900.00
TOTAL	**Rs.**	**96,836.00**

TOTAL CAPITAL INVESTMENT

Total Fixed Capital	Rs.	6,81,000.00
Total Working Capital for 3 Months	Rs.	2,90,508.00
TOTAL	**Rs.**	**9,71,508.00**

TURNOVER/ANNUM

1. 1,35,00,000 Envelopes (Plain)
2. 4500000 Envelopes (self sealing type) **Rs. 16,65,000.00**

PROFIT = RECEIPTS - COST OF PRODUCTION
= 16,65,000.00 - 14,29,558.76
= 2,35,441.24

PROFIT SALES RATIO = Profit/Sales x 100 = **14.00 %**

RATE OF RETURN = Operating Profit/T.C.I. x 100 = **24.23 %**

BREAK EVEN POINT (B.E.P.) = 69.21 %

29

POLYTHENE BAGS WITH PRINTING

INTRODUCTION

Polythene bags are made of polythene sheets which is fast replacing cellulose acetate (cellophane film. Polythene sheet is transparent, tough non toxic, not affect by humidity and is chemically inert. Polythene bags are much suitable for packing purposes.

Polythene sheets has possibilities in the packing field where protection against moisture and monsoon condition are required. Polythene is available commercially in two specific types, a conventional branched low density polythene and a linear high density polythene has become familiar to common man due to its characteristics as exhibited in films sheeting plastic bottles plastic piping and tube dish pans baskets television antena wire and tublers etc.

The properties of polythene vary as to type and molecular weight, Polythylenes are among the lights in all of the plastics. In appearance they are a translucent white the conventional polythelene being a little more transparent than the linear type. In comparison with the well known plastic materials they are about midway between the extremely flexible vinyl plastics and the more rigid polystyrenes. The cut standing properties of polyethylene are listed below :-

1. Readily mouldable into various shapes and forms.
2. Food mechanical properties combining together, strength, flexibility and toughness.
3. Excellent electrical resistances.
4. Low moisture vapor transmission.
5. High resistance to most solvents and chemicals.
6. Wide range of moulds form highly flexible film to rigid moulded forms.
7. Tasteless and odourless.
8. Good water resistances.

MANUFACTURINGPROCESS

The manufacturing process has been considered in the automation which is composed of an extruder using polythene pellets, printer, cutter and bottom sealer. Through this system production efficiency has been made effectively high, operation cost, reduced, operation and quality of product made constant. The following operations are described in details.

Extrusion of Polythene sheet:

Polythene sheet is extruded in the extruder by charging polythene pellet into the hopper. For blowing the rubber film coming out of extruder, air is introduced at pressure through the die blowing the film to approximate two or three times. The air pressure should be carefully adjusted to obtain the desired sheet thickness. The thickness of sheet can also be adjusted through the control of the wind cut rate. Generally, the thickness are form 70 to 700 gauge.

The sheet is wound on a pictrolle which permit maintenance of the air bundle. The cooling is effected by placing a special air ring at a suitable position after the die. The die should be generally operated & gives clearer film,. The die should generally be operated in vertical position and die operating temperature 375-450ºF.

Cutting & Making of Bags:

Printed tabular film polythene is cut off from certain bag lengigation and the put pieces of film taken into the polythene bag making machine. Although heat sealing machines are also available by which the bags can be prepared but in this machine production capacity is little. In the heat scaling machine the bottom part of the tabular film is sealed with a heat sealer.

The polythene bag making machine is available in the different size viz. 18 inch 28 inch 36 inch and 42 inches. The width of making bag's and sealing depends upon the sizes of the machine. For instances, if you have a machine of 18 inch. You can only bags of maximum upto 18 inch width the sealing.

Inspection and Packing:

The finished product is inspected thoroughly to see the thickness, uniformity. Some times due to improper air flow the thickness is not uniform. If it is so the attention should be paid immediately and trouble should be removed. The product should be removed. The product should be sorted and treated as waste.

Polypropylene Bags Printing:

Polythene Bags may be printed by Flexographic/Rotogravure printing machines or by other printing methods may be applied for the same. All the machines are fluently available in all over india.

SUPPLIER OF RAW MATERIALS

Polypropylene:

Polylefines Industries Limited
Mafathalal House,
Backbay Reclamation,
Mumbai - 400 001

MANUFACTURERS AND SUPPLIERS OF PLANT AND MACHINERY

New Kailash Engineering Works
5/31, Kirti Nagar Industrial,
New Delhi - 110015

Extruder:

Manjit Brothers
J-135, Vishnu Garden,
New Delhi - 110018
Ph.: 5430417, 534709
Fax: 91-11-5449682

Lal Engineering Works
A-805, Shastri Nagar,
New Delhi - 110052

K. S. Enterprises
201, Sector - 22,
Faridabad - 121 005
Haryana
Ph.: 0129-230654, 232762
Fax: 91-129-231942, 234844, 230654, 232762

PLANT ECONOMICS OF POLYTHENE BAGS WITH PRINTING

Rated Plant Capacity = 150.00 Kgs./Day

COST OF LAND & BUILDING

(Total land area required 250 sq. mtr.) Rs. 5,15,000.00

LIST OF PLANT & MACHINERY

1. Automatic bag making plant
(including extruder, die head, control board, air compressor, winder)
2. Cutting & Sealing machine
4. Stereo hydraulic press
5. Grinder
6. Weight for printed matter
7. Lab testing equipments

LIST OF RAW MATERIALS

1. L.D.P.E. Granules
2. Miscellaneous as (Bag handles printing ink etc.)

FIXED CAPITAL

Land & Building	Rs.	5,15,000.00
Plant & Machinery	Rs.	4,70,000.00
Other Fixed Assets	Rs.	65,000.00
TOTAL	**Rs.**	**10,50,000.00**

TOTAL WORKING CAPITAL/MONTH

Raw Material	Rs.	1,52,800.00
Salary & Wages	Rs.	31,562.50
Utilities & Overheads	Rs.	27,000.00
TOTAL	**Rs.**	**2,11,362.50**

TOTAL CAPITAL INVESTMENT

Total Fixed Capital	Rs.	10,50,000.00
Total Working Capital for 3 Months	Rs.	6,34,087.50
TOTAL	**Rs.**	**16,84,087.50**

TURN OVER/ANNUM

By sale of 45,000 kg. Polythene Bags	Rs.	36,00,000.00

PROFIT = RECEIPTS - COST OF PRODUCTION

= 36,00,000.00 - 30,59,699.25

= 5,40,300.75

PROFIT SALES RATIO = Profit/Sales x 100 = **15.01 %**

RATE OF RETURN = Operating Profit/T.C.I. x 100 = **32.08 %**

BREAK EVEN POINT (B.E.P.) = 59.82 %

30

PVC INSULATION TAPE

INTRODUCTION

Pressure sensitive adhesive tape are generally employed for the general purpose like wrapping, packaging, protection etc. and is coated with pressure sensitive adhesive.

The adhesive used attached the tape backing which may be of cloth, paper or plastic material like P V C etc. to the surface of some other material. The main requirement of pressure sensitive tapes are :-

1. They must provide instantaneous adhesion where applied by the use of light pressure.

2. The adhesive should be of such type that it can be clearly removed from the surface to which they been applied just be a light pull.

The adhesive used, should have in addition to the properties of tackiness and adhesiveness, the properties like internal strength, resillency, cushioning power, and its usefulness over a wide range of temperature.

The adhesive used here is usually rubber based otherwise specified the latex or other types of modified rubbers are mixed with plasticizers fillers, etc. Curved and thickned wide a suitable solvent to the desired consistency.

The adhesive acts with the evaporation of the solvent there by leaving the nearly dried film on the joint.

FORMULATIONS

Pressure Sensitive Grease Proof Adhesive:

Polymerized linseed oil	5.0
Chlorinated rubber	1.0
Micro-crystalline wax	0.5
Ethyl acetate	5.0
Toluol	1.0

Pressure Sensitive Filmor Tape:

Nitrocellulose	4.5
Blow castor oil	23.6
Acetone	5.0
Ester gum	3.5
Denatured alcohol	5.3
Benzol	58.1

USES & APPLICATIONS

The following are the main applications of pressure sensitive adhesives and tapes.

1. MASKING:

The means the protection of a portion of a surface during spray painting.

2. STENCILING:

During the painting of numbers and names on surfaces, a portion of the surface in protected by means of adhesive tapes.

3. PROTECTION:

Prevention of corrosion or abrasion of metals, wood, plastics etc. during the process of manufacture it is protected by means of adhesive tapes.

4. PACKAGING:

Bags, packages and boxes etc. are closed by means of such adhesive tapes.

5. SEALING:

Cracks or openings are sealed by means of the pressure sensitive adhesive tapes.

6. HOLDING:

Keeping doors etc. of refrigerators, stoves or any other such like articles closed during shipment. This is achieved by the use of such adhesive tapes.

7. IDENTIFICATION & MARKING:

Pipelines, cables, wires etc. are marked by such adhesive tapes of different colours for identification.

8. INSULATION:

Coils of electric motors are protected against electrolytic corrosion by covering with such adhesive tapes.

9. REINFORCING:

Leather and fabrics etc. are reinforced by means of such types of the manufacture of bags belts and shoes etc.

PROCESS OF MANUFACTURE

The process of manufacturing pressure sensitive adhesive tape may be divided into the following steps :

1. Preparation of PVC film of required thickness and size.
2. Preparation of adhesive.
3. Application of the adhesive.
4. Curing, if any,
5. Cutting and rolling.

PREPARATION OF PVC FILM

In the form of calendered, film, polyvinyl chloride is finding wide application. Transparent, translucent and coloured films of every description are available. The calender consists of two or more masssive steel rolls generally mounted vertically. The rolls are heated by steam and can be cooled by passing water through. The distance between rolls be very accurately controlled. The temperature of the rolls is very closely controlled.

Very smooth wide films of material of uniform thickness are obtained by its use.

P V C compositions may be calendered in a manner similar to that used for rubber. The PVC composition is formed into a soft dough on hot mixing rolls. It is then fed on to the calender, which is at a much higher temperature than with the rubber. Temperatures are of the order of 125-135^{0}C. Films from 0.0015 inches upto 0.125 inches can be made.

PREPARATION OF ADHESIVE

The adhesive as per the formulation No. 5 is prepared in a jacketed kettle. The rubber is first melted in the kettle and then other ingredients are added except the solvent. The mix is cooled properly and the solvent is added as required. The adhesives is now ready for the use of coating.

APPLICATION OF THE ADHESIVE ON P V C FILM

The equipment used for spreading the adhesive to the P V C film is similar to that which is used for a similar purpose in the rubber industry. A knife is supported at an adjustable height above the surface which supports the film. The adhesive paste is fed down in front of the knife and is carried forward udner the knife blade by the moving film. Thus film the adhesive paste is spread over the surface of the film, and the thickness of the coating applied depends the height of the blade above the film, the type of the film material used and the speed with the film is moving. The adhesive coating then set by solvent evaporation.

CUTTING & ROLLING :-

The coated film is then cut to a required lengths and width by a cutting machine and then rolled down on a cardboard spools or P.P. spools. These are then packed in a light card board box.

PLANT AND MACHINERY SUPPLIERS

Bombay -Industrial Engineers,
430, Hind Rajasthan Centre,
D.S. Phalke Road,
Dadar, (C.Rly),
Mumbai - 400 0014
Phone 4113999/4114275,
Fax: 22-4145846/2028798.

Jandu Engineening Vikash Marg,
Shakarpur,
Delhi - 110 092
Phone: 2242007/2247671,
Tlx: 3161266 RKG IN

PVC Film Suppliers:

Bhor Industries Ltd.,
16, Apollow Street,
Mumbai - 400 001

PVC Resin/Composition:

Calcio Mills (Chemical Division),
Anik Chamber,
Mumbai - 400 071

Rubber Chemicals Suppliers:

Bayer (India) Ltd.,
82, Veer Nariman Road,
Mumbai - 400 001

Latex Rubber:

Cahanpady Latex Manufacturing Units,
P.B. No. 22,
Kottayam,
Kerala

Carbon Black, Filler, White:

Bajaj Rubber Company
Khurshid Market,
Sadar Bazar,
Delhi - 110 006

Calcutta Carbon Mineral Supply Company Pvt. Ltd.,
Jackson Lane,
Calcutta - 1

Phillips Carbon Black Limited
Negaji Subhas Road,
Calcutta - 700 001

PRESENT MANUFACTURERS

A. S. Exports,
Unit No.4, 1st Floor,
Shiv Mandir Shopping Complex,
Chittaranjan Park,
New Delhi - 110 019
Tel: 011-6467186
Fax: 91-11-8924461.

Bhor Industries Ltd.,
4/24-A, Asaf Ali Road,
New Delhi - 110 002
Phone: 011-3269813
Fax: 91-11-3269040

PLANT ECONOMICS OF PVC INSULATION TAPE

Rated Plant Capacity = 100.00 Kgs./Day

COST OF LAND & BUILDING

(Total land area required 500 sq. mtr.) Rs. 6,90,000.00

LIST OF PLANT & MACHINERY

1. Jacketed kettle capacity 100 litres S.S.lined with stirrer
2. Adhesive paste spreading machine automatic
3. Cutting machine
4. Rolling machine
5. Mini boiler
6. Stainless steel tank
7. Drying chamber (15'X5'X8') with air heater and blower
8. Hand sealing machine
9. Miscellaneous
10. Automatic pouch packing machine

LIST OF RAW MATERIALS

1. Nitrile rubber
2. Phenolic resin
3. Rubber process oil
4. Antioxidant (Permanax WSL)
5. Calcium carbonate (pptd.)
6. Carbon black
7. Solvent naphtha
8. PVC film
9. Packaging material

FIXED CAPITAL

Land & Building	Rs.	6,90,000.00
Plant & Machinery	Rs.	10,59,000.00
Other Fixed Assets	Rs.	2,20,000.00
TOTAL	**Rs.**	**19,69,000.00**

TOTAL WORKING CAPITAL/MONTH

Raw Material	Rs.	2,03,060.00
Salary & Wages	Rs.	48,250.00
Utilities & Overheads	Rs.	84,375.00
TOTAL	**Rs.**	**3,35,685.00**

TOTAL CAPITAL INVESTMENT

Total Fixed Capital	Rs.	19,69,000.00
Total Working Capital for 3 Months	Rs.	10,07,055.00
TOTAL	**Rs.**	**29,76,055.00**

TURN OVER/ANNUM

By sale of 30,000 kg of pvc tapes (10 gm each)

TOTAL Rs. 60,00,000.00

PROFIT = RECEIPTS - COST OF PRODUCTION
= 60,00,000.00 - 49,79,328.10
= 10,20,671.90

PROFIT SALES RATIO = Profit/Sales x 100 = **17.01 %**

RATE OF RETURN = Operating Profit/T.C.I. x 100 = **34.05 %**

BREAK EVEN POINT (B.E.P.) = 60.34 %

31

RUBBER ERASER

INTRODUCTION

Rubber eraser can be made by extrusion or moulding process. They can be individually moulded or moulding can be carried out in desired thickness of sheet which can be then cut to size and finished. Pencil eraser don't damage the surface of paper and remove the graphite due to its adhesion to the rubber. The other constituents of the pencil eraser are first diluents and cheapening agents.

The manufacture of rubber eraser has good potential for development in small scale sectors. These are required in large numbers by school and college students. In addition to common type pencil eraser, there exists a good market demand for special type of eraser also, such as typewrite eraser, ink eraser etc.

The demand for items like eraser is closely linked with the growth of educational and industrial development. With the increasing number of schools, colleges, technological institutions, offices and other establishments, the market demand of eraser is expected to increase manifold.

USES & APPLICATION

School rubber or rubber eraser is mainly used by the students for erasing the pencil drawings and other pencil writings. This rubber is must for every college or school student. This rubber eraser is also used in by Artists, Draftsmen, engineers. it is also used in the offices, the commercial establishments.

The highest consumption of this type of rubber erasers is in schools, colleges and offices.

FORMULATION & PROCESS OF MANUFACTURE

1.

Corn Oil	4 lb. 6 oz.
Light MgO	2 1/2 oz.
Sulphur Chloride	12 oz.
Ground pumice (200 mesh size grounded)	1 lb. 80 oz.

Magnesium oxide and grounded pumice (passes through 200 mesh screen) are added to the corn oil and stirred until the solids are uniformly distributed through out the mass. Weighed quantity of [80 oz.] sulfur chloride is added slowly with vigorous agitations at such a rate that the temperature does not rise above 90ºF.

The mixture is now allowed to stand for 12 hr., whereupon the balance of the sulfur chloride may be added some what more rapidly than the initial quantity but with equally vigorous agitation.

Upon the addition of the second quality of sulfur chloride the mass thickness somewhat and is poured into wooden channel open at the top and having a cross section approximately one inch square.

The mixture is allowed to stand for several hours and is removed from the mold when solidified, cut into three inch length, imprinted and packed.

2.

	In Kg.
Palecrepe	450
Sulfur	87
Accelerator	18
Zinc Oxide	36
Stearic Acid	4.5
Light Calcined MgO	160
Ammonium Oleate	75
Eraser Crumbs	560
White Factice	1300
Whiting	1100
Titanium Dioxide	25
Fast Colours	18

The process of manufacture essentially consists of firstly mixing the various ingredients of the rubber compound and then moulding the same in the form of desired size of bars.

Palecrepe is first masticated in a mixing mill and then the remaining ingredients are added excepting sulfur. When the mixing is complete, sulfur is added and the rubber compound is dried in the form of a sheet of desired thickness.

The sheet is then pressed in mould in the hydraulic press. The moulded sheet is cut into the pieces of desired shape and size. Individual pieces are then stamped to have the brand name and then these are packed for marketing.

3.

Creepe Rubber	4
Starch	10
Petrolatum	4
Vulcanmized Waste Rubber	2
Factice	1
Abrasive	2
Lithophone	3
Sulfur	0.1
Accelerator	0.05

MANUFACTURING PROCESS

Manufacturing of rubber eraser consists the following processes.

1. Mixing of the ingredients
2. Moulding
3. Curing
4. Cutting of the rubber eraser pieces
5. Finishing stamping & packing

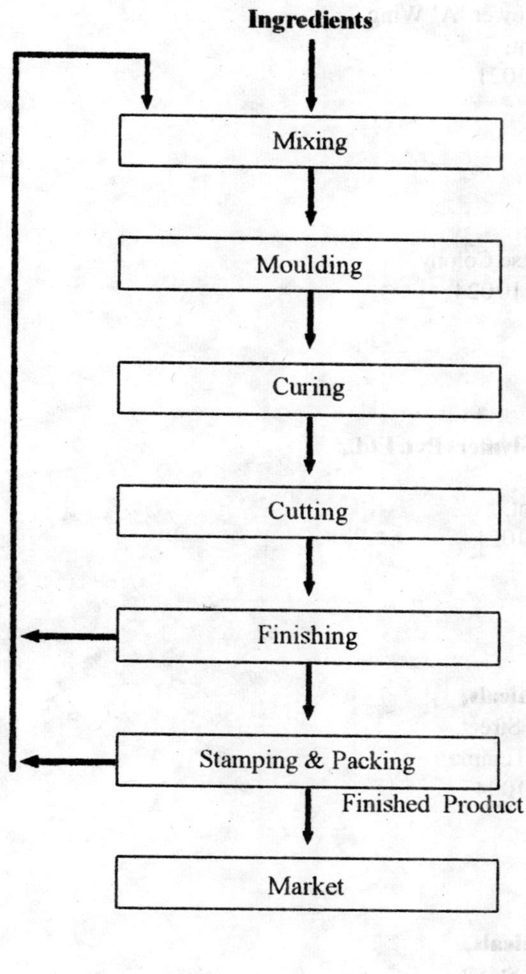

SUPPLIERS OF RAW MATERIALS

Rubber Chemicals:

Shama Rub-Chem Co. Pvt. Ltd.,
3-A, New Nai Niketan,
345, Mount Road,
Mazagaon,
Mumbai - 400 010

Rub-Chem Industries Pvt. Ltd.,
101, Mittal Tower 'A' Wing,
Nariman Point,
Mumbai - 400 021

Smoked Sheet:

Chemoplast,
C 362, Defense Colony,
New Delhi - 110 024

Factice:

Rishiroop Polymers Pvt. Ltd.,
65, Atilanta,
Nariman Point,
Mumbai - 400 021

Zinc Oxide:

Meera Chemicals,
89, Bhandari Street,
Near Round Temple,
Mumbai - 400 004

Stearic Acid:

Neera Chemicals,
89, Bhandari Street,
Near Round Temple,
Mumbai - 400 004

SUPPLIERS OF PLANT & MACHINERY

Mixing Mill & Hydraulic Press:

Bharat Enterprises,
Ashirwad Hevy Industrial Estate,
Building No. 3, Gala No. 20,
Ram Mandir Road, Goregaon (West),
Mumbai 400 104

Curtting Machine:

G. Engineering Works,
Howrah Anita Road,
Bankra Howrah - 71403

Testing Equipments:

P.S.I. Sales Pvt. Ltd.,
804, Hemkunt House,
6, Rajendra Place, New Delhi - 110 008

Boiler:

Indon Projects & Eqpt. Pvt. Ltd.,
D 170, Okhla Indl. Area,
Phase I, New Delhi 110 020.

Mixing Mill:

Muladhar Rubber Machines Pvt. Ltd.,
392, Shahabad, Daulat Pur,
Bawana Road, Delhi - 110 042
Ph. 594 798

Hydraulic Press:

United Engineering Co.,
Village Gokulpur, Sahi Mohalla,
Gokalpuri, Shahdara,
Delhi - 110 094

PLANT ECONOMICS OF RUBBER ERASERS

Rated Plant Capacity = 409.99 Grs./Day

COST OF LAND & BUILDING
(Total land area required 400 sq. mtr.) Rs. 7,20,000.00

LIST OF PLANT & MACHINERY

1. Mixing mill with chilled rolls and 25HP motor & red. gears batch
2. Hydralic press size 18"x18" 4 daylight with hydraulic pump
3. Cutting machine power operated
4. Rotating drum complete with 5 HP motor
5. Oil fired boiler
6. Packing machine
7. Laboratory testing equipment such as hardness testing balance, etc.

LIST OF RAW MATERIALS

1. Smoked sheet
2. Factice
3. Mineral oil
4. Antioxidant
5. Zinc oxide
6. Titanium calcined magnesia
7. Titanium oxide
8. Red oxide
9. Barytes
10. Kaolin
11. Whiting
12. Sulphur

FIXED CAPITAL

Land & Building	Rs.	7,20,000.00
Plant & Machinery	Rs.	6,12,000.00
Other Fixed Assets	Rs.	80,000.00
TOTAL	**Rs.**	**14,12,000.00**

TOTAL WORKING CAPITAL/MONTH

Raw Material	Rs.	91,475.80
Salary & Wages	Rs.	32,875.00
Utilities & Overheads	Rs.	41,000.00
TOTAL	**Rs.**	**1,65,350.80**

TOTAL CAPITAL INVESTMENT

Total Fixed Capital	Rs.	14,12,000.00
Total Working Capital for 3 Months	Rs.	4,96,052.40
TOTAL	**Rs.**	**19,08,052.40**

TURN OVER/ANNUM

By sale of 1,23,000 gross of Rubber Eraser	Rs.	38,13,000.00

PROFIT = RECEIPTS - COST OF PRODUCTION

= 38,13,000.00 - 25,74,483.12

= 12,38,516.88

PROFIT SALES RATIO = Profit/Sales x 100 = **32.23 %**

RATE OF RETURN = Operating Profit/T.C.I. x 100 = **64.41 %**

BREAK EVEN POINT (B.E.P.) = 43.70 %

32

RUBBER STAMP PAD & INKS

INTRODUCTION

Plastic rubber stamps are used in every commercial centre and office now the days. Due to fast development of trade, demand of pad inks are also increased enough. Pad inks mainly includes following three things.

i. Ink used on pad in less quantity but words should be marked dark and bright.
ii. Mark of ink should be very clear and dry soon on paper.
iii. The ink should not dry on pad or on stamp soon. There should be smell of any type.

But to keep all these three things together, it take much space and money. So authomatic stamp pad is one of the best among others. Pad ink is a thick fluid intended for marking with rubber stamps on paper, parchment or other material. It may be dye, solution, a pigment suspension or a mixture of solution and suspension of coloured substance in a suitable vehicle. Rubber stamp inks are usually solution of coal tar colour in glycerine. Alcohol is also used in some good quality pad inks.

Stamp - pad inks are widely used for a variety of purposes, such as, date stamping, marking standard instruction on a variety of surfaces, especially on paper. They are essentially non-drying inks and consists of basic dyes in an aqueous solution containing a high concentration of a hydroscopic agent, usually glycerol or diethylene glycol. The main necessities of these inks are described above. Drying of the pad is prevented by using high concentrations of glycerol. Hexylene glycol has been found suitable for sharp definitions of stamped impressions. Suitable basic and acidic dyes are used for colouring and their concentration vary between 2% to 8% according to the tinctorial strength of the dye used. Wide colour choice is possible in these inks. Sometimes, a small a mount of corrosion inhibitor like sodium borate and a rubber preservative chemical like thio-carbonilide may also be used.

USES & APPLICATIONS

Stamp - pad inks are widely used for a variety of purposes such as:

1. For date - stamping.
2. For marking standard instruction on variety of sources especially on papers.

Now a days as trade developed in every spheres the demand of such inks has also increased.

These inks are used in the houses, every offices, and commercial organisation.

PROCESS OF MANUFACTURE

Rubber stamp inks are of mainly two types,

i. Oil based.
ii. Glycerine based.

Oil based inks are those in which colour is dissolved in oils and glycerine based inks are those in which colour is dissolved in glycerine. Oil effects on rubber and so the oil based inks are in less use now-a-days.

Pad inks are found in various colours but purpal colour is in maximum use. Blue, green & red pad inks are also used but in very less quantity.

Purpal Colour *(Oil Based)*:

Purpal colour	:	3 parts
Oleic acid	:	5 parts
Castor oil	:	92 parts

Procedure:

Mix purpal colour in oleic acid stir it well, after that mix oil in this mixture and heat it on water bath.

Similarly different colours inks can be made by mixing respective colour soluble in oils by same procedure as described above.

Blue Ink:

Blue colour	:	3	parts
Oleic acid	:	6	parts
Castor oil	:	94	parts

Stamp Pad Moulding:

Stamp pad moulding machines are used for the production of stamp pad. The principle is to produce a “parision” - a tube of malten material-and close a mound around it, and introducting air to expand the parison into the shape or the mould. A measured quanitity of the moulding powder is put in tylinder, the feed end being of a sufficiently low temperature, being at the nozzle. The material should issue form the nozzle as a smooth slimy mass free from bubbles and lumps. A mould is closed around it and by introducing air it is expanded to the shape of the mould. The mould is opened and the piece thus formed is removed and given for finishing.

In injection moulding, the cylinder which is heated electrically is filled with the material and a mould is clamped tightly after centering it around the nozzle. The article is ejected after cooling. Usually solid toys are produced by the moulding process. But hollow toys can also be produced by first making two halves of a stam pad and then joining them by a suitable cement.

Cooling and Mould Release :

Some further time is allowed to elapse for cooling of the moulded article in the mould until it is sufficiently rigid to be ejected without any risk of deformation taking place subsequently. Control of mold temperature is also important if the quality of the article is to be maintained uniform and consistent through out the entire range. The mold temperature control systems allow the mold temperature to be raised to its optimum value before start up, so that during the initial period of production, the manufacture of highly strained parts from a cold mold and wastage of material due to short shots is avoided.

The mold is then opened to eject the molding and is closed again to receive the plasticized melt for the next cycle of operation.

Time Cycle :

The basic steps and operations of injection molding process are common in all injection molding machines, i.e, taking a quantity of plastics material, softening it in a cylinder by heating, forcing it under pressure by means of plunger of screw into a mold, cooling and plasticized melt in the mold, and ejectiong it out by opening the mold.

SKETCHES OF AUTOMATIC STAMP

Front View

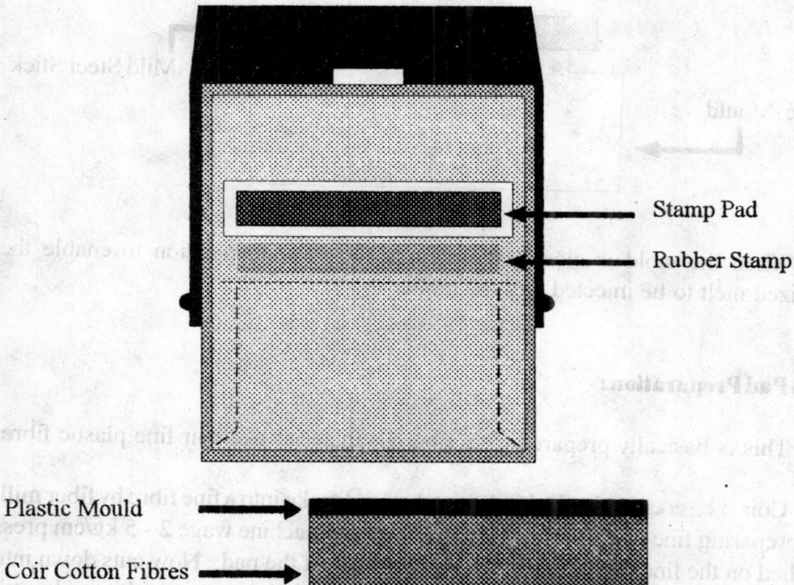

Mechanical Clamp of Rubber Stamp

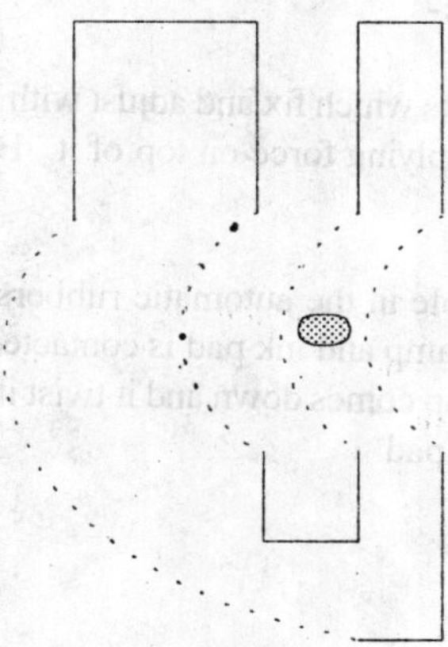

RubberStamp

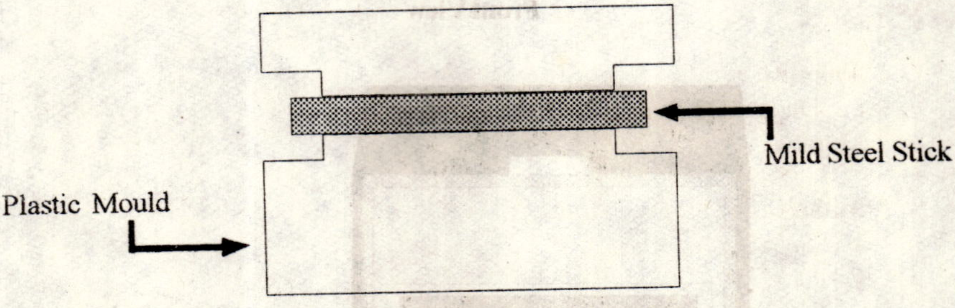

When the mold is closed, the cylinder is ready in position to enable the plasticized melt to be injected into the mold.

Stamp Pad Preparation :-

This is basically prepared from fiberous material like coir fine plastic fibre.

Coir (i.e., coconut husk) has been taken and make into a fine fibre by fiber mill. After preparing fine fiber it is pass through to press machine wage 2 - 5 kg/cm press is applied on the fine fiber, then it is formed a body of the pad. Now cuts down into a required size of pad, then pad is tightly fitted in a cloth bag stitched it, and put it in the thin plastic bag.

Now pad is ready to work. According to pad size, pad box also prepared wage is pad is kept. Now pad is ready for marketing.

Automatic Plastic Stamp:-

It is mainly two parts which fix and adjust with a clamp and fix rivet. Rubbers stamp is movable with applying force on top of it. Both these moulders are of fine plastics.

Ink pad is adjustable in the automatic rubbers stamp. Ink can be poured as required in it. Rubbers stamp and ink pad is contacted with each other. By applying force on it the rubber stamp comes down and it twist its sides. Stamp pad can be kept out from it for inking the pad.

SUPPLIERS OF RAW MATERIALS

Dyes:

Colour Chemicals Ltd.,
22, Dadabhai Naoroji Road,
Mumbai.

Sudarshan Chemical Industries (P) Ltd.,
162, Welleseley Road,
Poona - 1.

Ethylene Glycol:

Chemo India.,
24, Jambulwadi, Dadashaw Building.,
Ist Floor, Dhobi Talab,
Mumbai - 400 002

Glycerol:

Arun Rasyan Udyog,
Off 488, Katra Ishwar Bhavan,
Khari Baoli, Delhi - 110 006

Metal Sheets:

Mudra Dhatu Udyog (Bombay) Pvt Ltd.,
B-60, Bindal Industrial Estate,
Andheri-Kurla Road, Sakinaka,
Mumbai - 400 072

Rubber Chemical:

Bharat Adhesives
A-36, Mayapuri Indl. Area,
Phase - II, New Delhi - 110 064
Tel/Fax: 5407160, 5400710

Vimal Resin Pvt. Ltd.,
83, Anand Indl. Area, Mohan Nagar,
Sahibabad, Ghaziabad (U.P.)
Tel/Fax: 732993

PLANT AND MACHINERY SUPPLIERS

The A.P.V. Equipment Co Ltd.,
Hamilton House, 3, Graham Road,
Ballard Estate, Mumbai - 400 038

A.P.V. Texmaeo Ltd.,
2 Jessor Road, Dum Dum,
Calcutta - 700 028

Sheets Cutting Machines:

Bajaj Machinery Corporation
C-184, Naraina Indl. Area,
Phase - I, New Delhi - 110 028
Tel/Fax: 5797557 / 91-11-7525854

PRESENT MANUFACTURER OF PLANT AND MACHINERY

Tanks:

S. K. Engineering Company
C-7/4, Site - I, Indl. Area,
Bulandshahar Road, Ghaziabad (U.P.)
Tel/Fax: 711111

Boiler:

Sita Boiler Company
195-B, Libaspur Road, Samey Pur,
Delhi - 110 042 Tel/Fax: 729 4347, 7291044

Three Roll Mill:

Atlas Engineering Works,
8, Dewan Hall, Chandni Chowk,
Delhi - 110 006

Plastic Moulding Machinery:

Neoplasts Engg. P. Ltd.
Plot No. 43, GIDC Est Vmizo,
Vativa Ahemdabad.

33

SCREEN PRINTING ON PAPER/CARDS

INTRODUCTION

Like many areas in science and technology ,printing technology has undergone a process of revolution during the last 10 years. Not only has there been a radical improvement in the machineries but also in the various back-up service areas which makes the technological scenario of the printing industry equally exciting, sophisticated, if not little complex in nature.

This has been the result of the introduction of computer and electronic aided mechanisms have made into print technology and its related service areas. The magnitude of development in print technology has been quite phenomenal during the decade.

As the world is becoming faster in communication for the growing demand of corporate world, use of paper, visiting cards, greeting cards is increasing.

To meet the growing demand of printed paper, visiting cards, greeting cards a faster and accurate system was urgently needed. For this purpose computerised screen printing was introduced. The process of screen printing with computer has got many advantages like.

1. The reproducability of print, shade is very good.
2. Copying rate of prints is faster and can be varied.
3. The whole process is heat and clear compared to conventional screen printing.
4. Fine and complex prints can also be obtained with ease.
5. It saves labour.
6. It saves time at many-a-places in the process of printing.
7. Overall cost of production is low.

USES AND APPLICATIONS

The use of printed paper, visiting cards, greeting cards is even increasing. A system sophisticated with computer for screen printing on paper will be definitely useful. Printed paper, visiting cards, greeting cards are used at places well known to common people.

1. In corporate and administrative office.
2. In publicity of some article.
3. Greeting cards etc. for various occasion, festivals by people.

Better the quality and low cost of printing more the people will be attracted to use such facilities.

PRESENT MANUFACTURERS

Adographica
B-267, Okhla Phase I,
New Delhi - 110020
Phone : 684 1686

ABI Overseas Ltd.
G-76, Basement,
Kalkaji.
New Delhi - 110019
Phone : 646 1682

Cartolabs Enterprises
T 5, Bagrumpur,
Malviya Nagar,
New Delhi - 110017
Phone : 643 0124

Lynx Printers
4B, Tamoor Nagar,
New Friends Colony,
New Delhi - 110065
Phone : 683 7072

COMPUTERISEDSCREENPRINTINGPROCESS

The computerised screen printing can be divided into two parts. First part is making image on computer and taking out "Print out" and the second part is taking out copies of the "print out" by screen printing machines.

Part One :-

There are three main steps in "print out" from computer

1. The personal computer in which text and/or graphics are entered or transferred into it from other sources, like importing of files (from floppy) from other frames. This is done by the acceptance of images via. scanners and digitisers

2. The complete desktop publishing system will support output to a variety of devices including a laser printer, using a Xerographic technique to output directly on plain paper.

The output device, typically a laser printer supporting a standard page description language should allow the printing of combined text and graphics.

3. Page layout or typesetting software allowing screen based cut-and -paste from a variety of software sources and lending full support to the page description.

Part Two :-

Screen printing process is employed successfully for printing on all kinds of paper. With screen printing light color appear paper and more brilliant when printed on colored stock. It is also possible to print on silver, gold, bronze and other metallic papers if the ink is mixed with appropriate binding varnishes to reduce its brittleness upon drying. Bright colour do not hold well and are liable to get scratched or chipped. If the paper is more porous like blotting it is recommended to use a stiffer ink. Like paper, there are many varieties of card which can be used for screen printing. There are two method available for it.

1. Hand Printing or Silk Printing.
2. Automatic Printing Machine.

Cut a window in the cardboard so that the glass sheet fits exactly in it. While printing place the glass sheet inside the cardboard. This way when the glass sheet is surrounded by a cardboard of more or less the same thickness, the squeegee can be pulled evenly and smoothly across the screen and over the glass sheet without the screen mesh coming in contact with the glass edge, thus avoiding any possibility of damage to the screen mesh. In case due to some reason it is not practical or desirable to cut a window in a thick sheet of cardboard, there is another device. Cut two 'L' shaped pieces of cardboard of the same thickness, so that when placed together they form a window. Of these two pieces, one piece say 'X' may be fixed to the printing table using gum tape the other piece, say 'Y' being left loose and movable. While printing keep the glass sheet in position, one edge touching the fixed piece of 'X,' place the loose piece of 'Y' against the other edge of the glass sheet before lowering the frame. After printing, the loose piece 'Y' should be moved aside to remove the printed glass sheet.

Some form of build-up is necessary while printing on any thick material with shape edges. The usual fitting of the screen frame, as for printing on paper, will not serve for printing on a thicker material. For this purpose, the height of the screen surface will have to be slightly raised so that when the frame is lowered, it will rest evenly and flat on the surface to be printed. Besides, the underside of the screen fabric should be reinforced with cellotape for additional protection.

FLOWSHEET

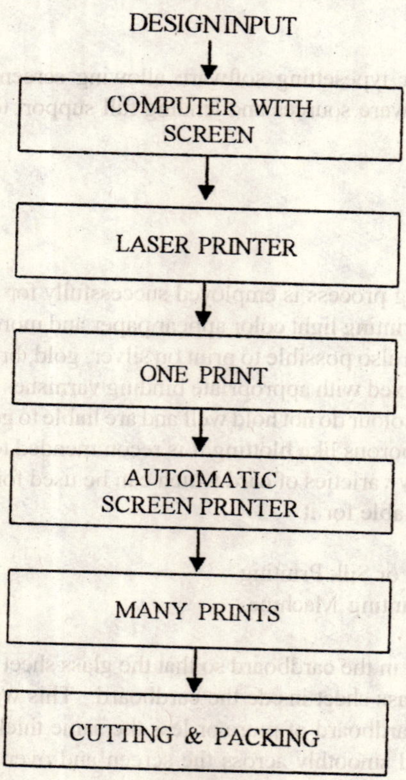

SUPPLIERS OF RAW MATERIALS

Papers :-

Om Prakash Jitendra Kumar & Company
63, Darya Ganj,
New Delhi - 110 002
Phones : 326 9680, 327 1380

Narain Paper Mart
4034/3, Haryana Market,
Chawri Bazar, Delhi - 110 006
Phone : 291 5135

Himgiri Paper Products
B-24, Indl. Area Lawrence Road,
New Delhi - 110 035
Phone : 718 9005

Inks - Toners etc. :-

Viram Dichen Corporation
281 - A, Samuel Street
Mumbai - 400 003
Phone : 329168

Kusum Enterprises
44 Gaya Building , 4th Floor,
109, Yusuf Mecharali Road,
Mumbai - 400 003
Phone : 345521

Printers Emporium
Connaught Circus,
New Delhi - 110 001

Khanna Printers Stores
Chata Bazar,
Mathura (U.P.)

Art Printing Inks Company
104, Site-4, Indl. Area,
Sahibabad, Ghaziabad, (U.P.)
Phone/fax : 767882

SUPPLIERS OF PLANT AND MACHINERY

Desk Top Publishing Systems :

Software Packages :-

A.T.E. Enterprises Limited (Marketed By)

Mumbai Telephone	:	287 2245, 636 6626, 636 7859
Delhi Telephone	:	371 2747, 371 2929
Bangalore Telephone	:	648760
Calcutta Telephone	:	287289
Chennai Telephone	:	75820
Coimbatore Telephone	:	33286

Solustan Electronics Systems Pvt. Ltd. (Developed By)
NIDC, Nr. Lambha,
Post Narol,
Ahemedabad - 382 405
Tel: 8335721, 832346

Gautam Gupta
PC Quest,
D-74 Panchsheel Enclave,
New-Delhi - 110017
Tel: 6433999, 6435999, 6413938

Inderjit Moulik
Sonata Software
36, Ganesh Chandra Avenue
Calcutta - 700 018
Tel. 279747/279749.

Hardware (Computer, Mouse, Printer etc) :-

Raba Contel (P) Ltd.
6 th Floor, Qutab Hotel,
New Mehrauli Road
New Delhi - 110016
Tel: 686 3901

Esskayjay's Kreation Pvt. Ltd.
7 B, Kiron Shankar Roy Road,
2nd Floor, Calcutta - 700001
Phone: 28 3903

Dealer :-

Team Computers Pvt. Ltd.
B - 12, Somdutt Chambers - 1
5, Bhikaji Cama Place,
New Delhi - 110 066
Ph: 609775, 674246

Screen Printing Machine :-

Lolita Manufacturing Works,
93-40, Katra Ganga Bishan,
Gaushalla Road, Krishanganj,
Delhi - 110 006 (Near D.C.M Ram Lila Maidan)

"Pricol " Automatic Screen Printing Machine
Premier Instruments & Controls Ltd.
Post Box No - 6331,
1087 Bec Avanashi Road,
Coimbatore - 641 037

Solar Machines Pvt. Ltd.
22 - D, Wadia Charities Buildings,
2nd Floor Brelvi Road,
Fort, Mumbai - 400 023

Ahuja Graphic Machinery Pvt. Ltd.
Prabhadevi Industrial Estate,
Veer Savarkar Marg,
Mumbai - 400 025
Phone : 422 8515

Inter Press Equipments & Machines Pvt. Ltd.
A - 16, Nariana Industrial Area - II
New Delhi - 110 028
Phone : 5704450/51/52

Print Link ,
Unit No. 31, Ist Floor,
Laxmi Industrial Estate,
Off Eastern Ceramics Ltd.,
Bangur Nagar, Goregaon (West),
Mumbai - 400 090
Phone : 672 7166

PLANT ECONOMICS OF SCREEN PRINTING ON PAPER/CARDS

Rated Plant Capacity = 10000.00 Nos./Day

COST OF LAND & BUILDING

(Total land area required 300 sq. mtr.) Rs. 2,10,000.00

LIST OF PLANT & MACHINERY

1. Complete Desk Top Publishing System (including computer, laser printer, mouse, floppies etc.)
2. Automatic Screen Printing Machine
3. Symphony Air Condition Cooler for Computer
4. Miscellaneous

LIST OF RAW MATERIALS

1. Printing Ink
2. Screen
3. Paper For Visiting Cards, Greeting Cards And Other Type
4. Miscellaneous

FIXED CAPITAL

Land & Building	Rs.	2,10,000.00
Plant & Machinery	Rs.	2,82,000.00
Other Fixed Assets	Rs.	1,02,000.00
TOTAL	**Rs.**	**5,94,000.00**

TOTAL WORKING CAPITAL/MONTH

Raw Material	Rs.	1,30,000.00
Salary & Wages	Rs.	14,125.00
Utilities & Overheads	Rs.	7,620.00
TOTAL	**Rs.**	**1,51,745.00**

TOTAL CAPITAL INVESTMENT

Total Fixed Capital	Rs.	5,94,000.00
Total Working Capital for 3 Months	Rs.	4,55,235.00
TOTAL	**Rs.**	**10,49,235.00**

TURNOVER/ANNUM

1. Paper Cost (Recovery)
2. Printing Charges(a) Visiting Cards

Rs. 28,50,000.00

PROFIT = RECEIPTS - COST OF PRODUCTION

= 28,50,000.00 - 21,17,516.70

= 7,32,483.30

PROFIT SALES RATIO = Profit / Sales x 100 = **25.70 %**

RATE OF RETURN = Operating profit / T.C.I. x 100 = **69.31 %**

BREAK EVEN POINT (B.E.P) = 36.05 %

34

SEALING WAX

INTRODUCTION

1. This is used in letters and envelopes, for impressing, seals on documents, parcel and insured covers.
2. Black sealing wax is commonly used in post offices and Railways.
3. Coloured sealing wax are used in other offices to seal the parcels etc.
4. Sealing is essential for the safety of the matter contained in the sealed package so the application of sealing wax is increasing very rapidly.

MANUFACTURINGPROCESS

The manufacturers of sealing wax consist the following process:

1. Melting of shellac.
2. Mixing of other ingredients.
3. Moulding
4. Testing

First of all required amount of shellac is fed into the melting pan. Generally melting pan is made of copper. The temperature for the melting of shellac is kept around 75-80oC. When the shellac is completely melted the heated rosin is fed into the melting pan. The whole mass is now stirred with a rod or using stirrer. Now the required amounts of fillers such as kaolin, barytes etc. are fed into the pan. The care should be taken that the filler should be finest one. After mixing of fillers the whole mass is again stirred for the homogeneous mass. Now small amount of bees wax and castor oil is added. Bees wax and castor oil imparts plasticity in the sealing wax. Now the colours are added. For mixing of colour the paste of colour is made with spirit or turpentine oil. Now this molten material is then poured in the metal moulds made of aluminium or gun metal. The marks of the lines of Junction of the mould box may be afterwards removed by holding the sticks over a clear fire, it passing them over a blue gas flame. The sticks of the sealing wax is now tested for its quality. After quality test it is then packed in cartons containing 500 gms. of sticks. Then it is stored and send to the market.

PROCESS DIAGRAM FOR MANUFACTURE OF SEALING WAX

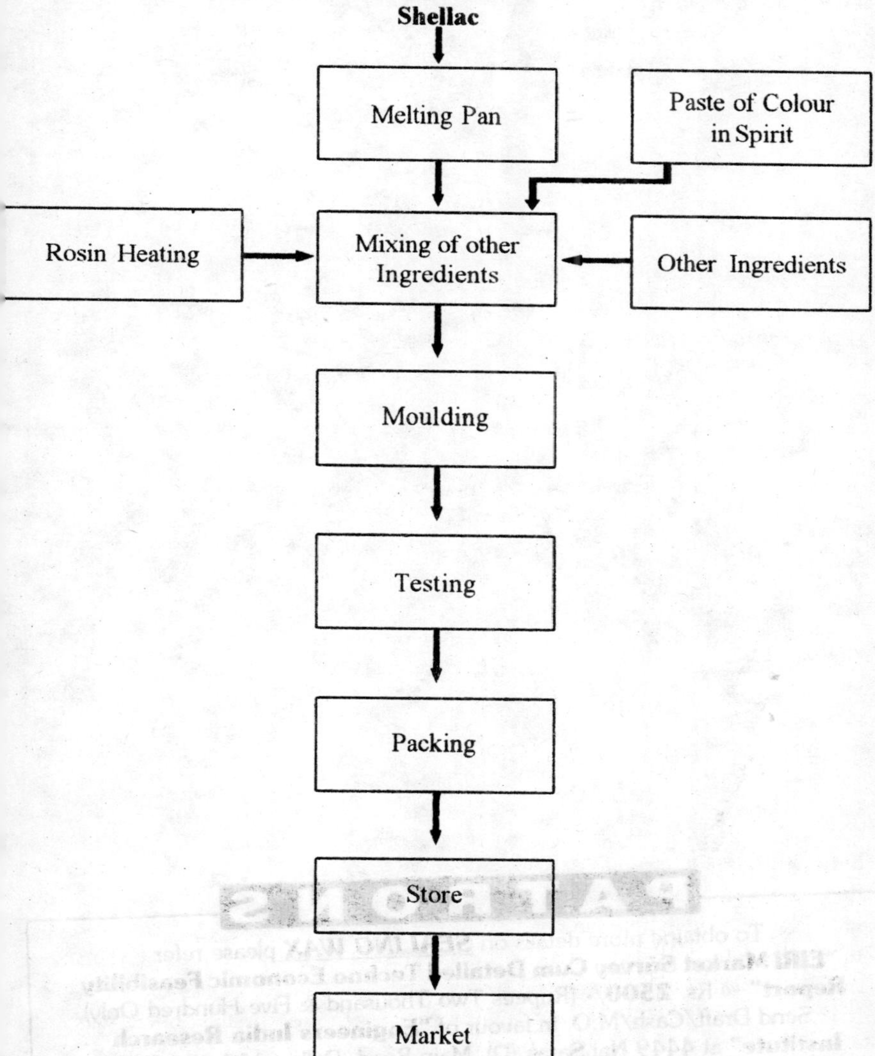

FORMULATION

Shellac	40%
Kaolin	20%
Barytes	20%
Rosin	20%
Bees wax + Castor oil	q.s. (0.5%)
Colours	q.s.

35

STAPLES, GEM CLIPS & PAPER PINS

INTRODUCTION

Paper pins are known to most of the people as these are used widely for pinning paper sheets in offices schools etc. The paper pin is made of mild steel wire of 20-22 SWG with a pointed end at one side and a well formed head on the other end. The pins are plated so as to make them reristant to rusting and corrosion, immediately after mechanical forming. In the growing economy like ours, where establishments (both in public and private sectors) are growing in up by leaps and bounds to cope with development programmes, stationary articles like gem clips and paper pins stapples, being an intimate of parts office stationery, will have a bright future.

Gem clips and paper pins are used to hold two or more papers together, in every office. There are so many papers in an office related to a correspondence, typed in loose pages, that they may get mixed up leading to confusions, so to keep them together some device was needed to hold them together. This job is done by paper pin and stapples etc. Gem clip present a number of advantages over the allpins. Gemclip does not damage the paper. It just holds the papers with spring effect, while pins make holes in the paper. But, paper pins provide a greater reliability in withholding papers together and just by removing the pin paper can be freed easily when so required.

Gem clip is made of nickel polished steel wire. This is folded at fourplaces.

All pins, Gem clips and Staples Pins are used to hold two or more papers together. The only difference being that an all pin and Gem clip can be removed easily when papers are needed to be separated, while a staple pins, if needed to be removed, is destroyed and can not be reused while an all pin can be removed and used again & again. An all pin is a straight pin with flattened head which never deserts papers tied with it unless & until some outer force is applied from the pointed size to push it headward.

USES AND SCOPES

Gem clips and pins are used at every place where paper work is done. As the industrialization proceeds ahead, the use of these items will also increase. It is used some what more due to its specific characteristic features, It holds the paper without damaging it. Any of the papers can be added without any difficulty. More over, it is easy to handle.

The consumption or rather its demand can be estimated by approximating the use of stationer in offices. Even if there are 10,00,000 offices in india, where much paper work is done in a day, and so many schools & colleges together, several tons of allpins must be consumed daily.

The use of staple pins & all pins is very simple and known to every body. In every Govt. or Private office, they are extensively used. As described earlier, an all pin is generally used where papers are to be separated after a particular interval of time and all pins can be used again and again, while a staple pin is used for permanent coupling of papers and if removed can not be reused. shop keepers also use stapler pins after packing the item in the paper bags or polythene bags.

Steel Wire for Staples:-

The cross sectional dimensions of various sizes of rectangular wire and their tolerances are given as :-

Thickness (mm)	**Width** (mm)	**Tolerance limits** (mm)
0.35	0.50	0.05
0.45	0.70	
0.55	0.75	
0.55	0.80	

Sizes and tolerances of wires of shapes other than round & rectangular are supplied as per agreement between supplier & purchaser.

The material specifications prescribed for staple pin wire, vide IS: 4224 - 1972, has under gone certain modifications in the chemical composition & mechanical properties.

Physical Properties of Staple Wires:-

Tensile test of steel wire is performed as per IS: 1521 - 1960. Values of tensile strength of cold drawn steel wires are given below :-

Light duty staples	:	590/880 N/mm^2 = 60/90 kg/mm^2
Heavy duty staples	:	1175/1570 N/mm^2 = 120/160 kg/mm^2

Note :- 1 N/mm^2 = 0.1020 kgs/mm^2

One tensile test is carried on a coil selected out of 10 coils of staple pinwires. Reverse bend test is essential for assessing the wires formability during staple making. One bend test is carried out for every 5 tons of finished wires of staple pin belonging to the same size group & lot. Bend tests are carried in accordance with IS: 1716 - 1971.

Three forward & backward bends through 180°. Over a diameter equal to six times the wire-diameter/cross section is supposed to be sufficient if it does not show any sign of failures.

Each coil or bundle of the wire is tied or fastened compactly and a tag with legible marking is attached with each coil. The tag contains details of wire size, type, finish, length, weight, manufacturers name & BIS certification marks etc.

Staplers using Standard Staples:-

The paper fastening office type staplers using staples or staple pins of the given specifications, are specified by the Bureau of Indian Standards under IS:5348 - 1969.

These staplers or stapling machines are of the following types :-

Desk type :-

1. Light duty,
2. Heavy duty,
3. Heavy duty long reach.

Plier type:-

Operating lever, hinge, staple channel, staple magazine, spring, spring follower, staple driver, vertical chute, chinching anvil, and base of the machine are the important parts of a stapler.

Taiwan - A Potential Supplier of Technical Know-how:-

Staple pin, gemclip and paper pins making machines of Taiwanese origin are very much successful.

In a move to attract increasing investment & tie-ups with Taiwan, Indian Govt. has made it possible for Taiwanese businessmen to visit India and interact with our businessman . Eleven Indian diplomatic missions abroad have been authorized to issue visas to Taiwanese nationals for business visits, as & when called for, if they produce a letter of invitation from an Indian businessman. Several more missions will soon be authorized for the purpose.

The decision to allow easy entry for Taiwanese businessmen into Indian business is significant. The Taiwanese are considered a big spenders in the world today having a large surplus. they are also faced with the critical condition that Hongkong is going to be transferred to China in 1997. Therefore, they need to spread their international links separately before the transfer of Hongkong. These are welcome situations for Indian businessmen to improve business relations with Taiwan. The other overseas country whose machineries for gem clips, paper pins and staple pins are preferred, Germany. The business relation with Germany is already congenial.

Thus, the entrepreneurs have a choice to select the capital equipments for mfg. these stationery hardwares from any one of these two technological giants.

PROCESS OF MANUFACTURE

Pin Manufacture:-

All pins are made on semi-automatic machine. These machines differ greatly in size and in design, but the principle of operation is much the same in all of them. Pins are made in a machine by five distinct operations of automatic nature.

Namely:

1. Forming the head.
2. Feeding the wire.
3. Pinching the wire.
4. Cutting the wire and forming the point.
5. Expelling the pin.

The head is formed by compressing and flattening against a die. The portion of the wire which project beyond this die remains after the precisely formed pin has been cut from the wire. This compressing and flatlening is done by a hammer which is attached to a reciprocating member, called a hammer stock, which in turn is actuated usually by a crank pin. The amount of wire which projects beyond the die, governs the size and thickness of the head and is regulated by adjusting the cutting knives to the proper distance form two dies.

Feeding the wire:-

Wire coil hangs on the decoiler stand. Its one free end is fed into the machine where the pin-head forms. After the head is formed, the hammer moves away from the die, and the die opens up and allows the feed mechanism to push the wire with a nail-head. At the end, the correct distance is adjusted through the die, to give a nail of the required length. The feeding mechanism is driven by an adjustable crank on the flywheel of the machine and by adjusting this crank various lengths can be obtained. The feed mechanism also pulls the wire through a series of staggered rolls as it leaves the steel, to straighten it.

Pinching:-

When the hammer has reached the end of the stroke, the wire has been fed the correct amount for the pin required and the die closes to pinch the wire. This thin action is motivated by crank at the crank shot.

Cutting Length:-

Immediately after the wire is pinched, two knives each attached to a lever come together and cut the wire. These cutting knives are ground to form the point of the pin. At the same time, that the cut is made, this point is formed by pressing the wire into the shape required and in doing so, some of the metal is squeezed out or protrudes between the knives and is cut off by the machine. These cut-offs are called whiskers.

Ejection of ready pin :-

Sometimes, because of dull knives or in sufficiently close adjustments the pin will still adhere to the wire, when the cutting knives open up. The cutting knives opening the return stroke of the hammer and in order to remove this adhering nail, an expeller comes into action, knocking the pin downward out of the die cavity, or else, the next stroke of the hammer will break it.

Nickel Polishing:-

After all mechanical operations, nickel polish is done as the clips and pins polish done in Barrel type set-up.

Bright Nickel plating, which deserves the name, have been employed for barrel plating. Electrolytes are available which can be used with the same efficiency in open-ended and immersed barrels as the modern plating solutions employed in still baths.

The composition of solution used in barrel plating are similar to those used for still plating, although earlier solutions used to have much lower metal concentrations.

Concentrations of 100 gms/ litre nickel sulphate used to be regarded as high and 150 gms/litre nickel sulphate as very high. Apart from nickel sulphate, earlier solutions also contained ammonium chloride, sodium sulphate, magnesium sulphate, magnesium chloride and sodium chloride etc.

Typical brighteners for barrel Nickel plating solution are:-

1. Acetylene derivatives
2. Derivatives of oxypyrinidine
3. Quaternary ammonium compounds.
4. Amines.
5. Pyridine derivatives.
6. Dye stuffs e.g. fuchsine and uninare dyes.

The PH of barrel nickel plating solutions used to be maintained is below 4.

Barrel nickel plating solutions operate at room temperatures between 40 and 60°C.

Current densities of between 1 & 1.5 A/dm² or more in some cases may be considered.

The deposition rate of Nickel in a barrel plating bath is normally higher in an emerged barrel unit than in an open ended barrel.

Plating Solutions:-

The main characteristic of a & bright nickel plating solution is that it contains special addition agents which effect the deposits agents which effect the deposition of bright nickel. Bright nickel plating solution bath contained cobalt sulphate, nickel formate and formaldehyde as addition agents and is used cut with following composition

	gms/litre
Nickel Sulphate	240
Nickel Chloride	30
Boric Acid	30
Nickel Formate	45
Cobalt Sulphate	2.6
Formaldehyde	2.5
Ammonium Sulphate	0.8

The PH of the solutions is maintained at 5.5 to 4.5 and the temp. is 60°C.

The manufacturing process of staples is completely semiautomatic. The wire of required thickness is purchased from outside and is fed into the machine. The wire is cut and bent at 90°C on two points and come out. The pins are then packed manually and dispatched.

PROCESS FLOW SHEET

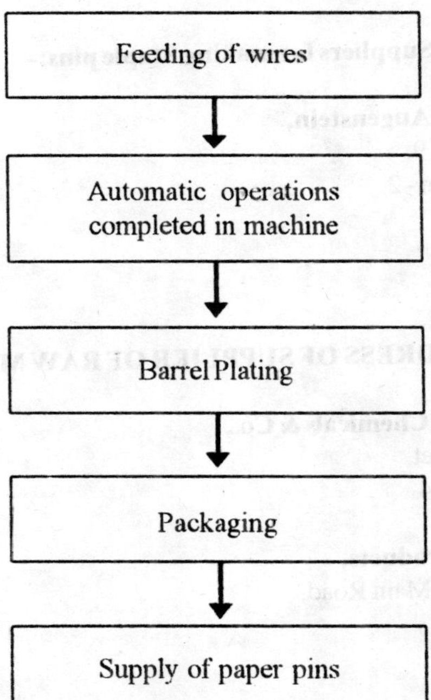

PLANT & MACHINERY SUPPLIERS

Paper Pin Machine & Drier Drum:-

Burma Industrial Corpn.,
G.T. Road, Putlighat,
Amritsar (Punjab).

Plating Equipment & Plating Salts:-

S.Singh & Company
Gandhinagar,
G.T. Road,
Ludhiana.

Complete Plant Supplier:-

S.B. Machine Tools,
23/4, Street No. 11,
New Rohtak Road,
New Delhi - 110 005

Overseas Machinery Suppliers for making Staple pins:-

Friedrich Karl Augenstein,
Flieder Street - 19,
D - 7531, Keltern - 2,
Germany

NAME & ADDRESS OF SUPPLIER OF RAW MATERIALS

Mehta Manmal Chemicals & Co.,
87 - 88 Kika Street,
Mumbai - 400 004

Eastern Wire Products,
223, Manickolla Main Road,
Calcutta - 11

RAW MATERIALS

(requirement per month)

1. Nickel Plated M.S. Wire (20 & 22 swg sizes) for Gem clips & Allpins(paper) 1000 kg.
2. Electroplating Materials & others

Note :-

Since the capacity of the plant is considered in weights of 'all pins' and 'gem clips' (i.e. 20 kgs each/day), the weight of M.S. wire taken as raw material will be divided equally between the two products.

PLANT ECONOMICS OF GEM CLIPS, PPER PINS & STAPLE PINS

Rated Plant Capacity = 60.00 Kgs./Day
= 18000.00 Kgs./Annum

COST OF LAND & BUILDING

(Total land areq required 150 sq. mtr.) Rs. 2,00,000.00

LIST OF PLANT & MACHINERY

1. Gem clips & paper pins producing machine semi-automatic with dies and accessories
2. Wire Stand & wire straightener with tensioning system
3. Automatic Stapler Pin making machine with all accessories
4. Electroplating unit with all the standard accessories
5. Testing & Inspection Equipments Working tools, fixtures, weighing and counting machine

LIST OF RAW MATERIALS

1. M.S. wire (20 & 22 swg sizes) for Gem clips & Allpins (Paper pins)
2. Electroplating Chemicals and additives, Pickling Chemicals, etc.
3. Imported Staple pin wires (as per specifications)
4. Packaging materials (i.e.; different sizes of printed card board/paper boxes)
5. Miscellaneous stores

FIXED CAPITAL

Land & Building	Rs.	2,00,000.00
Plant & Machinery	Rs.	4,00,000.00
Other Fixed Assets	Rs.	1,00,000.00
TOTAL	**Rs.**	**7,00,000.00**

TOTAL WORKING CAPITAL/MONTH

Raw Material	Rs.	59,250.00
Salary & Wages	Rs.	24,843.00
Utilities & Overheads	Rs.	35,600.00
TOTAL	**Rs.**	**1,19,693.00**

TOTAL CAPITAL INVESTMENT

Total Fixed Capital	Rs.	7,00,000.00
Total Working Capital for 3 Months	Rs.	3,59,079.00
TOTAL	**Rs.**	**10,59,079.00**

TURNOVER/ANNUM

1. By selling 15000 Kgs.(3.0 crores) Gem Clips
2. By selling 15000 Kgs. (2.4 crores) Paper Pins
3. By sales of 4 lakh packets of Staple Pins of all sizes

Rs. 24,70,000.00

PROFIT = RECEIPTS - COST OF PRODUCTION
= 24,70,000.00 - 17,62,916.38
= 7,07,083.62

PROFIT SALES RATIO = Profit/Sales x 100 = **28.63 %**

RATE OF RETURN = Operating Profit/T.C.I. x 100 = **66.26 %**

BREAK EVEN POINT (B.E.P.) = 47.16 %

36

STENCIL PAPERS

INTRODUCTION

Stencil papers are used for the purpose of duplicating copies. There are mainly two types of stencils which are in use these days i.e. typing stencils and pen stencils.

The stencil papers which are coated with a compound of nitro-cellulose are mainly used for duplicating and these stencil papers can produce more than thousand copies per stencil paper.

The estimated demand of the stencil papers in the country is reported to be in the order of 25 lakhs quires. The main consumers are the different Governmental Institutions offices, establishment and various Government semi-government under-taking. They consume more than 59% of the total demand in the country. The rest being consumed by various commercial establishment. Being a consumable item , there appears to be a good scope for this item in the country. The estimated increase in demand in every year as shown in the market position.

The demand is reported in the tune of 15%. There is good export potential for this item in the middle cast, south East, Gulf and African countries.

Duplicating has grown rapidly in large part because of the use of high speed copies as xerographic copier duplicators producing hundreds & thousands of copies in a run-copier-duplicators, e.g. xerox 9200, 9400, 9500 Van Dyk 8000, Estman Kodak 150, do not duplicate from a master, they remage at every cycle and for every copy. They are customarily used with a panoply of feeders, sorters staplers etc.

USES AND APPLICATIONS

The coated stencil paper are used in following field:-

a) In school, colleges and Govt. of ices for printing immediate documentations.
b) It is used for the purpose of duplicating copies.
c) There are used types of stencil one bind is used for typing stencil and other type is pen stencil.
d) With the help of these stencil paper, the necessary work can be done within a limited time.

B.I.S. SPECIFICATIONS

1. **Scope**

This standard prescribes the requirements and the methods of sampling and test for waxless stencil papers used on duplicating machines

2. **Terminology**

For the purpose of this standard, the definitions given in IS : 4395 - 1967 shall apply.

3. **Requirements**

(1). Description:

A. The stencil paper when cut on the typewriter on by a stylus by hand, shall be capable of rendering impressions when worked on a duplicating machine with duplicating ink. The impressions shall be of good definition and shall be free from patches, pin-holes, marks etc.

B. The stencil paper shall be free from any pronounced and disagreeable odour.

C. The stencil paper shall permit visibility of guides placed under it.

(2). Material:

The stencil paper shall be of suitable fibrous tissue coated with non-wax-based film forming material.

(3). Elongation

The average elongation of both directions shall be not more than 6% when tested by the method prescribed in 12.3 of IS : 1060 (Part I) -1966.

(4). Tensile Strength

The average tensile strength of both direction shall be less than 0.35 kg/cm width when tested by the methods prescribed in 12.3 of IS: 1060 -1966(Part I)

(5). Burst Factor

The brust factor shall noteless than 7.5 when tested as prescribed in 12.5 of IS : 1060 (Part I) - 1966

(6). Mass of coating

The mass of the coated stencil paper shall be not less than 48 g/m^2 and mass of the solution casting shall be not less than 35 g/m^2.

(7). Cut-outs & Filling

The stencil paper shall withstand the cutouts & filling test.

(8). Use with Stylus

The stencil paper shall show clear & uniform cutting with a stylus pen having a round (not sharp) point . It shall not tear or pull the paper at the time of writing with stylus pen using a writing plate with normal uniform pressure & shall not show any feathering.

(9). Performance

The stencil paper shall be capable of producing not less than 750 clear copies and then, after three days, another 500 copies without distortion, cracks of other failures that impairs legibility. The cuts of the stencil shall allow the ink to flow readily to give clear impressions.

(10). Leqibility of Typing

The stencil paper shall be such that the cut stencil can be read easily against a lighted background .

(11). Moisture Resistance

The stencil paper shall withstand the moisture resistance test.

(12). Keeping Quality

The stencil paper shall be capable of retaining its survivability under normal storage conditions for not less than two years from the date of manufacture which shall be tested by the acclerated ageing test.

(13). Backing Sheet

Each sheet of stencil paper shall be properly backed with a backing sheet confirming to I.S : 3301 - 1965. The backing sheet shall be suitably punched to enable it to be properly fitted to the respective duplicating machine for which the punching has been intended.

(14). Interleaving Sheets

Each stencil paper shall be interleaved with a grease-proof paper of a sheer of carbon paper (singleside of double side) as agreed to between the purchaser and the supplier. In case of interleaving with grease proof paper, eight extra sheets of carbon paper of appropriate size shall be provided for every 25 stencil papers.

(15). Sizes

The size of the stencil paper shall be as agreed to between the purchaser and supplier.

(16). Scale

The limit up to which the cutting can be done for different sizes of stencil papers including A3 or A4 size, as the case may be , shall be indicated on the stencil.

4. **Packing & Marketing**

(A). Packing - Stencil sheet shall be securely packed in packets of 25, 50 or 100 grams required.

(B). Marketing :- Each packet shall be marked with the following information.

a) Name & size of the material.
b) Number of sheets in the packet & the type of interleaving.
c) Name of the manufacturer & for recognized trade-mark, if any.
d) Month & year of Manufacture, &
e) Batch number in code or otherwise, to enable the lot of manufacture to be traceed from records.

(C). The packets may also be marked with the ISI Certification Mark.

5. Samplings

The method of drawing representative samples of the material, number of tests to be performed and the criteria for conformity of the material to the requirements of this specification shall be as prescribed in Appendix S.

MANUFACTURING PROCESS

The process of manufacture of the stencil papers is carried at in two steps. First step involves the prehiaration of the paper coating solution / paste and in the second stage coating the solution over the tissue paper.

The manufacture of the stencil paper coating solution is carried art with utmost precision and prescribed formulation. Any variation of the raw material may have adverse affect on the properties of the paper.

Initially all the ingredients are weighed and measured according to the formulation . Batch process is preferred as the proper formulation can be easily controlled. All the contents, according to the formulation are carefully measured into the reaction mixing vessel. The contents are mixed homogenous in order to have maximum reaction products. Later the contents are fed to the three rod mill so that it becomes into a thick paste form. Three roll mill is a continuous unit containing 3 parallel rolls of equal diameter maintained in a rigid frame work. The rolls run at different speeds, the receiving rolls being the slowest and the discharge roll being the fastest.

The clearance in between the front roll, back rolls and the middle rolls is adjusted independently. The pigment with the oil is placed in between the first and second rolls. The grinded and dispersed paste is removed from the last roll by a tapered delivery chute fitted with a scrapper pan.

The resulting paste obtained from the triple roll mill is charged into highspeed mixer with nitrocellulose ether and spirit, titanium dioxide etc. for atleast 1 hour.

In mixers the blades at the bottom of the vessel scoop the batch upward . The high shearing stress and the blade impact easily reduce agglomerates and aid the intimidate dispersions. Now the paste is ready to be coated over the tissue papers.

The coating of the paste over the paper is carried art with the help of stencil tissue coating machine. Solution coating requires a smoothing device of post metering set such as metering rod of air knife. Generally the application roll operates in the web direction, however it can also operate in the reverse direction if additional coating is desired .

Such coated paper roll is then further taken to stencil paper collecting machine. Later this paper is pasted to the backing tissue paper duly printed and ent to size. The size of paper is selected according to the demand. Further the prepared paper is send for packaging.

The final stencil papers are tested according to the standard as mentioned in the Indian standard of customers desired.

SUPPLIERS OF RAW MATERIALS

Indian Tissue Paper Suppliers:-

Ajanta paper and General Products Ltd.,
Vadavali Road,
Kalyan.

Alok paper Industries,
F/7, Industrial Estate,
Polo Ground, Indore (M.P)

For Import Papers:

Hoseph & Company
I.M.F. Rolling Mill,
Compound Vikhoroli,
Mumbai - 400 083

Jessop & Co. Ltd.,
I.M.F. Rolling Mill,
Compound Vikhorolli,
Mumbai - 400 083

For detail Content at:-

Department of Industrial Development
(Foreign Collection Section)
Udyog Bhavan,
New Delhi - 110 001

Supplier of Various Chemicals:

Desai Chemicals, Sagar
Talkies Building, Abid Road,
Hyderabad.

High Speed Mixers:

Ferro-Tech Engineers
Pratap Bhawan, Ground Floor,
5, Bahadurshah Zafar Marg,
New Delhi - 110 002
Ph.: 3351848, 3351830, 3318213
Fax: 91-11-3324082

Tripple Roll Mills:

Ferro-Tech Engineers
Pratap Bhawan,
Ground Floor,
5, Bahadurshah Zafar Marg,
New Delhi - 110 002
Ph.: 3351848, 3351830, 3318213
Fax: 91-11-3324082

Power Press:

Basant Industries
369, Basant Road,
Indl. Area-B,
Ludhiana - 141 003
(Punjab)
Ph.: 0161-534573
Fax: 91-161-533317

Sher-E-Punjab Engineering Works
CB-385, Indra Market,
Ring Road, Naraina,
New Delhi - 110 028
Ph.: 3298229/3298059
Fax: 91-11-3298229

Bajaj Machinery Corporation
47, Shradanand Marg,
(G.B. Road.)
Delhi - 110 006
Ph.: 7525854, 525861, 5797557
Fax: 91-11-7525854

Boilers:

Thermofab India
A-14, Sector - 57,
Noida - 201 301,
Distt. Ghaziabad,
(U.P.)
Tel/Fax: 8-530046

Ovens:

Ganapati Tractors
C-17, Sector-10, Noida - 201 301
Distt. Ghaziabad. (U.P.)
Tel/Fax: 554893

Ferro-Tech Engineers
Pratap Bhawan, Ground Floor,
5, Bahadurshah Zafar Marg,
New Delhi - 110 002
Ph.: 3351848, 3351830, 3318213
Fax: 91-11-3324082

Water Treatment Plants:

Apurva Water treatement Plants,
14-A, Byculla Service Industries,
Sussex Cross Road,
Byculla, Mumbai - 400 027

Reaction Vessel:

M. D. Engineering Company
117, M.I.E. Bahadurgarh,
Distt. Rohtak (Haryana)
Ph.: 8-311431
Tel/Fax: 91-8-314546

Paper Cutting Machine: (Fully Automatic)

H. G. Engg. Industries,
8 Sharad Indl. Estate,
Lake Road, Bhandup,
Mumbai - 400 078

Paper Varnishing Machinery:

Paper Board Machinery Company
Plot No. 115, Part - I,
DLF Industrial Area,
Faridabad - 121 003

PLANT ECONOMICS OF STENCIL PAPERS

Rated Plant Capacity = 6000.00 Quire.(10 Pcs.)/Day

COST OF LAND & BUILDING

(Total land area required 3000 sq. mtr.) Rs. 44,50,000.00

LIST OF PLANT & MACHINERY

1. **Production Unit:**
   Tripple roll mills 15 x 16 complete with motor, starter etc.
2. High speed mixers complete with motor, starter etc.
3. Stencil tissue coating machine (8 x 4 x 10)with drying arrangement
4. Vertical (Inclinable) power press with electric motor
5. Stencil collecting machine (carton type 14 x 4 x 5)
6. Boiler 500 kgs. steam per hour
7. Testing equipments
8. Oven with hot air blowing arrangement
9. Chemical balance and other chemical
10. Glass equipment and apparatus etc.
11. Miscellaneous equipments including pipes and fittings
12. Waste water treatment unit
13. Reaction Vessel (S.S) with jacket, with stirrer.

LIST OF RAW MATERIALS

1. Tissue paper
2. Nitro cellulose
3. Oleyl alcohol
4. Backing sheet
5. Interlinning paper
6. Carbon paper
7. Ether
8. Spirit
9. Titanium dioxide
10. Pure castor oil
11. Shell canea oil
12. Butyl alcohol
13. Butyl acetone
14. Dibutyl phthalate
15. Ethyl acetate
16. Glue
17. Ink
18. Packaging material

FIXED CAPITAL

Land & Building	Rs.	44,50,000.00
Plant & Machinery	Rs.	55,65,000.00
Other Fixed Assets	Rs.	23,25,000.00
TOTAL	**Rs.**	**1,23,40,000.00**

TOTAL WORKING CAPITAL/MONTH

Raw Material	Rs.	32,70,260.00
Salary & Wages	Rs.	1,54,320.00
Utilities & Overheads	Rs.	2,91,000.00
TOTAL	**Rs.**	**37,15,580.00**

TOTAL CAPITAL INVESTMENT

Total Fixed Capital	Rs.	1,23,40,000.00
Total Working Capital for 3 Months	Rs.	1,11,46,740.00
TOTAL	**Rs.**	**2,34,86,740.00**

TURN OVER/ANNUM

By sale of 18,00,000 quires(10 pcs) Stencil Paper **Rs. 6,30,00,000.00**

PROFIT = RECEIPTS - COST OF PRODUCTION

= 6,30,00,000.00 - 5,04,23,661.19

= 1,25,76,338.81

PROFIT SALES RATIO = Profit/Sales x 100 = **19.71 %**

RATE OF RETURN = Operating Profit/T.C.I. x 100 = **53.05 %**

BREAK EVEN POINT (B.E.P.) = 38.50 %

37

STICKER MAKING AUTOMATIC PLANT

INTRODUCTION

Paper stickers are quite popular both for consumer and industrial applications because of their good adhesion and easy to apply properties and their ability to import display characteristics to the surfaces which otherwise cannot be labelled or printed. Besides paper stickers , plastic stickers are also entering in the market. However , the demand for paper stickers & labels is quite substantial.

Product identification,information & graphics on glass, plastic and metal containers can be achieved via labels preprinted onto a label stock or by printing directly onto the container. i.e. stickers and labels .with both methods , printing can be accomplished using offset , letterpress , rotogravure, flexography(using rubber or newer plastic plates) or silk-screening.

Labelling is a means of performing the communication function of packaging ,by which contents are identified , the customer is encouraged to buy , & the low with regard to consumer & carrier protection is satisfied.

MANUFACTURINGPROCESS

There are following steps and sections during the manufacturing of stickers.

1. Coating section.
2. Drying section.
3. Release coating.
4. Printing section.
5. Quality control section.

The various section are gives here in detail.

Coating Section:

Prior to sending the paper for coating , it is necessary to check the physical appearance and fitness of paper so that the ultimate product could be of good quality. For stickers , 100 GSM Maplitho paper 30" are used . The sheets of 100 GSM Maplitho paper 30" width are fed to a coating unit where a pressure sensitive adhesive is applied on it. The pressure-sensitive adhesives are prepared initially. These are special type of adhesive applied on the base paper.

Drying Section:

Adhesive coated sheets are than passed through a tunnel drier (drying chambers) .The paper sheets are passed through the dries . The chain conveyer is applied for this purpose. Temperature of the drying can be controlled via thermo-stat , fitted, fitted with the drying chamber .

Release Paper Coating:

The dried adhesive coated paper sheets are now laminated in this section . The lamination is done to give maximum protection and aesthetic appeal , compatibility and bonding possibilities between the layers , and the salability of the surface.

Printing Section:

The laminated paper sheets are now sent for printing . In this section , desired printing can be employed.

Quality Control & Inspection:

Ultimate section is the quality control and inspection the products upto standard level are passed for packing and rest under standard product is rejected. The final product is packed and then ready for dispatch for marketing.

PLANT AND MACHINERY SUPPLIERS

Automatic Sticker making Machine:

Matex Snc.
Via Encrico Mattei 1/5,
36040 Brendela - Vicenza,
Italy.
Tel. 0444/770366-770991
Telex - 480823 MATEX I

Narendra Company (p) Ltd.,
273, Mysore Road,
Bangalore - 560 026
Phone : 622177/622178
Telex - 0845-8251, PEAKIN

Coating Machine:

Master Mechanical Works
Master House, Plot No 54,
Phase-II, Road No. 15 . MIDC,
Moral Indl. Area,
Andheri (E),
Mumbai -400 093

RAW MATERIAL SUPPLIERS

Silicon Paper:

Pyloff Packaging (P) Ltd.,
5th Floor, Maneekji Wadia Bldg.,
127, M.G.Road, Fort,
Mumbai -400 023

Maplitho Chrome Paper:

Om Prakash Jitendra Kumar & Co.,
63, Darya Ganj,
New Delhi - 110 002
Ph. : 326 96 80, 327 1380

Narain Paper Mart,
4034/3, Haryana Market,
Chawri Bazar, Delhi - 110 006
Ph. : 291 5135

Adhesives:

Adhesives & Allied Products,
12, Netaji Subhash Road,
Calcutta -700 001

Printing Ink:

Ajanta Ink Company
Basai Road, Gurgaon.
(Haryana)
Phone/Fax : 8-330028

Art Printing Inks Company
104 Site-4, Indl. Area,
Sahibabad, Ghaziabad.
Phone/fax : 767882

38

STRAPPINGS

INTRODUCTION

Strapping is applied to a group of packages or a package before final shipping. Strapping reinforces the package and allows a thinner or lighter corrugated or wooden bulk containers. It also allows a group of boxes, crates etc. to be combined into a large package which is easier to handle than the separate packages.

Strapping may be made of steel or plastics e.g. nylon, polypropylene and rayon. Strappings are applied under tension to hold the package tightly. Steel strapping is dimensionally stable under all but very high tensions. Steel does not creep or stretch appreciably under tension.

Steel strappings may be cold rolled, heat treated or hot rolled. Plastic strappings are resilient and less dimensionally stable. they may continue to stretch for a time under tension. But they have the advantage that because of their resilience they remain tight even when the package shrinks.

Strappings are generally flat in form but steel strapping may be in the form of wire or oval shape and nylon strapping is the form of cord. Steel strapping is generally of 10 mm. width and 0.35 mm. thickness; nylon and polypropylene strappings are of 12 to 13 mm. width and 0.50 mm. thickness. Rayon cord may be of about 20 mm. dia. Other sizes are also available.

Strappings may be applied to packages either with the help of hand tools or semi or fully automatic machines. Steel strappings are joined at the ends by snap-on. thread-on, push type and magazine fed seals; that may also be welded. wire, oval or narrow steel strappings may be joined by twisting. Plastic strappings are joined with the help of buckles or they may be friction welded or heat sealed. Power operated strapping machines may strap from 10 to 30 straps per minute.

Cushioning Materials:

Cushioning materials are required to protect the package from vibration and shock during handling and transportation. Cushioning materials are especially important in the packaging of fragile or delicate products e.g. glassware, electronic instruments, précision instrument, television etc.

A variety of cushioning materials are available e.g. animal hairs, rubber foam, blown vinyl flexible foam, honeycomb kraft paper, corrugated board, polyethylene foam, polystyrene foam, cellulose wading, cotton, fiber glass, and shredded paper. Selection of cushioning material depends on the fragility of the item, the hazards involved in transportation and the characteristics of the cushioning material. In addition effect of temperature and humidity on cushioning material and the effect of cushioning material on the product should also be taken into account.

Different items can withstand different amount of shock. The capacity of an items or withstand shock is expressed in terms of G-factor which is the minimum force required for damage, given as the number of g, where g is the acceleration due to gravity. Manufacturers of cushioning materials supply GVS static pressure carves where stative pressure is the weight of the article divided by the area to be supported by cushioning. It is possible to find the required thickness of cushioning material from these curves if we know the G-factor and the static pressure for the item to be supported.

Foamed polystyrene can be obtained in the form of moulded, extruded or fabricated insert, pads, blocks, strands and sheets. Moulded parts are produced from expandable bead in a metal mould in densities of 0.5 gm/cm^2. Sheets are produced by extrusion of beads or granules in densities of 2 to 10 gm/cm^2. Fabricated products are produced from moulded or extruded slabs by slicing, cutting, stamping, drilling etc. in densities of 0.5 to 2.5 gm/cm^2. Strands are extruded and then expanded to 0.15 to 0.40 gm/cm_2 density.

Polyurethane foam of rigid and flexible types are available in densities ranging from 0.75 - 1.5 gm/cm^2 to very high upto 20 gm/cm^2 but high density foam is used for packaging only rarely. Polyurethane foam articles can be moulded or fabricated from slabs. One advantage with polyurethane is that it can be foamed-in-place around the product to be packed or cushioned; the liquid components of the polyurethane are poured or sprayed and then foamed in place in the presence of a catalyst and blowing agent.

39

TABLE OFFSET & DESK TOP PUBLISHING

INTRODUCTION

The revolution in desktop printing started in 1985. Though the technology is just 12 years old, already plenty of hardware and software options are available. Johann Gutenberg installed a successful printing press in the fifteenth century. Since then, publishers have been booking for a better, cheaper and faster way to get words and pictures on paper. It took years to make even the slightest improvement on the printing press, but DTP keeps advancing at an accelerated pace. Like any other computer system the three main components of DTP are hardware, software and printer.

Book is an important source of knowledge. Increase in standard of living further leads to develop interest in studying of course not always true. With increase in industrialization, the demand for books has to increase.

To sum up, desk top publishing has come to stay. But its full potential and applications can only be realised by those conversant with the various packages available and prepared to study the combinations there of.

DESKTOPPUBLISHINGSYSTEMS

Laser Printers and Digitizers:

Desk Top Publishing involves many components, but without good output devices, all the effort that goes into designing and laying out pages is wasted. Currently, the primary high-resolution output device in a desk top publishing operation is the laser printer. Most good looking documents that result from desk top publishing are more than just nicely formatted type.

Laser Printers and digitizers as much as computers and software - makes desk top publishing a personal rather than a strictly corporate or industrial endeavor.

Laser Printers:

A laser printers is essentially a photocopier. In fast, many such printers use the same technology that photocopiers do, the photo sensitive drum temporarily holds an electric charge in the shape of an image transferred to it by a computer-driven laser beam. the charge and the image carried within it are transferred to a sheet of paper as it rolls across the drum. The paper then attracts the toner (plastic ground into a fine powder) and heat bonds the toner to the paper.

Digitizers : Producing Graphic Images:-

A digitiser transforms an image into digital information you can store in a computer memory or on a mass storage device.

SOFTWARE

Two main types of DTP software are : the page make-up program and the typsetting program. Such programs combine the conventional roles of the typesetter and the pasteup artist. Text can be typed, arranged in columns and blocks on a page. It is also possible to break up the text, add headlines, captions and subheads. Some programs provide the facility of inserting graphics within and around the text. The graphics may be as simple as a box or a line, or as complex as aline drawing, schematic or digitised photograph.

Macintosh page make-up programs are : Ready Setgo, PageMaker and MacPublisher. They allow mixing of text and graphics freely and are compatible with other Mac progrems such as Mac Write, MacWord, MacDraw and MacPaint.

PAGEMAKE-UPPROGRAMS

Page Maker:

Aldus Corp's Pagemaker for Mac got DTP off the ground. It has simple menu commands, WYSIWYG (what you see is what you get) displays, the ability to incorporate text and graphics from other programs and to output to high resolution printers and typesetters.

Page Maker permits working on a WYSIWYG view of a page in three different sizes - normal reduced and enlarged. Each view gives presentation of what appear at the laser printer.

A page is treated as a windowpane on the screen. Only a portion of the page is seen at a time. There are no scroll bars to move the page. To move to a different part of the page SHOE PAGE command is used. A miniature version of the page is displayed on the screen, with a dotted box within it. Place the box at the required spot, exit; the SHOW PAGE window, and the selected part of the page is now on the screen. Obviously, during heavy editing, the system will be very slow.

There are four blocks - text picture, solid and frame. Using text, a square block of 2.54 cm * 2.54 cm is created and can be resized to anything. Resizing requires grasping the lower right corner of the text block and tugging it. It is difficult to grab the right spot but some practice makes block manipulation scheme simple.

MacPublisher-II:

This program divides the screen into many windows. The right hand of screen contains the page which cannot be moved, resized or scrolled. Lower left corner has dog-ear flaps which enable to flip through the pages of the publication. Documents up to 96 pages can be created but disc space and number of documents in an average publication make this limit about 30 pages.

PFS:

ClickArt Personal Publisher. ClickArt has drop-down menus, dart text and graphics on a light screen background, mouse operations (optional), an I-beam text cursor, an arrow pointer and MacPaint like graphics tools.

The program lists most commands under the eight drop-down menus across the top of the screen. These commands are executed using a keyboard or mouse. Text can be typed directly from ASCII text files, and fonts can be selected for both of them.

Ventura Publisher:

Ventura allows to control character spacing and line spacing in decimal increments. It will automatically number the chapeters, and up to right levels of headings, as well as footnotes and figures. Minimum number of lines to be isolated in windows or orphans can be specified. Text can be imported in six different file formats.

PAGE DESCRIPTION LANGUAGES (PDL)

PDL enables a printer to construct a page grom a combination of text, fonts and graphics. The computer system can specify complete page images rather than small inked areas. The page is sent in the form of ASCII text and graphics 'Primitives' basic codes that describe the size and shape of graphic objects. PDL compiler in the laser printer intercepts this information, converts it into dots and processes it into an image ready for printing.

Post Script:

The most common PDL is post script. the computer talks to postscript with Engligh like commands. All programs that support a post script printer programs that support a post scrip printer drive will work with any post script compatible output device.

Interpress:

Interpress's files are in binary form. For debugging, binary codes can be translated into a more readily recognisable and readable form.

DDL:

DDL is the most recent PDL and includes most of the elements of the two other langauges. It is programmable like post script and has document control features superior to those of tinerpress.

OFFSETPRINTINGPRESS
TABLEOFFSETPRINTINGM/CSPECIFICATION

Specification:

Plate Size	Punched 1/2" pinbar 381*254mm - 15"*10" strength edge upto381*254mm-15"*10"punched12.5mm368*250mm-14.5"*8*1/8"
Printing Area	330*341mm/13"*9.5"
Paper Sie-Maximum	368*257mm-14.5"*10*1/8"
Minimum	150*114mm-5*7/8*4.5"
Paper Substance	40-190 gsm(depended on quality)
Speed	3600-7200 impression per hour
Damping	Automatic Rotafount or intergated fount system
Electric Supply	220/240 V single phase 50 H. Full load running current 2 Amps. Other voltage and frquencies are available
Weight Apporox	120 Kgs/264 lbs
Width	635mm25"
Height	610mm24"
Length (incl. delivary tray)	940mm37"
Cabinet Width	607 mm 23"
Height	660 mm 26"
Length	965 mm 38"

SPECIFICFOLDINGMETHODS

Cross Association:

This technique is employed on double-width news presses and similar machines where double folders are in use. The idea is to feed all of the webs into one folder so that the number of pages oer copy is increased at the expense of the output of the other folder.

The webs on one side of the press are first taken down the appropriate former and then transferred across to the draw rollers of the twin folder. The webs from both sides of the machine will now be together at this point and will progress together as for a normal production run. Where cross association is used to produce tabloid papers, this will result in a larger, one piece newspaper indistinguishable from the usual product apart from the extra pages. With broadsheets, however, the papers will be produced in two sections. The two sections will be alinged back-to-back, but folded in together as they pass through the cross fold rollers.

SUPPLIERS' ADDRESSES

Paper Suppliers :

Om Prakash Jitendra Kumar & Company
63, Darya Ganj,
New Delhi - 11 00 02.
Ph. 326 96 80, 3271380

Narain Paper Mart,
4034/3, Haryana Market,
Chawri Bazar, Delhi - 11 00 06.
Ph. 291 51 35.

Himgiri Paper Products
B-24, Indl. Area Lawrence Road,
New Delhi - 110 035
Phone : 718 9005

Printing Ink:

Baluja Spectra
C-50 Okhla Indl. Area-II,
New Delhi - 110 020
Phone/fax : 6835715, 6835722

Ajanta Ink Company
Basai Road, Gurgaon (Haryana)
Phone/fax : 8-330028

Art Printing Inks Company
104 Site-4, Indl. Area,
Sahibabad, Ghaziabad, (U.P.)
Phone/fax : 767882

Inks India (Delhi)
C-49, Sector-8,
Noida-201 301 (U.P.)
Phone/fax : 523801, 011-8-557270

Van Inks & Chemicals (P) Ltd.
B-150, Phase-II,
Noida-201 305 (U.P.)
Phone/fax : 567141, 011-8-521507

Printing Material:

Alcon Graphic
1693/121, Shanti Nagar,
Tri Nagar, New Delhi - 110 035
(Rubber Blankets)

Graphichan Sales
Bhupin Das Bhawan,
Krishna Mkt. Pahar Ganj,
Delhi - 110 055

Process Chemical Co.
Shanti Mohan House,
16, Ansari Road,
New Delhi - 110 002

SUPPLIERS OF DTP SYSTEM

Zenith Electro Systems Pvt. Ltd.,
106, Mittal Chambers,
Nariman Point,
Mumbai - 400 021.

Pearl Digital Systems,
704, Rohit House,
Talstoy Marg,
New Delhi - 110 001.

CMS Computers Pvt Ltd.,
201, Arcodia,
Nariman Point,
Mumbai - 400 021

DCM Data Products,
4th Floor, Vikrant Tower,
4, Rajendra Place,
New Delhi - 110 008.

Wipro Information Technology Ltd.,
5th Floor, s.B. Tower,
88, M.G. Road,
Bangalore - 560 001.

LIST OF MANUFACTURERS OF PRINTING MACHINERY

MOI Engineering Ltd.
612-A, Chiranjiv Towers,
43, Nehru Place,
New Delhi - 110019
Phones: 6413093, 6450956

H.S. Enterprises
4852/24, Ansari Road,
Darya Ganj,
New Delhi - 110002

J. Mahavir & Co. Pvt. Ltd.
3620-21, Netaji Subash Marg,
Darya Ganj,
New Delhi - 110002

SID Mark Sales
186, Dr. Ambedkar Road,
Dadar, Mumbai.

Lakshmi Printers Store
3/3A, Asaf Ali Road
New Delhi - 110002

PLANT ECONOMICS OF TABLE OFFSET & DTP

Rated Plant Capacity = 200.00 Pgs./Day

COST OF LAND & BUILDING

(Total land area required 22.69 sq. mtr) Rs. 46,500.00

LIST OF PLANT & MACHINERY

1. Table-top offset printing machine with all the accessories (stand/storage cabinet & voltage stabilizer)
2. Computer(PC/AT-486) with all the accessories & Power suppliers
3. Laser printer
4. Dot - matric printer (132 column)
6. OA scanner
7. Air condition (cap 2 ton)
8. UPS (1 KVA) with batteries

LIST OF RAW MATERIALS

1. Plates - paper plates & typing or photocopying expenses for 125000 copies
2. Metal plates
3. Inks & solution
4. Rubber blankets
5. Stationary
6. Floppy diskettes & misc.

FIXED CAPITAL

Land & Building	Rs.	46,500.00
Plant & Machinery	Rs.	5,62,000.00
Other Fixed Assets	Rs.	1,00,000.00
TOTAL	**Rs.**	**7,08,500.00**

TOTAL WORKING CAPITAL/MONTH

Raw Material	Rs.	10,430.00
Salary & Wages	Rs.	19,200.00
Utilities & Overheads	Rs.	6,500.00
TOTAL	**Rs.**	**36,130.00**

TOTAL CAPITAL INVESTMENT

Total Fixed Capital	Rs.	7,08,500.00
Total Working Capital for 3 Months	Rs.	1,08,390.00
TOTAL	**Rs.**	**8,16,890.00**

TURNOVER/ANNUM

1. By Printing 8,00,000 Sheets with paper plate
2. By Printing 7,00,000 Sheets with metal plate
3. By Composing 60,000 pages

TOTAL **Rs. 9,58,935.00**

PROFIT = RECEIPTS - COST OF PRODUCTION

= 9,58,935.00 - 7,22,892.20

= 2,36,042.80

PROFIT SALES RATIO = Profit / Sales x 100 = **24.62 %**

RATE OF RETURN = Operating Profit/T.C.I. x 100 = **28.65 %**

BREAK EVEN POINT (B.E.P) = 63.33 %

40

TAGS, LABELS AND SEALS

INTRODUCTION

Label is one of the important components of any package. The primary purpose of the label is to identify the name of the product, the quantity of the product and the name of the manufacturer. In addition the label may identify the important ingredients of the product in some cases and in the case of hazardous products warnings may be displayed on the label. However, the label also serves as a vehicle for advertising and sales promotion. The sales value of the product can be increased many times by proper design of the label.

In many cases the container or the product may be labeled directly by printing, screen, embossing or hot-stamping processes. However, in this section we are concerned only with labels, tags or seals of printed or embossed per, films or foils that are applied or attached to a container or the product.

Labels may be obtained in a variety of types and sizes depending on the form of container. Labels for cylindrical cans are of wrap around type. Frozen food and bakery products usually have a wrap around or overwrap type label. Glass containers usually have vandwraps or spot labels which cover only a portion of the container. Neck bands or shoulder labels may also be applied on glass containers. Other types or labels include caup labels, end label, face label, insert label, rider label, tab label, top label etc.

Labels are supplied to users in either cut or in rolls. Cut or sheet labels may be either straight-cut (guillotinecut) or die-cut. Guillotine-cut labels can have only straight parallel edges but die-cut labels can be produced in any shape and design. Die-cut method produces very accurate dimensions but is costly.

Paper is the most widely used material for making labels because of its fine printing qualities, flexibility and low cost. A variety of coated and uncoated grades of paper are available for different applications. Foil-paper laminations are often used because of the protective properties and- sale appeal of the foil. film or plastic labels are used to some extent on cosmetics and gift and speciality items.

MANUFACTURINGPROCESS

Printing and Decoration:

Labels can be printed by any of the basic printing processes. Letter press, offset lithography and flexography are most widely used printing processes. Flexography is cheapest and can be used for short runs. Gravure process is economic only for long runs. Hot stamping and screen printing are also used in special cases.

Varnish, lacquer or synthetic coating can be applied over printed labels to protect the surface of the label, to make it moisture and frost resistant and to improve its appearance. Metallic inks and metallic powders mixed with coatings are used to achieve special effects. Embossing is used to give a three dimensional effect and a luxury appearance.

Adhesives:

Starch, dextrin, animal glues, casein and synthetic adhesives are used for fixing unglued labels. Selection of the adhesive depends on the material of the label and the substrate on which it is to be applied. Glass and plastic containers require special adhesives. In some cases the adhesive must be able;e to withstand impression of the container in water e.g. beverage bottles. Similarly sometimes labels have to be applied on oily, hot or wet containers and the adhesive must work under these condition. Some adhesives are alkaline in nature and may cause staining of the label; neutral or acidic adhesives may be used in such cases.

Gummed Labels:

Labels may be gummed or glued during manufacture and these labels are remoistened before applying to the containers. These labels are generally made from papers. Adhesives used are similar to those used on gummed paper tapes. Paper used for labels may be white, coloured, coated, metallized and specially finished and may range in substance from 60 gsm to 90 gsm or even higher. The amount of adhesive may range from 20 gsm to 40 gsm. these labels are generally used for labeling small runs, re-labeling or supplementary labeling.

In the manufacture of gummed labels, the roll is first gummed as in case of gummed tapes. After the gumming operation the sheets are 'flattened' and then printed. The film of gum must be properly broken to make the sheet flat enough to be fed into the printing presses.

A roll of gummed paper with the gummed side out, is passes over a bar under tension at a 45° angle. It is then necessary to pass the sheet over another bar, making a 90° angle with the first bar. Without the second bar, the sheet would curl from one end to the other. The second bar removes this curl. In this flattening process care should be taken to ensure that the ungummed side of the sheet is not roughed up and thus mar the printing surface. The flaking of the glue film should also be avoided. the finishing operations are similar to those used in finishing ordinary coated paper. Machine finished papers are usually calendered, depending upon the finish desired. The regular multiple trimmers and cutters are used for the remainder of the finishing. Trimming is done to size, usually 17 x 22-500 or 20 x 25-500. these rolls are then packed in moisture proof bags e.g. polythene bags.

Heat-Activated Labels:

Heat-activated labels are coated with a specially formulated adhesive which is activated by heat. the adhesive is activated by hear before applying the label on the container. the adhesive may be quick action or delayed action type. Delayed action type adhesives are preferred for labels. These labels may be activated on a simple hot-plate and applied by hand or special semi-automatic or automatic equipments may be used.

These labels are used on metal or glass containers, of film wrapped bakery products, as labels on supermarket products e.g. cheese and meat wrapped in films. these labels are also used for closing film bags; the label is folded across the top and sealded to the bag under heat and pressure.

Heat-seal adhesives eliminate many problems associated with conventional adhesives. However, these adhesives create other problems when hot, cold or wet bottles are to be labeled or when the bottles are coated with silicone or contaminated with grease, dirt etc. Small or odd shaped bottles may also cause trouble and in this case a thin label made from 70 gsm paper should be used. For hot bottles a quick action adhesive should be used; for wet bottles a water-resistant adhesive is recommended.

Paper used for these labels may be of substance 70 gsm or less or even upto 140 gsm. Heavier paper is used for bag headers because the label must withstand the weight of the contents in the bag. these labels should be stored in dry, cool place at temperature below 32°C.

Pressure Sensitive Labels:

Pressure sensitive labels are versatile. These labels are easy to use because no glue pot or water moistening or heat activation equipments are required. They can be used for identification, name plates, assembly marking, price marking, service labels, product guarantees and many other purposes. These labels are specially suited for plastics and other difficult surfaces; they are also suitable for delicate and fragile items and instruments and gifts where easy removal is desired. However, these labels are costlier than other types of labels.

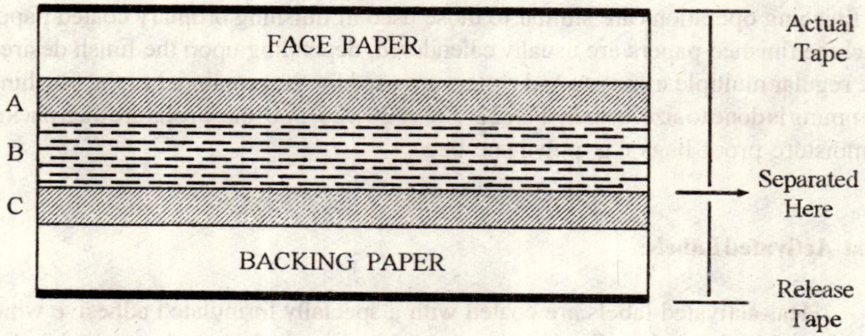

Pressure Sensitive Label System

The construction of pressure sensitive label has been shown already in figure. The base substrate (paper, film, foil or cloth) is printed, coated with adhesive and the release paper. Sometimes, the printed side is coated with a protective transparent ink, varnish or plastic coating. These labels are available in sheet, roll or fan fold forms. these labels may be removable or permanent depending on the formulation of the adhesive. Paper used for these labels may be of 70 gsm to 140 gsm substance. Foil in generally of 0.05 mm. to 0.125 mm. and film of 0.025 mm. to 0.10 mm.

Seales, Stickers and Tags:

Seals are special purpose labels produced by dies that print, emboss and die-cut in a continuous series of operations. these are produced in "French-edge" seal presses. These seals have a narrow embossed border. These are used on bottles or jars of food products, textiles, hosiery, sports goods, glass-ware and other products. They are used to convey a rich appearance on costly items e.g. cosmetics, gift items, instruments, watches, jewellery, pens, ties etc. Seals are generally made from aluminium foil laminated to paper but paper alone can also be used. Seals may be supplied without adhesives or with adhesives. The adhesive may be water moistenable type, heat-activating type or pressure sensitive type.

Sticker are small labels with adhesive applied to them. They are, generally, used for advertising purposes on cars, scooters, buses and shop windows, sales counters on glass panels or other surfaces. they have a pressure sensitive adhesive applied on the back of the label. Stickers have now-a-days become very common because of their ease of application.

Tags are special purpose labels that are attached to a container or product by string, wire, fibbons, holes, slots etc. They are generally applied as products or packages which cannot be labeled otherwise e.g. electrical appliances household items, clothings, tools, instruments, luggage. Slot tags are attached to shirt buttons. Ribbon tags are used on jewellery or perfumes. Tags are generally made from paper and foils.

41

TRACING PAPER

INTRODUCTION

Tracing paper is defined as a paper with sufficient transparency to allow to design to be traced through and reproduced.

There are two types of tracing papers:

(a) Natural and
(b) Prepared

Natural tracing papers are made transparent by highly beating the pulp and then super calendering. The sheet made out of it. Prepared tracing papers are obtained by tracing papers with oils, resins, waxes etc. To render them transparent and suitable for use with ink of oil.

USES & APPLICATIONS

Tracing paper as it is clear by its name is mainly used for tracing drawings of various engineering machines, tools as well as for making drawings of buildings etc. These drawings are further used for making a number of blue prints on a special type of paper. This is known as ammonia printing. This process is very simple and saves a lot of time for getting a number of blue prints.

Apart from thus this paper has various other uses, it is also used in craft work, in some cases for packaging etc. but its major use in in engineering drawing only.

MANUFACTURINGPROCESS

Tracing paper is defined as a paper with sufficient transparency to allow a design to be traced through and reproduced. There are two types of tracing papers (a) Natural and (b) prepared. Natural tracing papers are made transparent by highly beating the pulp and then super calendering the sheet made out of it. Prepared tracing papers are obtained by treating paper with oils, resins, waxes etc., to render them transparent and suitable for use with ink and or oil. The base paper is strong and durable and is manufactured out of all rags or substantial quantity of pulp. While all rag paper is manufactured wholly out of rages. 'rag contents paper' contains not less than 25 percent rag pulp.

The function of the paper when viewed by transmitted high should be uniform throughout and it should normally have a ground glass appearance. An acceptable tracing paper should be free from hard sports wrinkles, pin holes and other defects which normally effect adversely its use. The natural paper is bold as smooth, ultra smooth or with a mat finish. Some of the major operations which are carried out for the manufacturing of tracing paper are discussed below.

Stock Preparations:

Stock preparation denotes the several operations that must be undertaken in order to prepare the furnish from which paper is made. During the stock preparation steps, paper making pulps are most conveniently handled as aqueous slurries, so that they can be conveyed, measured, subjected to desire mechanical treatments and fixed with non fibrous additives before being delivered to the paper machine.

Beating and Refining:

Virtually all pulps are subjected to certain mechanical actions before ring formed into a paper sheet. Such treatments are used to improve the strength and other physical properties of the finished sheet and to influence the behavior of the system during the sheet-forming and drying steps. Beating and refining may be considered synomynous. During refining, the cellulose fibers are swollen, cut, macerated, and fibrillated.

Filling and Loading:-

Materials, i.e.; mineral pigments for filling and lading, are added to the pulps slurry to make the paper making furnish. Pigments are used in varying amounts, depending upon the grade of paper, and may comprise 2-40 wt.% of the final sheet. Fillers can improve brightness, capacity, softness, smoothness, and ink receptivity. They almost invariable reduce the degree of sizing and the strength of the sheet.

Sizing:

Sizing is the process of adding materials to the paper in order to render the sheet more resistant to penetration by liquids, particularly water. Unsized or waterleaf paper freely absorbs liquids. Writing and wrapping papers are typical sized sheets, as contrasted with blotting paper and facial tissue which usually are unsized. Rosin, various hydrocarbon and natural waxes starches, glues, casein, asphalt emulsions, synthetic resins, and cellulose derivatives are some of the materials which are used as sizing agents.

Other Beater Additives

Beater adhesives are employed widely to enhance fiber to fiber bonding. Starches probably are used in the greatest tonnage natural gums e.g. our and locuslbean, also are used as are modified celluloses e.g. the carboxymethyl and hydroxethyl derivatives. Urea formaldehyde and melamine formaldehyde polymers provide wet strength to the finished paper sheet.

Other natural and synthetic materials are used to alter the paper properties and to influence the behavior of the system during sheet forming and drying.

Sheet forming, Pressing & Drying:

Sheet forming:

Continuous sheet forming and drying came into use in 1800. The equipment was of two types: the cylinder machine and the Fourdrinier machine.

Sheet Pressing:

The sheet leaving the wet end contains approximately four parts of water per part of fiber; however, it is possible to remove additional water mechanically without adversely affecting sheet properties. This is achieved in rotary presses, of which there may be one or several on a given paper machine. The press rolls may be solid or perforated and, often, suction is applied through the interior.

The sheet is passed through the presses on continuous felts (one for each press), which act as conveyers and porous receptors of water. They are essential to the effectiveness of water removal. The water content of the sheet usually can be reduced by pressing to 1.9-1.2 parts of water per part of fiber without deleteriously affecting product quality.

Sheet Drying:

At a water content of 1.2-1.9 parts of water per part of fiber, additional water removal by mechanical means is not feasible and evaporative drying must be employed. This is at best an efficient but costly process and often is the production bottleneck of paper making. The dryer section most commonly consists of a series of steam-heated cylinders. Alternate sides of the wet paper are exposed to the hot surface as the sheet passes from cylinder to cylinder.

RAW MATERIAL SUPPLIERS

Caustic Soda :

Alkali & Chemical Corporation of India Ltd.,
P.O. Rishra Distt.
Hoogly, West Bengal.

D.C.M. Chemical Works,
P.B. No, 1211 E,
New Delhi - 110 015

Lime :

Burma Lime & Chemical Co. Ltd.,
Taratolla Road,
Garden Road,
Calcutta - 700 001

SUPPLIES OF PLANT & MACHINERY

Pheroz Industrial Manufacturing & Engineering Company Pvt. Ltd.,
1167, Sector 33-C,
Chandigarh - (Punjab)

Aceme Machinery Company,
233 Zaveri Bazar,
Mumbai - 400 002

42

WATER PROOF INK

INTRODUCTION

According to most historians, ink was first prepared and used by the chinese and the Egyptians as early as 2600 B.C. in the form of writing ink. These early inks were probably composed of carbonaceous materials such as lamp black or soot mixed with animal glue or vegetable oil vehicles. With the evaluation of civilization and technology different type of ink come in existence. Writing ink formulation became a highly developed art under the Chinese, who were printing from hand - cut blocks Gutenburg introduced movable type in Europe. Writing inks differ from printing inks in that the latter are generally applied to a substance by means of a printing press. With the development in science and technology now it is possible to make numerous types of inks, such as fleno graphic ratogravene publication ink, synthetic inks used in ball point pens and toner inks. Water proofing inks which are frequently called indelible ink are in corrodible or indestributable inks. These inks are used for writing important documents on paper, film and drawing, marking purposes. These inks are used generally with the help of fine pens e.g. tico type pens.

The manufacture of water proofing inks are similar to that of other general ink manufacture. Grinding of different ingredients in fine pulverized form and mixing them with the bare to make the homogeneous solution.

As the raw material and plant and machinery are indigenous and early available. The manufacture of water proofing ink faces no major problem. As the ink industry comes under small and cottage scale industries. The facilities of for S.S.I. units are also available to its.

USE & APPLICATION

Water proofing inks are generally used for writing important documents as well as in drawing marking with the help of them films for fine sketching. Artists generally use there inks for letter making sketching the fine lines and design making.

These inks are also used for writing on textile fabrics. It goes without saying that these inks resist washing and are unaffected by immersion in water. These inks are also used for printing labels for battles and marking on films paper. These are also used in cyclostyle printing as well as in marking on tracing papers.

PROPERTIES

As the name suggest, these inks do not spread or removed from the substiate on coming in contact with water. These inks should quality the following tests.

1. Test For Water Proof Quality and Solvent Resistance:

The test shall be carried out with a clean line pen.

Draw few lines (0.5 mm.. thick, 5mm. apart and 150 mm. long) or figures or both on the matt side of (a) cellulose acetate transparent medium for tracing drawing. (b) drawing paper, (c) tracing cloth, and (d) tracing paper. Mark off the draw into two equal parts, allow to dry for 12 hours. Make the tests on sections selected from each one of the two equal parts.

Place four drops of water and spream them over the drawing for a length of about 25 mm. applying no rubbing or friction. Allow the drawing to dry normally. There shall be no spreading of the ink nor shall it show more than a faint stain.

Soak the drawing for length of about 25 mm with water by a sponge and then bolt it with a clean piece of blotting paper. There shall be no stain on the bottling paper.

Place four drops of petrol, benzene, or carbon tetrachloride and spread them over the drawing which has been allowed to dry for a further period of 12 hours, to a length of about 25 mm. applying no rubbing or friction. Repeat the operation if necessary to keep the surface wet for at least 5 minutes. There shall be no spreading of ink or reduction of colour.

FORMULATIONS

1. Black

Aniline Oil	41.0 Kg.
Potassium Chlorate	2.4 Kg.
Distilled Water	21.2 Kg.
Hydro Chloric Acid (Sp. gr. 1.124)	32.8 Kg.
Copper Chloride (Pure)	2.6 Kg.
	100.00 Kg.

2. Blue

Gum lac	8 Kg.
Boiling Water	80 Kg.
Borax	4 Kg.
Gum Arabic	4 Kg.
Indigo Blue	4 Kg.
	100.00 Kg.

MANUFACTURING PROCESS

Aniline oil, potassium chlorate and 12 kg of water are mixed and heated in a vessel on a water bath, (steam jacketed reaction vessel also can be used) at a temperature of 80°C - 95°C. Until the chlorate is completely dissolved. Then add half of the hydrochloric acid (16 Kg) and heating is continued until the mixture begins to take on a darker colour. Then a solution of copper chloride, remaining water and acid is prepared and added into the reaction vessel. The vessel is then heated till the mass acquires a fine red-violet color.

The entire mass is now poured into a flask with a well fitting ground glass stopper (Big glass bottle like vessels with tight stoppers are used for this purpose). The liquid is kept for several days. When the sedimentation of precipitate is over, seperate out the clear liquid from the sedimented precipitate.

Ink optained thus will have good resistance to water, oil, alcohol, oxalic acid, alkalies etc. It is assumed that 90 Kg of Ink is obtained from 100 kg of ingredients.

MANUFACTURES OF RAW MATERIALS

Aniline Oil:

Ajay Organic Pvt. Ltd.,
9/11, Homi Modi Street,
Fort,
Mumbai - 400 001

Hindustan Organic Chemicals Ltd.,
(Marketing Division),
Rasayani P.O.,
Raiga Distt.,
Maharashtra - 410 207

Gums:

Bhiwani Gum and Guar Factory,
Prop. Express Dairy Co.,
198 Bjipen Dey Road,
Behala,
Calcutta - 34

Pigments:

Geo Chem Industries,
59, Jailash Nagar,
658, Tardev Road,
Mumbai - 400 007

Borax:

Arun Rasayan Udyog,
588, Katra Ishwar Bhawan,
Khari Baoli,
Delhi - 110 006

Copper Chloride & Potassium Chlorate:

Rohit Services (P) Ltd.,
E A - 21,
Inderpuri (FF),
New Delhi.

PLANT & MACHINEROES

Boilers:

ACC- Vickers-Babcock Ltd.,
Express Towers,
18th Floor,
Nariman Point,
Mumbai - 400 021

Mixer:

Amar Bhart Fabricators,
6th, Mile Kanak Pura Road,
Bangalore - 11

Tanks:

Acmec India Corpn.,
16, Manu Mansion,
Old Custom House Road,
Mumbai - 400 001

PLANT ECONOMICS OF WATER PROOF INK

Rated Plant Capacity = 100.00 Kgs./Day

COST OF LAND & BUILDING

(Total land area required 250 sq. mtr.) Rs. 4,15,000.00

LIST OF PLANT & MACHINERY

1. Tank (S.S) capacity 150 litres
2. Mixer (Dough type) equipped with all the accessories
3. Filter
4. Furnace (simple)
5. Aluminium tanks fitted with fine tap capacity 60 kg. each
6. Miscellaneous equipments

LIST OF RAW MATERIALS

For Blue Ink :

1. Gumlac 210 Kg.
2. Water 2100 kg.
3. Borax 105 kg.
4. Gum Arabic 105 Kg.
5. Indigo Blue 105 Kg.

For Black Ink:

6. Borax 150 kg.
7. Shallac 450 kg.
8. Water 2500 kg.
9. Lamp black 112.5 kg.

FIXED CAPITAL

Land & Building	Rs.	4,15,000.00
Plant & Machinery	Rs.	2,17,000.00
Other Fixed Assets	Rs.	15,000.00
TOTAL	**Rs.**	**6,47,000.00**

TOTAL WORKING CAPITAL/MONTH

Raw Material	Rs.	87,847.50
Salary & Wages	Rs.	17,908.00
Utilities & Overheads	Rs.	13,480.00
TOTAL	**Rs.**	**1,19,235.50**

TOTAL CAPITAL INVESTMENT

Total Fixed Capital	Rs.	6,47,000.00
Total Working Capital for 3 Months	Rs.	3,57,706.50
TOTAL	**Rs.**	**10,04,706.50**

TURN OVER/ANNUM

1. By sale of 30,000 kg of Blue Proofing ink
2. By sale if 37,500/- kg of Black ink **Rs. 22,50,000.00**

PROFIT = RECEIPTS - COST OF PRODUCTION

= 22,50,000.00 - 16,72,690.17

= 5,77,309.83

PROFIT SALES RATIO = Profit/Sales x 100 = **25.53 %**

RATE OF RETURN = Operating Profit/T.C.I. x 100 = **57.46 %**

BREAK EVEN POINT (B.E.P.) = 41.40 %

43

WAX CRAYON

INTRODUCTION

The wax "Crayon" as originally defined covered a drawing material, generally in the form, employed by the artist for drawing. The crayons are made in black, white and red colours, the black and red used for outline and shading, the white to high ten light. Crayons are now for the most part artifically prepared mixtures of a base of prepared chalk, and pipe or china clay with prussian blue, chrome yellow vermilion, ochers, ambers, and other pigments, cemented together, by the introduction of some weak adhesive, usually gum Iragacanth. Calcium gypsum stealite, and compound of magnesium bismuth and lead are occasionally used as base.

Two types of crayons are produced in India-chalk crayons and marking crayons.

Chalk Crayons:

The raw materials required are gypsum, calcium carbonate, and pigments. Washed and powdered gypsum, freed from earth and other associated impurities, is heated to remove water of hydration (loss in wt. 15%). The product is powdered and sieved (80-100 mesh), mixed with water containing gum and bleaching powder, and poured into greased brass moulds. When set, the moulds are opened and the crayons removed to wire gauge trays and dried in the sun.

For collard chalk crayons

The ground material is dry-mixed with neutral pigments, red ochre, yellow ochre, Prussian blue (Chinese blue), yellow chrome, ultramarine blue, etc. and the mixed powder moulded as in the case of white chalk crayon.

The equipments required are brass mould in 2 sections, each section containing a number of semi-circular grooves. When the 2 parts are brought into juxtaposition, a number of holes of circular cross section are formed.

Crayons are packed in dealwood boxes holding 1 gross pieces. One maund of gypsum gives 8 gross pieces of crayon.

Marking Crayons

Marking crayons are made in many colours and in many grades of hardness. Clay, Plaster of Paris, Pigments, and dyes are mixed in mixing machines, pasted with water and the dough squirted through a machine. The resulting sticks are dried, and one end sharpened.

Pastels

The chief raw material for pastels is china clay, which should be neither too smooth nor too gritty. Clay of the required quality is available in Gwalior, Delhi and Bikaner, in Bihar and Orissa, and in Madhya Pradesh. The clay is washed in tanks to free it from gritty materials and mica, mixed with neutral pigments-red ochre, yellow ochre, ultramarine blue etc., and made into a dough with water. It is kneaded in rollers and squirted into thin cylinders. The cylinders are spread over stone slabs in lengths of two feet and dried. They are cut into smaller lengths, one of the ends shaped to a point with a pencil knife, and packed in cardboard cartons.

MANUFACTURING PROCESS

The manufacture of crayons consists of preparing and moulding the coloured mass. The first step in the process is to mix the powdered colour and stealite, or its equivalent together with a suitable amount of the stearic acid base in a closed rotating cylinders or ball mill and the rotation is continued until the mixture is uniform in colour. The amount of colour used is proportional to wax and varies according to the hue, and its colour strength between 8 to 25 kgs. of colour, are used to each 100 kgs. of base wax. Tints are made by using the pigment lithopene is used alone.

The mixture from the ball mill is then made in to paste is them compressed in a horizontal brass or bronze cylinder having at one end a plate to which the crayons are to be made. The paste is of such a consistency that slight pressure will force it out of orifice in front of the cylinder at a regular rate. The piston is put in position and the mass forced by uniform gentle pressure out of the narrow opening.

The conveyer belt must move away at the same rate at rod is ejected from the cylinder, so that a long stick of crayon mass rests upon it. This stick is stick of crayon mass rests upon it. This stick is cut by a blunt knife, in to uniform lengths, which are dried upon boards with an absorbent paper. The rods shrinks some what on drying, and when dry they are enclosed in casing similar to those of the ordinary lead pencil.

There is another process in which a thick paste is molded in to blocks of the length of crayons. These block are slowly dried at a uniform temperature and sawed by a fine saw into thin rods which are enclosed in a wooden case. The powder from the sawing is used in the next batch. The disadvantage of this method is that it is difficult to avoid cracks in drying in the blocks and a large number of the sawed rods break, even with the most careful treatment.

Moulding may also be done manually in moulds. These moulds are made of aluminium one mould contain 64 pastels. This moulds cost about Rs. 250/- only. On cottage scale manufacturing 3-4 moulds are sufficient. Waxes are melted in a container and moulds are dipped in cold water and when it is solidified, the crayons are taken out.

The colour used in crayon manufacture include lamp black, dip black, chrome yellow, primrose yellow, Indian red, Tuscan red, Prussian Blue, raw number, burnt sienna, American Vermilion French ocher, rose pink, vandyke, brown rose, lake ventain red and chrome green (light medium and dark).

Colours used for different coloured crayons are:

White: Zinc oxide, lithopene, Titanium oxide,
Black: Carbon bone black,
Blue: Prussian Blue, Ultramarine blue,
Yellow: Chrome yellow,
Red: Iron rod oxide.

Colours are also composited to produce other hyses, for example purple lake, para red, and lithopene are combined to give a purple of desired tone.

Formulation for crayon used by children is given below:

	Ingredient	%
1.	Stearic acid	40
2.	Paraffin wax	45
3.	Bees wax	10
4.	Carnauba wax	5
5.	Colour	9.5 (2-2.5 parts)

Pastels:

Pastels are crayons that are made of colouring materials diluted with a white base. They are made into cylinders or pencils with the last amount of gum necessary to hold the particles of colour together in the highest possible manner so that a touch of the pencil on the surface of the paper leaves an impression.

Pastels for the used by artists, are sold in a series of tone, usually six in number of the darkest pencils of the series are mixed with white to a greater degrees as they second the scale towards the lightest. Thus artist can select a certain number of tone ready to use at one. A pastel can be applied as a pencil by means of lines for short strokes, or it may be rubbed using the tip of the finger as a pad.

What is commonly known as a wax drawing pastels is some what different from the original artists pastel crayon. The composition may consist of hard soap wax and colour. Bees wax and sper maceti are suitable wax materials. The melted waxes and the hard soap are mixed with the pigment and the mass ground until smooth in a heated mill. The finely ground pasty mass is then poured in to water so as to secure binding of the colour wax materials. In white ground mass, white lead, zinc white, pearly white or titanium oxide may be used to intensify the whiteness. Although is a common agglutinant, glue and gum senegal are also used. Oils, fats, and wax serve as agglutinant and products glass when so desired.

Ethyl cellulose laurate have been proposed as wax adjusts which will strengthen the crayon in the longitudinal direction by providing small stringly particles. These cellulose derivatives can be dissolved at an elevated, temperature is in stearic acid or in mixture of wax cerosion, carnauba, bees wax, paraffin etc. In one crayon a filler and a pigment are united by a binder. That includes water soluble etherized cellulose and also small straingly particles of water insoluble etherized cellulose and a waxy substances composed, of mix water insoluble etherized cellulose, and a waxy substance composed of a mixture of stearic acid and a wax.

Formulation for wax drawing pastel block is given here:

	Ingredient	Parts by Weight
1.	Hard soap	80
2.	Bees wax	60
3.	Sper maceti	28
4.	Carbon black	14
5.	Burnt Umber	5
6.	Prussian Blue	4

Marking Crayon:

A crayon that is used exclusively for marking is made in a different manner from the artists crayon and usually of much cheaper materials. The manufacture of cheap wax crayon with paper wraps is not unlike that of the manufacture of candle, both in procedure and materials. Marking crayons are made of different compositions in accordance with the materials to which they are applied, e.g. leather, cloth, metal, glass, etc. A fresh Crayon for ground marking is prepared from colophony styrene, yellow wax and chrome yellow. A crayon for marking textile fibers is formed of stearic acid, barium sulphate and starch. A tailors marking crayon requires a hard wax like carnauba blended with paraffin wax and pure white tale. A glass, marking crayons must be fairly soft is made from paraffin, a little stearic acid and para red or other colour. A luminous writing stick may be composed of japan wax, socerite, paraffin and petroleum jelly together with a small proportion of lumen scent sulphide.

CHILDREN'S WAX CRAYONS

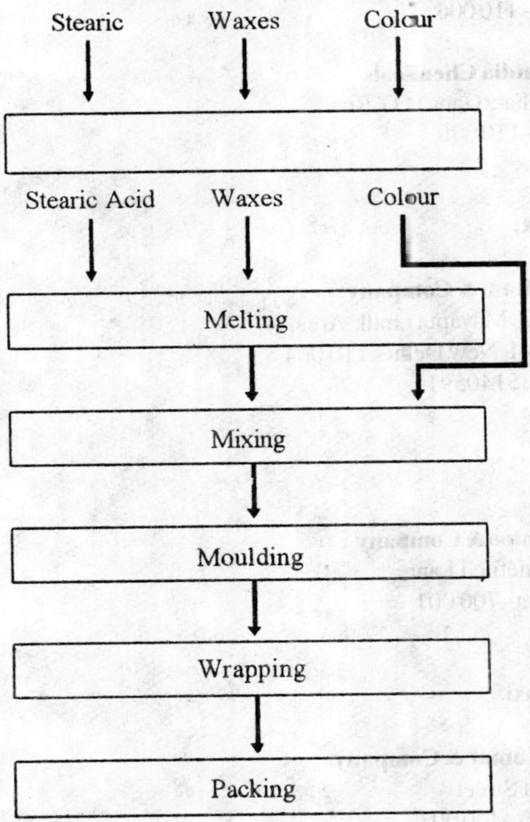

SUPPLIERS OF PLANT AND MACHINERY

Asian Engg. Industries
275/297, Bellasis Road,
Mumbai - 400 003

Indian Moulding & Engg. Works (P) Ltd.,
2 Church Lane,
Calcutta.

SUPPLIERS OF RAW MATERIALS

Stearic Acid:

Anantram Lachmandas Aggarwal,
6692/1, Khari Baoli
Delhi - 110 006

New India Chemicals
1433, Faiz Ganj, B.G. Road,
Delhi - 110 006

Paraffin Wax:

Ralla Ram & Company
A-28/2, Mayapuri Indl. Area,
Phase - I, New Delhi - 110 064
Phone : 5140591

Bees Wax:

M. Mintoo & Company
26, Bonefiled Lane,
Calcutta - 700 001

Carnauba Wax:

Kirti Kumar & Company
50, Isaji Street
Mumbai - 400 003

44

XEROX PAPER

INTRODUCTION

People require paper to meet the basic needs of modern life because it has may diverse uses.

The paper & paper board industry has a major role in the economic development of the country. Apart from its applications as writing and printing paper, it has a distinguished record of service in the packaging & other related industries at present there are 42 varieties of paper are being produced in our country and these can be listed into the following categories :-

1. Printing paper
2. Writing paper
3. Packing & Wrapping papers
4. Other varieties (Cigarette paper, Xerox paper, Base paper etc.)
5. Other boards

ELECTROGRAPHIC OR XEROX PAPERS

Electrography is also known by the trade names, viz. Electrofax, and better known in India as "Xerography", Electrophotographic machines are used for copying or printing by electro-optical methods in contrast to contact printing or to conventional chemical photograpic process. The electro-optical method is based on electrostatics and photo conductivity & requires no chemical processing. The most consumer form of automatic electro photographic machine used a sensitized coated paper which is conducted & coated with an emulsion of photo conduct or like Zinc oxide, a binder and a sensitizer. This paper is changed with the corona device charging system or the machine and era booted to the document in the dark.

The corona operates between 6-10 KV During the exposure, its light (in the form of image) falling on this paper dissipates the charge forming an electrostatic latent page of the document Electrostatic latent image is developed by insertion in a liquid developer containing oppositely charged lower particles which when dried in an air blast give dry copy making of this copy of a document takes few seconds.

In xerox equipment a cylinder made up of special Vitreous selemium layer coated onto aluminium. The dry toner powder is attracted to the latent electrostatic image on the drum and this powder is then transferred to the final receiving sheet. The transfer of the powder is affected by the applications of a voltage of opposite polarity to the toner charge sign while the cylinder is in close contact with the paper. The drum is cleaned of residual toner and repeats the cycle. In this Electrofax system based on zinc oxide/resin coatings, the latent electrostatic image is formed directly on the coating surface on this not subsequently transferred. It is developed either by toner method as described before or by a dispersion of toner particles in a dielectric liquid medium.

REQUISITES OF A GOOD XEROX PAPER

1. The quality of this paper should be as good as that of a photographic paper.
2. The solvent hold out should be high to permit the application of a smooth to uniform thickness of oxide/retin coating.
3. The base paper should be covered with barrier layers, which should be smooth and free from pin - holes.

SPECIFICATIONS OF THE PRODUCT

The sensitized Zinc oxide coated paper is required to attain the acceptance potential of 340 volts at a relative humidity of 40-60 %. The dark decay rate should be less than 5 volts per second. Exposure of charged paper to 450 to 650 mm light should dissipate the charge is less than a second.

Zinc :- The production of zinc in our country has been on increase are ever since independence in 1947. In 1950, the production of zinc concentrates was 666 tons only By 1985 it has risen to 87,082 tons i.e. in 22 years the output multiplied 131 times.

However in recent years the rate of rise in production of zinc slowed down. In 1980-81, the total output of zinc in our country was estimated at 45526 tons by 1988-89, it had risen to 89000 tons thus, output rose by 95.4 percent in eight years. Even though new deposits of zinc are being discovered the total output of zinc is not likely to rise 100,000 tons by this end of current century.

RAW MATERIALS & THEIR - AVAILABILITY

In the manufacturing of Xerox paper, some of chemicals used are special grade Zinc oxide, organic solvents like. Toluene, and alcohol, sensitizer, electroconductive resin binder rising and paper. These materials are available abundantly in our country.

SUPPLIERS OF ZINC OXIDE

Ashkin Chemicals
Bhatwada Dholi Kui,
Opp. Hanuman Tample,
Near Vasn Bazar,
Baroda : 290 001

Chembond Chemicals Pvt. Ltd.,
B-23, Todi Industrial Estate,
New Sun Mils Compound,
Lower Parel,
Mumbai - 400 013

PLANT ECONOMICS OF XEROX PAPER SHEETS

Rated Plant Capacity = 140000.00 Paper sheets/Day
= 42000000.00 Paper Sheets/Annum

COST OF LAND & BUILDING

(Total land area required 200 sq. mtr.)	Rs.	6,65,000.00

LIST OF PLANT & MACHINERY

1. Paper coating plant
2. Mixing equipment
3. Testing & Calibration equipment
4. Electrometer

LIST OF RAW MATERIALS

1. Paper
2. Zinc oxide
3. Organic solvents (Toluene and alcohol etc.)
4. Sensitizer
5. Electroconductive resin (binder resin)

FIXED CAPITAL

Land & Building	Rs.	6,65,000.00
Plant & Machinery	Rs.	4,25,000.00
Other Fixed Assets	Rs.	1,08,000.00
TOTAL	**Rs.**	**11,98,000.00**

TOTAL WORKING CAPITAL/ANNUM

Raw Material	Rs.	90,00,000.00
Salary & Wages	Rs.	8,47,500.00
Utilisation & Overheads	Rs.	4,50,000.00
TOTAL	**Rs.**	**1,02,97,500.00**

TOTAL CAPITAL INVESTMENT

Total Fixed Capital	Rs.	11,98,000.00
Total Working Capital for 3 Months	Rs.	25,74,375.00
TOTAL	**Rs.**	**37,72,375.00**

TURN OVER/ANNUM

By Sale of 4,20,00000 Sheets per annum @ Re. 0.35/- per sheet

Rs. 1,47,00,000.00

PROFIT = RECEIPTS - COST OF PRODUCTION
= 1,47,00,000.00 - 1,12,79,097.50
= 34,20,902.50

PROFIT SALES RATIO = Profit/Sales x 100 = **23.27 %**

RATE OF RETURN = Operating Profit/T.C.I. x 100 = **90.68 %**

BREAK EVEN POINT (B.E.P.) = 30.49 %

DIRECTORY SECTION

(INDIAN & OVERSEAS)

✓ **MACHINERIES**

✓ **RAW MATERIALS**

✓ **TECHNOLOGIES**

Aditya Poly Pack

27/G, Laxmi Industrial Estate, Link Road,
Versova, Andheri (W), Mumbai - 400 058

Phone : 6263257,6294521
Fax : 91-22-6271919

Products : Plain & Printed LD/LLD/HM/HD pouches & rolls for all types of consumer products

Aditya Laminators Pvt. Ltd.

17/J, Laxmi Industrial Estate, New Link Road,
Andheri (W), Mumbai - 400 058

Phone : 62632576294521
Fax : 91-22-6271919

Products : Rotogravure printing machines, Coating for Wrappers, Double/Triple film laminates & Other consumer products for Hand & Automatic machines.

Anjana Machinery Manufacturers Pvt. Ltd.,

206, Udyog Bhawan, Sharma Indl. Estate,
Goregaon (E), Mumbai - 400 063

Phone : 6730146
Fax : 91-22-6148897

Products : Packaging machinery for Gumming, Label gumming, Label printing, Corrugation board and box making complete plant, slitting and Rewinding machine, Coating and Laminating machine, Flexographic printing machines.

Anu Enterprises

125, Universal Induatrial Estate, J.P. Road,
Andheri (West), Mumbai - 400 058

Phone : 6230523

Products : Automatic case sealers, corrugated carton machine with BOPP tape.

Bhagwati Paper Industries

C-13, South Side of G.T. Road,
Indl. Area, Ghaziabad (U.P.)

Phone : 8-48097

Products : Paper converting machines.

Compack Systems

E-211, Flatted Factory Complex,
Okhla, New Delhi - 110 020

Phone : 6831545,6914067
Fax : 91-11-6841307

Products : Shrink & stretch wrapping machines and materials specially in shrink polythene.

Continental Crowns & Closures

B-154, DDA Shed, Okhla Indl. Area,
New Delhi - 110 020

Phone : 6812655
Fax : 91-11-6434734

Products : Cap sealing machines

Dashmesh Mechanico

14, Gali No. 8, Anand Parbat Indl. Area,
New Delhi - 110 005

Phone : 5737112,5754774

Products : Corrugated box making machines.

D. F. Industries

8, Apurva Indl. Estate, 88 Makwana Road,
Marol Naka, Andheri (E),
Mumbai - 400 059

Phone : 6344730,6325888

Products : Manufacturers & Exporters of Stitching wire.

Duotone Corporation

30, Laxmi Indl. Estate, New Link Road,
Andheri (W), Mumbai - 400 053

Phone : 6320439,6266943
Fax : 91-22-6266535

Products : Magic seal bag/Zip lock bag making plant.

Eagle Manufacturing Company

C-19, Ghatkopar Indl. Estate, L.B. Shastri Marg,
Ghatkopar (W), Mumbai - 400 086

Phone : 5170543,5171732
Fax : 91-22-5170370

Products : Semi automatic P.P. box strapping machines.

Graphic Sales

4E/8, Jhandewalan Extension,
New Delhi - 110 055

Phone : 7524665,737090,8522130
Fax : 91-11-7524665,8522130

Products : Thread sewing machine, filling systems and process equipments.

Hindustan Inks

2803/2, Third Phase, GIDC,
Vapi - 396 195, Gujarat.

Phone : 02638-30782,30786,30787
Fax : 02638-30781,30788

Products : Flexo/Gravure inks, Lamination adhesives, Offset and Screen inks, Process inks, Spot colours, Heatset or IR inks & News inks or Custom inks.

Innovative Technologies

Mahavir Industries Building,
Sunmill Compound,
Lower Parel, Mumbai - 400 013

Phone : 4937252,4941411
Fax : 4461290

Products : Glueing machines, Book pressing machine and Paper drilling machine.

Ivory Paper Traders

4859, Chowk Bara Tooti,
Sadar Bazar,
Delhi - 110 006

Phone : 3542143,7773849,7512676

Products : All kinds of Papers & Boards.

Jangir Sons

25/7, Gali No. 9, Anand Parbat Indl. Area,
New Delhi - 110 005

Phone : 5730101

Products : BOPP, PVC Surgical tape, Micropore tape, Silicon plant, Slitting machines, Tape plant machinery.

J. K. Engineering Corporation

19A, Rajendra Nagar, Indl. Area,
Mohan Nagar, Ghaziabad.
(U.P.)

Phone : 720934

Products : Corrugated board & box making machines, All types of cable machine, Lamination machine, Stitching wire making machine.

Kalsi Machinery Company (P) Ltd.,

121, East Mohan Nagar, Indl. Area,
Amritsar. (Punjab)

Phone : 231139,231805,230595
Fax : 0183-231805

Products : Thread book sewing machines, Box stitchers, Paper folding machines.

Kapoor International

22, 23, Vishnu Indl. Estate, Masrani Lane,
Halao Pool, Kurla (W),
Mumbai - 400 070

Phone : 5142594,5168891
Fax : 91-22-5141878

Products : Packing master shrink wrapping machines for PVC/LDPE.

K.U. Sodalamuthu and Co. Pvt. Ltd.,

428, Mettupalayam Road,
Coimbatore - 641043.

Phone : 441223,441805,448346
Fax : 91-422-431279

Products : Plant and machinery for Paper cones, P.O.Y. Tubes, Cores, Composite Cans, Fibre Drums, Pulp Moulded Products etc.

Kuru Engineering College

Chinnavedampatti P.O.,
Coimbatore - 641 006

Phone/Fax: 0422-212957

Products : Paper cone and Paper tube making machinery.

Lakshmi Industries (Regd.)

124, Indl. Area A,
Ludhiana - 141 003
(Punjab)

Phone : 662313

Products : Ball pen & refill making machinery.

Leo Pharma Automation

4, Ashok Indl. Estate, L.B.S. Marg,
Mulund (W), Mumbai - 400 080

Phone : 5617372
Fax : 5612165

Products : Screen Printing Machinery

Madras Type Foundry

38, Jones Street,
Chennai - 600 001

Products : Cutting machine, Perforating, Punching, Proof press, Rubber Stamp making, Rule cutting & Bending & Hot stamping machineries.

Manjeet Enterprises

H-14, Indl. Area, Govindpura,
Bhopal.

Phone : 580175

Products : Rotogravure multicolour printing machines, P.U. & PVC Coating, Lamination embossing, Coagulation plant, Curing oven and Tripple roll mills.

Marsons Print-Graf Machines Pvt. Ltd.,

D-9, Udyog Sadan No. 2, Opp. ESIC Hospital,
Central Road, MIDC, Andheri (E), Mumbai - 400 093

Phone : 8320174, 8301581, 8369362 Fax : 91-022-8369359

Products : Rotogravure & Flexographic printing machines, Adhesive coating & Dry/Wet lamination plant, Slitting & Rewinding machine, Self adhesive tape coating machines (BOPP/PVC), Bag making machines, P.P. Box Strap printing machines, Self adhesive tape slitting & Rewinding machines (BOPP/PVC).

Micro Engineers (INDIA)

Fitwell House, L.B.S. Marg,
Vikhroli, Mumbai - 400 083

Phone : 5784425, 5784808, 5785368, 5781574
Fax : 91-22-5785725/5784801

Products : Manufacturing paper corrugated packaging machinery.

M. M. Industries

Hampton Court,
N. Parekh Marg,
Colaba, Mumbai - 400 005

Phone : 4951103

Products : Machinery of Coding/Marking & Labelling.

Neptune Plastic & Metal Industries

Jain Chambers 18, R.N. Mukherjee Road,
7th Floor, Calcutta - 700 001

Phone : 28-1979/2351/1991
Fax : 0091-33-282070/4046

Products : Multilayer films, Box strapping (PP, HDPE, Nylon), Refil/Straw, Bag makers, Film winders and PP Sutli plant.

Parekh Marketing Ltd.,

Ramakrishna Mandir Road,
Andheri (E),
Mumbai - 400 059

Products : Industrial adhesives for Packaging & Labelling, Lamination and Stickers.

Premier Instruments & Controls Limited

Post Box No. 6331,
Coimbatore - 641037
(INDIA)

Products : Foil stamping machines.

Printech Graphics

1, Motia Khan,
New Delhi - 110 055

Phone : 522016, 7512555
Fax : 7534555

Products : File punching machinery, Case making machinery and Paper drilling macines.

Pro Doing Industrial Company Limited

No. 47, 22nd Road, Taichung Industrial Park,
Taichung, Taiwan.

Phone : 886-4-359-7712
Fax : 886-4-359-7269

Products : Polycell bag making whole and PVC shrink label making whole plant equipments.

Samrat Engineering Works

F-133, Mayapuri Indl. Area,
Phase - II, New Delhi - 110 064

Phone : 5400814, 5492553

Products : Die cutting machines, Glueing machines (automatic carton pasting), Printing, Paper cutting, Stitching, Perforating machines, Paper cutting knives.

Shai-fa-ley Enterprises

21, Laxmi Indl. Estate, Goregaon (W),
Mumbai - 400 090

Phone : 8737557
Fax : 91-22-8725164

Products : Quality extruders & equipments for LLDPE, HM, PP, LD, PVC Film, Box strapping.

Sharma Engineering Works

Shop No. 40, Main Market,
Sultanpur Majra,
Nangloi, Delhi - 110 041

Products : Polythene making machines, Extruders-HM-LD-PP, Cutting & sealing machines.

Spirowind Machines Pvt. Ltd.

162/1, Jawahar Nagar, Goregaon (W),
Mumbai - 400 062

Phone : 8724832
Fax : 91-22-8733618

Products : Manufacturers of Exporters of Packaging machineries, Spiral paper tubes & cones.

Sud & Waren Pvt. Ltd.

72, Sector - 6, Indl. Estate,
Faridabad - 121 006 (Haryana)

Phone : 0129-242402,242342,241243
Fax : 91-11-6468991

Products : Continuous stationery presses, Envelope pasting, pneumatic reel lifter, Electronic web alignment, Carbon interleaving, File hole punching, Duplex punching & Cross turn bar.

Swastik Packaging

4 Dev Sadan Chimat Pada, Marol Naka,
Andheri (East), Mumbai - 400 059

Phone : 8324673,8392379,8341340
Fax : 91-22-8388192

Products : Polybag & any heat sealable materials, Liquid sealer, Impulse sealer, Heat shrink packing machine and Continuous bag sealer.

Tapping System

C-135, Ghatkopar Indl. Estate,
L.B. Shastri Marg, Ghatkopar (W),
Mumbai - 400 086

Phone : 5172224
Fax : 91-22-5170370

Products : Carton sealing machine and Economic solution for box taping.

Techno Engineering Works

D-17, Pushpanjli Enclave,
Pitampura, New Delhi - 110 034

Phone : 7019232,7010681

Products : Paper tubes & paper cones plants.

Vikrant Engineering Works

BE-103, Gali No. 3, Hari Nagar,
Near Radha-Krishna Mandir,
New Delhi - 110 064

Products : High speed packaging machinery, Automatic labelling machines etc.

Wonderpack Industries (P) Ltd.,

321, T.V. Indl. Estate, S.K. Ahire Marg,
Worli, Mumbai - 400 025

Phone : 4949580,4934736,4936496
Fax : 91-22-4938796/4363960

Products : Shrink wrapping machine and systems, L sealers & Web sealers.

Yenyeskay Machine Tools

23, Shastri Road No. 1, P. N. Pudur,
(Maruthamalai Road), Coimbatore - 641

Phone : 434288,443728
Fax : 0422-212130

Products : Paper gum tape plant, Film lamination machine, Disc ruling machin, Automatic paper bag making machine.

103. ALUM FOR WATER TREATMENT
104. ALUMINIUM PAINT
105. ALUMINIUM HYDROXIDE GEL
106. ALUMINIUM INGOTS FROM BAUXITE
107 AMLA PLANTATION
108. AMPICILLIN TRIHYDRATE IN CAPSULES WITH STRIP PACKING
109. AMMONIUM CHLORIDE TABLETS
110. AMMONIUM DI-CHROMATE
111. AMMONIUM SULPHATE
112 AMMONIA GAS
113. AMMONIA PAPER
114. AMMONIUM NITRATE
115. AMUSEMENT PARK
116. AMMONIUM CHLORIDE BLOCK
117. AMMONIA LIQUOR
118. AMINO ACID FOR POULTRY FEED
119. AMINES & ALLIED PRODUCTS
120. ANODIC ALUMINIUM LABELS
121. ANGORA RABBIT WOOL
122. ANTI CORROSION LUBRICANTS (No Costing)
123. ANTI SCALE COMPOUND for Adding Sugar Juce Boiling
124. ANTHRAQUINONE
125. ANTIMONY TRI-OXIDE
126. ANTI STATIC POLYTHENE BAGS
127. ANHYDROUS CALCIUM CHLORIDE
128. ANTIMONY
129. APPLE JUICE CONCENTRATE & DEHYDRATED FRUITS & VEG. MANUFACTURING
130. APPLE POMACE PECTIN
131. APPLE JUICES
132. AQUA CULTURE SHRIMP FARM (EOU)
133. AQUA CULTURE PRAWN FARMING (100% EOU)
134. ARTIST COLOURS
135. ARTIFICIAL FLOWERS
136. ARTIFICIAL FISH MEAL for PoultryFeed
137. ARMOURED CABLES
138. ASBESTOS CEMENT PIPE & Fitting for Bldg. Sewerage & Drainage
139. ASBESTOS RIDES & ROOFING SHEET
140. ASBESTOS CEMENT PIPES AND FITTING FOR BUILDING SEWIRAGE & DRAINAGE
141. ASPHALTIC ROOFING SHEET
142. ASH TRAYS FOR MARUTI CARS
143. ASBESTOS FIBRE MOULDED PRODUCTS
144. ASBESTOS GASKET SHEET
145. ASPIRIN
146. ASAFOETIDA (HING)
147. ATRAZIN PESTICIDE
148. AUTO CLUTCH PLATE
149. AUTO TUBE (All Type)
150. AUTO BULBS (HEAD & TAIL)
151. AUTO FLAPS
152 AUTO PISTON & PISTON RING (Piston Assembly - Al. Alloy)
153. AUTO SPOKES
154. AUTO TYRE, TUBE & FLAPS
155. ATTA (MINI FLOUR MILL)
156. AUTOMATIC BISCUIT PLANT
157. AUTOMATIC BREAD PLANT
158. AUTOMATIC BREAD & BISCUIT MAKING PLANT
159. AUTO CABLES
160. AUTO PINS
161. AUTO LEAF SPRING
162. AUTO TELEPHONE RECORDING & ANSWERING M/C.
163. AUTO GEARS ,
164. AUTO PART (Rubber)
165. AUTO FLOUR MILL
166. AUTO INJECTION MOULDED PLASTIC COMPONENTS

Readily available 15000 Detailed Project Reports

167. AUTO WIRES FOR 2/3 WHEELERS CLUTCH WIRES, BRAKE WIRES, SPEEDO METER WIRE & GEAR WIRES
168. AUTO VOLTAGE STABILIZERS
169. AUTOMOBILE FILTER
170. AUTOMOBILE BUSHES
171. AUTOMATIC BRICK PLANT
172. AUROMINE- O
173. AUTOMOBILE PAINTS
174. AUDIO CASSETTES ASSEMBLY & RECORDING
175. AUDIO & VIDEO CASSETTES
176. AUTOMATIC BOOK BINDING
177. AUTOBODY BUILDING
178. AUTOMOBILE REFRIGERATORS
179. AUTOMOBILE RADIATORS
180. AUTOMATIC VOLTAGE STABILIZER
181. AUTOMOBILE BRAKE SHOES
182. AUDIO MAGNETIC TAPES
183. AUTOMOBILE WORKSHOP & SERVICE CENTER
184. AUTOMOBILE PISTON RINGS
185 AUTOMOBILE PISTONS
186. AUTOMOBILE CYLINDERS FOR TWO WHEELERS
187. AUTOMOBILE WIRES FOR TWO/THREE WHEELERS, CLUTCH WIRE, BRAKE WIRE, SPEEDO METERS WIRE & GEAR WIRES
188. AUTOMATIC PLANT FOR TOFFEE/CANDY MANUFACTURE
189. AUTOMATIC CANDLE UNIT
190. AUTOMATIC VENDING MACHINE FOR HOT & COLD BEVERAGES
191. AUTOMOBILE POLISH
192. AUTOMOBILE BLINKERS
193. AUTOMOBILE GASKET
194. AUTOMOBILE PARTS FOR MARUTI VEHICLE
195. AUTOMOBILE GARAGE/ WORKSHOP FOR TRUCKS (12-15 TRUCKS)
196. AUTOMOBILE PARTS
197. AUTOMOBILE RUBBER PARTS
198. AUDIO CASSETTES SCREW
199. AYURVEDIC MEDICINES
200. AYURVEDIC SHARBAT
201. AYURVEDIC PAIN BALM OINTMENT
202. AZO-DYE STUFFS
203. BABY DIAPERS
204. BACTERICIDA FOR CANE JUICE
205. BADMINTON RACKETS
206. BADMINTON SHUTTLE COCKS
207. BAKELITE MOULDED PRODUCTS
208. BAKERS YEAST
209. BAKELITE SHEETS (PHENOLIC SHEETS) ELECTRICAL GRADE
210. BAKELITE ELECTRICAL ACCESSORIES (SWITCH, SOCKET, PLUG)
211. BAKERY UNIT (BUNS, BREAD, PASTRY, CAKES & TOFFEES)
212. BAKING POWDER
213. BALL POINT PEN REFILLS (100% EOU)
214. BALL POINT PEN REFILLS & INKS
215. BALL BEARING
216. BALLOONS (All Type)
217. BAMBOO STICKS FOR AGARBATTIES
218. BANANA & ITS BYE PRODUCTS

Price Rs. 2500/- for each "Detailed Project Report" Payable in advance through Draft/Cash/M.O. in favour of "ENGINEERS INDIA RESEARCH INSTITUTE". Or Ask by V.P.P. PH.: 291 8117, 291 6431, 292 0361 Fax: 91-11-291 6431 (24 Hrs.)

354. CAMERA (35 M.M)
355. CARTONS FOR DISTILLERY
356. CASHEWNUT SHELL LIQUID & KERNELS (CNSL)
357. CARPET WOOLLEN YARN DYEING
358. CASTOR OIL HYDROGENATION
359. CASTOR OIL REFINING
360. CANDLE (Semi Automatic)
361. CAST IRON POWDER
362. CASEIN BASED PIGMENTS USED IN SPORT INDUSTRY
363. CASHEWNUT (Dried & Fried)
364. CARD/GREY BOARD
365. CANDLE (NON DRIP)
366. CATTLE FEED BY TAPIOCA
367. CAUSTIC SODA/CHLORINE PLANT MEMBRANE CELL
368. CARBOXY METHYL CELLULOSE
369. CANNING & PRESERVATION OF FRUIT & VEGETABLE
370. CANNING & PRESERVATION OF FRUITS & VEGETABLE WITH COLD STORAGE & RAISIN (KISMISH MAKING)
371. CASSETTE TAPES (COVER)
372. CANVAS SHOES, JUNGLE BOOT, RUBBER KNEES & BOOT COMBAT
373. CALCIUM SILICATE
374. CALCIUM GLUCONATE
375. CANVAS SHOES
376. CASTOR OIL EMULSIFIER
377. CASEIN FROM MILK
378. CARPET WEAVING
379. CABLES FOR CABLE NETWORK
380. CABLE (FLAT/RIBBEN)
381. CABLES FOR AUTOMOBILE
382. CABLES (PVC WIRE)
383. CABLES-ARMOURED
384. CABLES-TEFLON COATED
385. CABLES-TELEPHONE
386. CABLES- XLPE/PVC
387. CABLES-WELDING
388. CABLES-OPTICAL FIBRE
389. CANNING OF ROSGULLAS IN METAL CANS
390. CALCIUM NITRATE
391. CATIONIC SOFTENER
392. CANNING & BOTTLING OF FRUITS & VEGETABE PRODUCTS
393. CATECHU (KATTHA) - CHEMICAL PROCESS
394. CATTLE BREEDING
395. CARPET DRY CLEANING
396. CAR AIR CONDITIONERS
397. CARBOXY METHYL CELLULOSE (C.M.C.)
398. CARD BOARD MATCH BOXES
399. CARDINAL FROM C.N.S.L.
400. CAPACITOR DISCHARGE IGNITION (CIDI Unit)
401. CASHEWNUT KERNEL EXTRACTION FROM CASHEWNUT FRUIT
402. CARBON ZINC CELL (DRY CELL)
403. CANDY HARD BOILED
404. CASHEW FENI (WINE DISTILLATION FROM FRUITS & CASHEWNUT)
405. CARD BOARD BOXES & CARTONS (SYSTEM PACK)
406. CAR PAINTS
407. CAR POLISHES
408. CASTOR OIL DERIVATIVE OLEORESIN
409. CANNED FRUITS & VEGETABLES
410. CANNED FRUITS & VEGETABLES
411. CANNED FRUITS & VEGETABLES
412. CERAMIC INSULATOR
413. CERAMIC CORES & TUBES
414. CEMENT PLANT
415. CHEESE (Processed)
416. CEMENT ROOFING TILES
417. CERAMIC TILES (GLAZED)

418. CELLULOSE ACETATE
419. CEMENT WATER PROOF COMPOUND
420. CEMENT PAINT
421. CEMENT PLANT (800 TPD)
422. CEMENT COLOUR/LIME COLOUR (SYNTHETIC RED IRON OXIDE) USED FOR FLOORING
423. CEMENT FROM RICE HUSK
424. CEMENT (CLINKER)
425. CEMENT FROM FLY ASH AND LIME
426. CEILING FAN
427. CENTRIFUGAL PUMP
428. CELLULOSE POWDER & MICRO CRYSTALLINE CELLULOSE POWDER
429. CELLULOSE ACETATE MOULDING POWDER
430. CERAMIC NOVELTIES
431. CERAMIC TRANSFERS (FOR PRINTING ON CERAMICS)
432. CERAMIC COATED ALUMINIUM THREAD GUIDE
433. CERAMIC THREAD GUIDE
434. CERAMIC FIRING/ DECORATIVE TILES
435. CEMENT POLE, JALLIE & TILE
436. CHEMICAL LABORATORY
437. CERAMIC CROCKERY WARE (Bone China - Hitkari)
438. CHEMICAL RESISTANT IRON & STEEL
439. CERAMIC GLAZED TILES
440. CEMENT GRINDING
441. CEMENT OXIDE
442. CERAMIC MAGNET
443. CEMENT TILES (LAYING OVER RCC ROOFS)
444. CHINA CLAY
445. CHOKES, TRANSFORMERS & ELIMINATORS
446. CHOLORINATED PARAFFIN WAX
447. CHICKEN/MUTTON (SHEEP MEAT) PROCESSING
448. CHICKEN/MEAT PROCESSING AND PACKAGING
449. CHROME PLATED (C.P.) BATH ROOM FITTINGS
450. CHOKES & PATTIES
451. CHAIN LINK FENCING OUT OF PVC COATED WIRE
452. CHEWING TOBACCO
453. CHROMIC ACID
454. CHINESE SOYA SAUCE
455. CHROMIC ACID
456. CHEWING GUM
457. CHLORAM PHENICOL
458. CHELATED ZINC (Zn-EDTA)
459. CHILLI POWDER
460. CHOCOLATE
461. CHEWING GINGER & AMLOKI
462. CHROME PLATING
463. CHOKE & STARTER
464. CHOKE OF FLUORESCENT TUBES
465. CHEMICAL ETCHING OF STAINLESS STEEL
466. CHEMICAL LAMINATION OF PHOTO
467. CHLORINATED RUBBER BASED PLANT
468. CITRONELLA OIL
469. CINEMA HALL
470. CIGARETTES
471. CIGARETTES- HERBAL
472. CINNAMON BARK OIL
473. CINE-ARC- CARBON
474. C.I. CASTINGS (FOUNDRY) BY INDUCTION FURNACE
475. CITRIC ACID BY MOLASSES
476. CIGARETTE & BIDI
477. CIDER PLANT (APPLE WINE)
478. CITRONELLA OIL
479. C.I. POWDER BY GRINDING PROCESS
480. CLOVE OIL
481. CLOTH (COTTON PROCESSING & FINISHING OF CLOTH)
482. CLUTCH WIRE FROM DRAWN WIRE
483. CLEANING OF COOLING SYSTEM & BOILER

484. CLAY PLATES FOR ELECTRIC HEATERS
485. CLUTCH PLATE FOR 4 WHEELERS
486. CLUTCH PLATE FOR 3 WHEELER
487. CLEANING POWDER (VIM)
488. CLUTCH FACING & BRAKE LINING
489. CLEAR TRANSPARENT LACQUER FOR COATING ON BRASS BANGLES TO MAKE IT WEATHER RESISTANT
490. CLINICAL THERMOMETER
491. C.N.S.L. BASED RESIN IN LIQUID & Powder Form
492. COPPER WIRE DRAWING & ENAMELING
493. CORDLESS PHONE
494. CONCENTRATION OF MANGANESE ORE
495. COPPER & BRASS TUBES
496. CORRUGATED SHEET BOARD & BOXES
497. COPPER BOTTOM STAINLESS STEEL UTENSILS
498. COOLING COILS FOR AIR CONDITIONERS
499. COLOUR LAB (QSS-PHOTO)
500. COMPUTER CONTINUOUS STATIONERY
501. COMPUTER ASSEMBLY
502. COMPUTER MONITOR
503. COMPUTER RIBBON
504. COMPUTER RIBBON REFILLING & REINKING
505. COMPUTER MONITOR TUBE & T.V. PICTURE TUBE (B/W)
506. COMPUTER SOFTWARE (100% EOU)
507. COMPUTER FORMS AND SECURITY PRINTING PRESS
508. COMPUTER FORM (COMPUTER STATIONERY)
509. COMPUTER JOB WORK
510. COMPUTER ATTENDANCE REGISTER
511. COMPUTER PRINTER
512 COMPUTER KEYBOARD
513. COMPUTER EDUCATION INSTITUTE
514. COMPUTER (MINI/ PERSONAL)
515. COMPUTER-LAPTOP
516. COMPUTER PERIPHERALS
517. COMPUTER STATIONERY AND IMPORTED HARDWARE PARTS
518. COOLANT ENGINE
519. COLLEGE
520. COLD DRINKS
521. COLD PROCESSED TYRE RETREADING
522. COLD STORAGE
523. COLD STORAGE & ICE
524. COLD ROLLING MILL
525. COLD PROCESSED TREAD RUBBER
526. COLD CREAMS
527. COLD ROLLING OF STEEL STRIPS
528. COLD ROLLED PRESSED STEEL DOORS, WINDOW FRAMES
529. COTTON ADHESIVE TAPES & PLASTER OF PARIS BANDAGES For Hospital
530. COLOUR & B/W TV
531. COLOUR TELEVISION
532. COSTUME JEWELLERY
533. COTTON SEED OIL
534. COTTON YARN
535. CONDUIT IRON PIPES (C.I.PIPES)
536. CONDENSED MILK SWEETENED
537. COIR FOAM (RUBBERIZED COIR) CUSHION & MAT ETC.
538. CONCRETE HOLLOW BRICK/ BLOCKS
539. CONDENSED MILK
540. COCONUT OIL
541. COFFEE PLANTATION
542. COBALT OCTOATE
543. COIR PITH
544. COPPER NITRATE
545. CONCENTRATE OF TOMATO (TOMATO PASTE)

546. CONFERENCE BAG, FOLDERS ETC. (PLASTIC)
547. CORN FLAKES
548. COATING ON PLASTICS
549. COPPER OXY-CHLORIDES
550. COPPER PHTHALOCYNINE BLUE & GREEN
551. COATED PAPER & BOARD
552. CONVERTER
553. COPPER CLAD LAMINATES FOR PCB'S (PAPER & FABRIC BASED)
554. COPPER RODS FROM SCRAPS
555. COLLECTION OF MILK & PACKAGING IN POLYTHENE POUCHES (MILK CHILLING)
556. COURIER SERVICES
557. CONFECTIONERY
558. CONFECTIONERY INDUSTRY-SEMI AUTOMATIC PLANT (TOFFEE & CANDY MANUFACTURING)
559. COAL BRIQUETTING FROM COAL
560. COAL BRIQUETTES FROM AGRO WASTE
561. COUNTRY LIQUOR
562. COPPER STRIPS COILS
563. CONCAST STEEL BAR
564. COATING & PRINTING OF LAMINATED PAPER POUCH
565. COATING & LAMINATION ON PAPER (HOT MELT FILM LAMINATION METHOD)
566. COUNTRY LIQUOR FROM MOLASSES
567. COSMETIC UNIT
568. COMPOSITE CONTAINER
569. COPPER BERYLLIUM ALLOY SPRINGS
570. COLOUR MASTER BATCH FOR VARIOUS PLASTICS
571. COMPACT DISC PLAYER
572. COMPACT DISC (CD)
573. COTTON FINISHING
574. CONSTANT VOLTAGE TRANSFORMER (C.V.T.)
575. CORROSION CONTROLLING CHEMICAL (PIPE LINE)
576. COPPER FOIL
577. COPPER & BRASS INGOTS
578. COMPRESSOR (HERMETIC) FOR AIR CONDITIONER
579. COATING ON PLASTICS & GLASS
580. COATING OF CLEAR TRANSPARENT LACQUER ON BRASS BANGLES TO MAKE IT WEATHER RESISTANT
581. COCONUT PLANTATION
582. COCONUT PRODUCTS & BYE PRODUCTS PROCESSING COMPLEX (WET FRESH) 100% EOU
583. CONVEYER BELTS
584. COPPER SULPHATE
585. COIR INDUSTRY
586. COSMETIC (HERBAL & SYNTHETIC)
587. COTTON & ACRYLIC YARN SPINDLES
588. CO-EXTRUSION MULTI-LAYER FILM
589. COLOURED FLAME CANDLE
590. COMMUTATOR FOR ELECTRIC MOTOR
591. COTTON BUDS/SWABS
592. COATING ON METALLIZED POLYE-STER FILM/ METALLIZED PAPER/ ALUMINIUM FOILS
593. COOLER BODY & TRUNK (FABRICATION UNIT)
594. COSMETIC, DETERGENT POWDER & PERFUMERY COMPOUND
595. COLOUR MASTER BATCHES FOR VARIOUS PLASTICS
596. COUNTRY LIQUOR
597. COBALT OCTOATE

598. CONDENSER FOR MOTOR
599. COAL GRINDING
600. COCOA POWDER
601. COTTON ROLLS
602. COSTUME/IMITATION/ ARTIFICIAL JEWELLERY (CHAINS & BANGLES)
603. CONCENTRATE OF ROSE, JASMINE & LILLY EXTRACT
604. COPPER WINDING FOR SUBMERSIBLE PUMP & MOTOR
605. COMPACT FLUORESCENT TUBES
606. CONE FOR SOFTY ICE CREAM
607. CORRUGATION OF PLAIN GALVANIZED SHEET
608. CORN FLAKES
609. COTTON GINNING & PRESSING
610. COMPUTER PERIPHERALS
611. COMPUTER HARDWARE
612. COMPACT DISC PLAYER (AUDIO/VIDEO)
613. CO_2 WELDING WIRE
614. COPPER POWDER
615. COPPER EXTRACTION FROM PCB WASTES
616. CRYSTAL TABLEWARE
617. CRUCIBLE BY FIRE CLAY
618. CRACKING OF KERNELS (DESHELLING/DECORTICAT-ING)
619. CRICKET BAT/BALL
620. CROCKERY WARES
621. CRAYON WAX
622. CRITICAL AUTO BODY SHEET METAL PARTS
623. CREPE BANDAGES
624. CUBICAL ELECTRICAL PANEL BOARD (SWITCH BOARD)
625. CUSHION COMPOUND, THREAD & VULCANIZING SOLUTION, FORMULATION AND MANUFACTURE
626. CUTLERY & SILVER JEWELLERY (GOLD PLATED)
627. CUTLERY (STAINLESS STEEL)
628. CURRY POWDER
629. CUTTING OIL
630. CYCLE & RIKSHAW FRAMES
631. CYANIDE ZINC BRIGHTENER
632. CYCLE TYRE & TUBES
633. CYLINDER LINERS FOR AUTOMOBILES
634. CYCLE HANDLE BAR GRIPS
635. CYCLE SPOKES
636. DAIRY FARM & PRODUCTS
637. DAIRY FARM AND DAIRY (MILK) PRODUCTS (PASTEURISED MILK, BUTTER, CAKE & PANEER)
638. DAIRY PRODUCTS
639. DAIRY PRODUCTS & MILK PACKAGING IN POUCHES
640. DALL/PULSE MILL
641. DAIRY FARM & MILK PDTS.
642. DAIRY PLANT
643. DETERGENT POWDER
644. DETERGENT CAKE & POWDER
648. DECORATIVE LAMINATED SHEET (SUNMICA)
649. DESK TOP PUBLISHING(DTP)
650. DEHYDRATED ONIONS & ONION POWDER
651. DEHYDRATION OF FRUITS & VEGETABLES
652. DEXTROSE SALINE
653. DEXTROSE FROM POTATO
654. DEHYDRATED GARLIC FLAKES
655. DEXTRIN & STARCH BASED ADHESIVE
656. DEXTRIN
657. DEXTROSE 5%
658. DEXTROSE (ANHYDROUS) FROM STARCH
659. DESICCATED COCONUT POWDER

660. DEXTROSE POWDER FROM STARCH
661. DEAD BURNT DOLOMITE
662. DETERGENT CAKE
663. DEXTROSE SALINE (I.V. FLUID) IN PLASTIC BOTTLES
664. DETERGENT WASHING POWDER (ARIEL TYPE)
665. DEHYDRATED CASTOR OIL
666. DENIM JEANS & JACKETS
667. DENIM CLOTH (INTEGRA-TED UNIT WITH BLEACHING, DYEING & PRINTING)
668. DETTOL TYPE ANTISEPTIC LOTION
669. DEPARTMENTAL STORE
670. DEHYDRATION OF VEGETABLES
671. DENIM CLOTH
672. DEHYDRATION AND CANNING OF FRUITS & VEGETABLES
673. DEHYDRATION OF FRUITS, VEGETABLES & NON-VEGETABLE PRODUCTS
674. DE-HULLING OF JAUN FOR BEER INDUSTRY
675. D.G. SET
676. DHOOP BATTI STICK
677. DISPOSABLE PLASTIC SYRINGES (STERILIZED)
678. DISPOSABLE PLASTIC CUPS, GLASSES, ETC.
679. DISTILLED WATER AMPOULES
680. DI-OCTYL PHTHALATE(DOP)
681. DISTRIBUTION TRANS-FORMER
682. DIRECT COTTON DYE (NO COST ESTIMATION)
683. DIARY EQUIPMENT
684. DIAZO COATING LUMINESCENT PIGMENT
685. DISTILLED WATER
686. DISPOSABLE CIGARETTE GAS LIGHTER
687. DISPOSABLE NEEDLES
688. DIE MAKING FOR SHEET METAL WORKING
689. DIAMOND TOOLS FOR CUTTING / DRILLING & POLISHING
690. DIRECT BLACK DYE
691. DISH ANTENNA
692. DI-CALCIUM PHOSPHATE FROM ANIMAL BONES
693. DI-CALCIUM PHOSPHATE FROM ROCK PHOSPHATE
694. DIGITAL ELECTRONIC WATCHES
695. DISTILLATION OF ROSIN AND TURPENTINE
696. DIAMOND IMPREGNATED SEGMENTS (METAL BONDED) FOR MARBLE SAWING
697. DI-NITRO CHLORO BENZENE (D.N.C.B.)
698. DI-ETHYL PHTHALATE (DEP)
699. DISH ANTENNA & SATEL-LITE EQUIPMENTS.
700. DIAMOND CUTTING & EXPORT
701. DI-ETHYL OXALATE
702. DISPOSABLE BABY DIAPER
703. DIAGANOSTIC CENTRE
704. DIESEL GENERATOR SETS
705. 4,4-DIAMINO STILBENE 2,2 - DISULPHONIC ACID
706. DOOR BELL
707. DOOR LOCKS/PAD LOCKS
708. DODECYCLE BENZENE SULPHONATE
709. DOUGH MOULDING COMPOUND
710. DRY ICE
711. DRY DISTEMPER & LIME COLOURS
712. DRY GINGER
713. DRY CELL
714. DRYING OF RED CHILLIES, HALDI, DHANIA, PEAS, AND GREEN PEAS
715. DROSS LEAD SCRAP, LEAD POWDER
716. DRY CELLS & STORAGE BATTERIES

Price Rs. 2500/- for each "Detailed Project Report" Payable in advance through Draft/Cash/M.O. in favour of "ENGINEERS INDIA RESEARCH INSTITUTE". Or Ask by V.P.P. PH.: 291 8117, 291 6431, 292 0361 Fax: 91-11-291 6431 (24 Hrs.)

717. DRUM CLOSURES
718. DRIP IRRIGATION
719. DRY FRUIT ROASTING & PACKING
720. D.T.P. & OFFSET PRESS
721. D.T.P. CUM TABLE OFFSET
722. DUPLICATING INK
723. DUPLICATING INK (BLACK) FOR GESTENER DUPLICATOR
724. DUPLICATING STENCIL PAPER
725. DUPLEX/FILE BOARD
726. DYE STUFFS
727. DYE INTERMEDIATE
728. DYE FIXING AGENTS
729. DYEING OF HANK YARN FOR POWER LOOM
730. EAF BASED STEEL
731. EARTH LEAKAGE CIRCUIT BREAKERS (ELCB)
732. EASTER GUM (NOCOSTING)
733. E.C.G/E.E.G. PAPER
734. EDIBLE & NON EDIBLE OIL
735. EDTA AND ITS SALT
736. EDIBLE OIL (MUSTARD OIL)
737. EGG POWDER
738. EGG POWDER (100% EOU - AUTOMATIC IMPORTED PLANT)
739. EGG TRAY
740. EHT TRANSFORMER
741. ELECTRICAL GLS LAMP
742. ELECTRIC FANS
743. ELECTRONIC SERVICE CENTRE
744. ELECTRONICCHOKE
745. ELECTRICAL APPLIANCES
746. ELECTRONIC FLASHER FOR AUTOMOBILES
747. ELECTRONIC TOYS
748. ELECTRONIC GAS LIGHTER (MULTI SPARK)
749. ELECTRONIC TIMER
750. ELECTRONIC ENERGY METER
751. ELECTRIC IRON
752. ELECTRICAL INSULATION TAPES (USING BOPP FILM)
753. ELECTRONIC BALLAST (CHOKE)
754. ELECTRICAL LAMP (GLS)
755. ELECTRONIC QUARTZ CLOCK/WALL CLOCK
756. ELECTRICAL STAMPING
757. ELECTRONIC INDICATOR
758. ELECTRONIC TELEPHONES
759. ELECTRO MAGNETICRELAY
760. ELECTROPLATING ON GOLD AND THEIR CHEMICAL TREATMENT IN GOLDEN COLOUR & SILVER THREAD
761. ELECTROPLATING SCHEME PLANT
762. ELECTROPLATING OF SILVER & SILVER
763. ELECTRICAL INSULATION TAPE (USING BOPP FILM)
764. ELECTRICAL LAMP (INCANDESCENT LAMP)
765. ELECTRICAL REPAIR
766. ELECTRICAL HORN FOR AUTOMOBILE
767. ELECTROPLATING BRIGHTNER
768. ELECTROLYTIC CAPACITOR (MOTOR START)
769. ELECTRIC HEATER CLAY PLATES
770. ELECTRIC LAMP ADHESIVE POWDER
771. ELECTRONIC FAN REGULATOR
772. ELECTRICAL ACCESSORIES (SWITCH, SOCKET, PLUG,)
773. ELECTRO CARDIOGRAM MACHINE (ECG MACHINE)
774. ELECTRIC PORTABLE TOOL
775. ELECTRO POLISHING OF STEEL
776. ELECTROPLATING CHEMICALS
777. ELECTRIC MIXER
778. ELECTRIC CABLES (POWER AND CONTROL CABLES, MINING CABLES, FRLS CABLES, INSTRUMENTATION CABLES, SCREENED CABLES, SUBMERSIBLE PUMP CABLE ETC.)

779. ELECTRONIC SECURITY SYSTEMS
780. ELECTRONIC T.V. TUNER
781. ELECTRONIC TEST & MEASURING INSTRUMENT
782. ELECTRONIC TELEPHONES
783. ELECTRONIC TIMER (PROCESSED CONTROL)
784. ELECTRO REFINING OF ZINC
785. ELECTRONIC FLASH GUN
786. ELECTRONIC MAIL (E-MAIL)
787. ELECTRICAL AND ELECTRONIC PANEL METER (ANALOGUE, DIGITAL, VOLTMETER ETC.)
788. ELECTRICAL MOTOR STARTER
789. ELECTRONIC FIRE ALARM
790. ELECTRIC SWITCHES, PLUGS, SOCKETS & OTHER ACCESSORIES
791. ELECTRIC WATER HEATER
792. ELECTRIC MOTOR WINDING (FOR FAN, MIXIES ETC.)
793. ELASTIC & RIGID TAPES
794. ELECTROPLATING BRIGHTNER FOR NICKEL
795. ELECTRICAL FIXTURES (CHOKES & STARTER, PATTIES LIGHTENING FIXTURES ETC.)
796. ELECTROPLATING UNIT
797. ELASTIC THREADS & TWINE
798. ELECTRIC GENERATORS
799. ELECTRIC MOTOR
800. EMERGENCY LIGHT
801. EMBOSSING POWDER OR RESIN COMPOUND
802. EMERY POWDER
803. EMPTY AMPOULES
804. EMULSIFIER FOR PESTICIDE
805. EMPTY GELATIN CAPSULES
806. EMERY PAPER CLOTH
807. EMULSIFIER FOR CUTTING OIL
808. EMULSION PAINTS
809. EMPIRE SLEEVINGS
810. ENAMELING OF COPPER WIRE
811. ENGINEERING WORK SHOP
812. ENAMEL WARE
813. ENDOSULFAN
814. ENGINE VALVE
815. EPABX/EPAX SYSTEM
816. EPOXY RESINS & METAL FILLING COMPOUND
817. EPOXY RESIN BASED PRIMER (PUTTY)
818. EPOXY TRANSFORMER (CURRENT & POTENTIAL)
819. EPOXY RESIN
820. ERW STEEL CONDUIT PIPE
821. E.R.W. PIPES
822. ERW TUBES
823. ESSENTIAL OILS
824. ESSENCE & SOFT DRINK CONCENTRATE
825. ETHYL ALCOHOL FROM MOLASSES
826. ETHYL ACETO ACETATE FROM ALCOHOL
827. ETHYL HEXANOL FROM ETHYL ALCOHOL
828. ETHYLENE GLYCOL MONO STEARATE ETHYLENE GLYCOL DI-STEARATE
829. ETHYL ACETATE
830. ETHYL ACETATE
831. ETCHING OF BRASS
832. ETCHING PROCESS
833. EUCALYPTUS OIL
834. EUCALYPTUS TREE PLANTATION
835. EXERCISE NOTE BOOK & REGISTER
836. EXPANDED POLYSTYRENE MOULDING
837. EXTRACTION OF OIL (CARDAMOM, JEERA ETC.)
838. EXTRACTION OF GLUE POWDER
839. EXPANDED POLYSTYRENE EXTRUSION PROFILE USED FOR MATCH BOX MAKING

840. EXTRACTION OF ALKALOID FROM SOLANIUM KHASIANUM
841. EXTRACTION OF GOLD, SILVER & COPPER
842. EXTRACTION OF ESSENTIAL OIL AND PACKING OF GROUND SPICES (100% EOU)
843. EXTRACTION OF EDIBLE OIL FROM OIL SEEDS (EXPANDER - EXTRUSION COOKING PROCESS)
844. EXTRACTION OF ACID OIL FROM SOAP STOCK
845. EXHAUST FAN
846. EXTRACTION OF OIL FROM WAX, GENERATED AS A BYE PRODUCT FOR PETRO CHEMICALS
847. EXTRACTION OF JASMINE ESSENCE
848. EXTRACTION OF ALKALOIDS FROM VINCA ROSEA
849. EXTRACTION OF CHEMICAL FROM D.M.O
862. FAST COLOUR
863. FATTY ACID FROM WASTE VEGETABLE
864. FASTENERS (NUTS, BOLT, RIVET & WASHER)
865. FERRO ALLOYS
866. FERRIC ALUM
867. FERRO CEMENT
868. FERROUS SILICATE
869. FERRO MANGANESE ON ALUMINA THERMIC PROCESS
870. FERRO SILICON
871. FERRITE COURSE
872. FERRIC CHLORIDE
873. FEED MILLS (CATTLE & POULTRY FEED)
874. FERRO ALLOYS (OF NIOBIUM, MOLYBDENUM, TITANIUM, TUNGSTEN & VANADIUM)
875. FIBRE BASED BITUMINOUS WATER PROOF FELT
876. FROZEN FOODS, FRUIT & VEGETABLE PROCESSING WITH BACKWARD LINKAGES(100% EOU)
901. FLEXO GRAPHIC & ROTO GRAVURE PRINTING INK
902. FLOURSPER BRIQUETTES
903. FLUSHING CISTERN
904. FLOPPY DISKETTES
905. FLORICULTURE (CUT FLOWER) -100% EOU
906. FLORICULTURE (CUT FLOWER) WITH GREEN HOUSE TECHNOLOGY
907. FLUORESCENT TUBE
908. FLY ASH BRICKS
909. FLOOR POLISH
910. FLUORESCENT TUBES & GLS LAMPS
911. FLUSH DOOR, CHIP BOARDS, INSULATING BOARDS & HARD BOARD
912. FLOAT GLASS
913. FLOOR COVERING SHEET
914. FLOUR MILL (ROLLER)
915. FLOUR MILL (GRINDER/ PULVIRIZED)
916. FLUORESCENT TUBE & CHOKE
917. FLUORESCENT POWDER FOR FLURESCENT TUBES

850. EXTRACTION OF SOYBEAN OIL FROM SOYBEAN (EXPANDER EXTRUSION - COOKING PROCESS) WITH SOYA GRITS
851. EXTRACTION AND FILTRATION OF EDIBLE OIL
852. EXTRACTION &FILTRATION UNIT FOR EDIBLE OIL
853. EXTRUDED ALUMINIUM SECTION
854. EXTRACTION & REFINING OF VEGETABLE OIL
855. FABRICATION WORKSHOP TO MANUFACTURE TRUSSES & TANKS (PRESSURE VESSELS)
856. FABRICATION OF STORAGE TANKS AND M. S. DRUMS
857. FAT LIQUOR
858. FAST FOOD PARLOR
859. FACSIMILE/FAX MACHINE
860. FABRICATION INDUSTRIES (WORKS) FOR S.S & M.S VESSELS WITH ELECTRO-PLATING UNIT (TOOLROOM)
861. FATTY ACID
877. FERRITE MAGNETS
878. FERROUS SULPHATE
879. FERRITE CORE TRANS-FORMERS
880. FERRO SILICON
881. F.H.P. MOTOR
882. FILE /DUPLEX BOARD
883. FILTERS FOR ALL VEHICLES
884. FIBRE REINFORCED PLASTIC
885. FISH FARMING
886. FISH CANNING & POUCHING
887. FISH OILS
888. FIRE BRICKS
889. FIBRE GLASS
890. FIRE WORKS & PYRO TECHNIQUE
891. FILM STUDIO (VIDEO)
892. FISH (PRAWN & OTHERS) & MARINE PRODUCTS
893. FISH MEAL
894. FISH NET
895. FIRE EXTINGUISHER
896. FLAT/RIBBON CABLES
897. FLUSH DOORS
898. FLOCK PRINTING
899. FLAVOURED MILK
900. FLIP TOP CANS
918. FLEXOGRAPHIC & ROTOGRAVURE PRINTING
919. FLEXOGRAPHIC PRINTING INKS
920. FOAM AND ITS PROD-UCTS AS MATTRESSES (CUSHION, PILLOWSHEET)
921. FORMALDEHYDE
922. FOOD COLOUR
923. FORGING (NON FERROUS)
924 FORGING PLANT (FOR MANUCATURING OIL/GAS PIPE FITTINGS
925. FOUNDRY & MACHINING JOB WORK UNIT
926. FORMIC ACID
927. FOOD GRADE CALCIUM CHLORIDE
928. FOODDEHYDRATION
929. FORMAL DEHYDE RESIN
930. FORMULATION FOR DDT, BHC, MELETHION
931. FORGING PLANT (FOR MANUFACTURING OIL/GAS PIPE FITTINGS)
932. FOUNDRY/C.I. CASTINGS
933. FOAM BOOSTERS

934. FRACTIONAL DISTILLATION OF D.M.O
935. FRACTIONAL DISTILLATION OF ESSENTIAL OIL & MEDICINAL PLANT EXTRACTS
936. FRUIT JUICES, SQUASHES, KETCHUP ETC.
937. FRUIT JUICE MAKING AND PACKING IN PLASTIC CONTAINERS (POUCHES)
938. FROZEN FRUITS & VEGETABLES
939. FRUIT DRINKS IN TETRA PACKS (FROOTI TYPE)
940. FRUIT JUICE MAKING & PACKING
941. FRP PRODUCTS
942. FRICTION DUST (LIQUID & POWDER) FROM CNSL
943. FRIED & ROASTED GROUNDNU, GRAM, PEA, ETC. IN POUCHES
944. FRUIT PULP & JUICE CONCENTRATE(i.e. MANGO AND PINEAPPLE PULP & CONCENTRATE)
945. FRENCH POLISH
946. FRUIT JUICES BOTTLING
947. FRUITS & VEGETABLE DRYING BY FREEZE DRYING METHOD
948. FRUIT JUICES, PICKLE PROCESSING & CANNING
949. FRUIT FLAVOURS (WHISKEY, VODKA, GRAPE, BUTTER SCOTCH & RUM)
950. FROZEN FINGER CHIP
951. FURNISHING FABRICS ON POWER LOOM
952. FURFURAL FROM RICE HUL
953. FUEL OIL
954. FUEL BRIQUETTES FROM AGRO WASTE
955. FUEL BRIQUETTES FROM JUTE CADDIES (BIO COAL FROM AGRO WASTE)
956. FURNACE OIL
957. GARLIC FLAKES
958. GAS PIPE (LPG)
959. GARLIC POWDER
960. GALVANIZED ERW PIPES
961. GAS LIGHTER
962. GALION THREAD
963. GAS FILLING OF LPG CYLINDER (LPG GAS BOTTLING PLANT)
964. GALVANIZING PLANT
965. GARLIC OIL & POWDER
966. GAS MANTLES
967. GAS DETECTOR FOR L.P.G.
968. GATE, GRILL, WROUGHT IRON & BRASS STAIRCASE, RODS & RAILING
969. GASKET SHEET
970. GENERATOR SET (PORTABLE)
971. GEMS & JEWELRY
972. GEMS MANUFACTURE
973. GEM CLIPS, PAPER PINS & STAPLE
974. GELATIN & OSSEIN FROM BONE
975. GEOMETRY BOX (MATHEMATICAL INSTRUMENTS)
976. GELATIN
977. GENERATOR (MUSICAL SOUND)
978. GENERATOR (D.G. SET)
979. GELATIN CAPSULES (HARD)
980. GRINDING UNIT (CEMENT)
981. G.I. WIRES
982. GINGER POWDER
983. GINGER OIL, SANDAL WOOD OIL, NAGARMUTHA OIL
984. G.I. PIPES
985. G.I. PIPE FITTINGS
986. GLAZED CERAMIC TILES
987. GLASS BOTTLE BY SCRAPS
988. GLS LAMPS & FLUORESCENT TUBE
989. GLASS SILVERING(MIROR)

990. GLACIAL ACETIC ACID
991. GLASS SHEET (AUTOMATICPLANT)
992. GLASSWARE
993. GLASS TUBES- Report - Rs.2500/-
994. GLOW SIGNS
995. GLASS BOTTLES
996. GLS LAMPS/BULBS
997. GLASS WOOL
998. GLUE FROM LEATHER WASTE
999. GLASS SHEET FOR WINDOW PANES
1000. GLUE EXTRACTION & GLUE WHITE POWDER
1001. GLUCOSE & GLUCOSE SALINE
1002. GLASS MARBLES
1003. GLUE & GELATIN
1004. GLYCERIN PURIFICATION
1005. GLYCERIN EXTRACTION PLANT FROM COCONUT OIL
1006. GLASS FLOORING TILES
1007. GLASS SYRINGES
1008. GLUE POWDER FOR TECHNICAL GLUE FLAKES
1009. GOSSY POL (POLY PHENOL)FROM COTTON SEED OIL- COST Rs.2500/-
1010. GOAT FARMING
1011. GOAT SLAUGHTERING & BREEDING FARM
1012. GOLD EXTRACTION USING CYANIDE SOLUTION & ACID
1013. GOBAR GAS (BIO GAS)
1014. GOLDEN COLOUR SHADE
1015. GOLD ELECTROPLATING
1016. GOLD PLATING ON GLASS
1017. GOAT & SHEEP FARMING
1018. GOLF COURSE
1019. GOLD, ROLLED GOLD & SILVER PLATING
1020. GOLD JEWELLERY
1021. GOLD ELECTROPLATING OR METALLIC JEWELLERY ARTICLE INCLUDING METALLIC WATCH STRAPS
1022. GOLD & SILVER PLATING ON PVC & NYLON
1023. GOLD SALT
1024. GOLD PLATED SILVER JEWELLERY
1025. GOLD PLATED SILVER JEWELLERY AND CUTLERY
1026. GOLD COLOUR (POWER) FOR MORE BRIGHTNESS PROCESS AND FORMULATION FOR OBTAINING MORE BRIGHTNESS AND YELLOW COLOUR FOR PRECIPITATED GOLD POWDER
1027. GOLD COLOUR ELECTROPLATING ON CHEAPER ORNAMENTS WITHOUT USING GOLD
1028. GOLD CYANIDE POWDER
1029. GRAPE DEHYDRATION
1030. GRAPE WINE
1031. GRINDING OF SPICES (TURMERIC, RED CHILLIES, MASALA)
1032. GRANITE SLAB / TILE
1033. GRAPHITE POWDER FROM GRAPHITE ORE
1034. GRANITE MONUMENT
1035. GRANITE CUTTING & POLISHING UNIT
1036. GREEN HOUSE, PLANT MICRO PROPAGATION
1037. GRANULES (PLASTIC) FROM WASTE
1038. GRANULES (PLASTIC) FROM RESIN
1039. GROUND NUT OIL MILL
1040. GROUND NUT OIL REFINING
1041. GREASES MANUFACTURE
1042. GRANITE & MARBLE TILES
1043. GREETING CARD BY OFFSET PRINTING PRESS
1044. GRAPHITE CARBON PLATES

Price Rs. 2500/- for each "Detailed Project Report" Payable in advance through Draft/Cash/M.O. in favour of "ENGINEERS INDIA RESEARCH INSTITUTE". Or Ask by V.P.P. PH.: 291 8117, 291 6431, 292 0361 Fax: 91-11-291 6431 (24 Hrs.)

1045. GRAPHIC DEVELOPER FOR GRAPHIC ART FILM AND GUM SOLUTION FOR PRINTING
1046. GHEE, BUTTER & PANEER
1047. GREASES FROM CASTOR OIL
1048. GRINDING WHEELS
1049. GRINDING MEDIA BALLS
1050. GRANITE CRUSHING
1051. GRAM DALS & FLOUR MILLS
1052. GRAM DALL/PULSE MILL
1053. GREENPEAS PROCESSING & CANNING
1054. GRAPHITE ORE BENIFICATION UNIT
1055. GRADED & M.I. CASTING
1056. GRADES OF GUAR GUM
1057. GRIPE WATER
1058. GRANULATED MIXED FERTILIZER
1059. GRAVURE PRINTING CYLINDER
1060. GUM FROM TAMARIND SEED POWDER
1061. GUAR GUM
1062. GUAR GUM POWDER
1063. GUNNY BAGS
1064. GUM FOR PASTING LABELS/OFFICE PASTE (GUM)
1065. GUAR GUM POWDER (FOOD GRADE)
1066. HAZMOLA TYPE AYURVEDIC TABLET
1067. HAWAI CHAPPAL (RUBBER)
1068. HARD RUBBER BATTERY CONTAINER
1069. HATCHERY FARMING (BROILER)
1070. HAND BLOCK PRINTING
1071. HAND TOOLS
1072. HAIR SHAMPOOS
1073. HAIR DYE IN CREAM FORM
1074. HAMMERS
1075. HAIR FIXER
1076. HALOGEN LAMPS
1077. HAIR DYE POWDER
1078. HARD CHROMIUM & NICKEL CHROMIUM PLATING
1079. HANDKERCHIEF
1080. HANDICRAFTS
1081. HARD GREASE
1082. HAIR DYE IN HAIR OIL FORM
1083. HARD & SOFT FERRITES
1084. HARD GELATIN CAPSULES (EMPTY)
1085. HANK YARN DYEING FOR POWER LOOM
1086. HAMMER TONE PAINTS
1087. HARD COKE
1088. HARD CHROMIUM PLATING
1089. HAND MADE PAPER
1090. HAND LOOM PRODUCTS-KHES, BEDSHEET, BED COVERS, FURNISHING
1091. HARD BOARD FROM RICE HUSK
1092. HARD BAORD FROM BAGASSE
1093. HAWAN SAMAGRI
1094. HACK SAW BLADE
1095. HYDRATED LIME
1096. HDPE/LDPE MANUFACTURING FROM ETHYL ALCOHOL
1097. HOLIDAY RESORTS
1098. HOSPITALS
1099. HOSPITAL (Rs. 100 Cr. PROJECT)
1100. HOSPITAL/NURSING HOME
1101. HOLLOW CONCRETE BLOCK/ Brick
1102. HDPE FILM / SHEET
1103. HOTEL (3 STAR)
1104. HOTEL (5 STAR)
1105. HOTEL (NO STAR)
1106. HOT ROLLING MILL

1107. HOSE PIPE (RUBBER)
1108. HING (ASAFOETIDA)
1109. HOT DIP GALVANIZING
1110. HYDROGEN PEROXIDE
1111. HDPE/LDPE PIPES
1112. HIGH VOLTAGE WIRE
1113. HOSIERY INDUSTRY (FOR MEN)
1114. HOSIERY INDUSTRY (for WOMEN -BRA & PANTY)
1115. HOSPITAL RUBBER GOODS & SHEETS
1116. HDPE/PP WOVEN SACKS (BAGS)
1117. HDPE PIPE & FITTING
1118. HDPE & LDPE PIPE FITTING
1119. HDPE TARPAULINS
1120. HDPE BOX STRAPPINGS
1121. HDPE/LDPE PIPES & FITTINGS
1122. HDPE PIPE
1123. HERBAL KUM -KUM ROLI
1124. HEAT TRANSFER LABEL FOR RUBBER
1125. HEXAMINE FROM FORMALDEHYDE
1126. HEAT TRANSFER LABEL by SCREEN PROCESS
1127. HEAT TREATMENT OF LEAF SPRING
1128. HELICAL SPRING (COIL SPRINGS)
1129. HELMET
1130. HEALTH CENTRE
1131. HERBAL MEDICATED CIGARETTES
1132. HERBAL COSMETIC
1133. HERBAL TOOTH PASTE & TOOTH POWDER
1134. HESSIAN BAGS (LAMINATED) WITH PRINTING
1135. HESSIAN CLOTH
1136. HEPTAL DEHYDE
1137. HERBAL SHAMPOO/CREAM
1138. HEALTH CLUB CUM BEAUTY PARLOUR WITH HAIR SALOON & SONA BATH
1139. HELMET FOR COAL MINES
1140. HEAT CHAMBER PAINTING
1141. HINGES (Piano Type)
1142. HINGES (M.S.)
1143. HIGH ALUMINA CERAMICS
1144. HIGH RUPTURING CAPACITY (HRC) FUSES
1145. HIGH TENSILE FASTENERS
1146. H.M BAGS
1147. HOMOEOPATHIC MEDICINES
1148. HOSIERY & TAILORS LABELS
1149. HOT DIP GALVAINZING
1150. HOSIERY PRODUCTS LIKE CHILDREN KNITWEAR, T-SHIRTS & ACRYLIC FIBRE
1151. HOMOEO & BIO MEDICINES WITH MOTHER TINCTURE
1152. HOT ROLLED (HR) COILS
1153. HOSIERY MERCERIZING
1154. HOSIERY CLOTH (COTTON) PROCESSING-BLEACHING, DYEING & FINISHING OF CLOTH
1155. HOIST & CRANES (MATERIAL HANDLING EQUIPMENTS)
1156. HOOKS & CLIPS (METAL)
1157. HOT MIX PLANT
1158. H - ACID
1159. H.T. & M.V. INDUSTRIAL CUBICAL SWITCH BOARDS
1160. HUME PIPES
1161. HURRICANE LANTERN/ STOVE
1162. HYDROGENATION OF CASTOR OILS

1163. HYDROCHLORIC ACID (HCL)
1164. HYDROGEN PEROXIDE BY AUTO OXIDATION PROCESS
1165. HYDRAULIC BRAKE CYLINDER
1166. HYDROFLUORIC ACID
1167. HYDRAULIC DOOR CLOSER
1168. HYBRID SEED
1169. HYDRATED CALCIUM SILICATE BRICKS
1170. HYPODERMIC NEEDLES FOR DISPOSABLE SYRINGE
1171. HYDRAULIC LIFTING DEVICES (FOR AUTOMOBILE SERVICING & REPAIR)
1172. HYDROGENATED CASTOR OIL
1173. HYDROGEN GAS PLANT (HYDROGEN & OXYGEN)
1174. IBUPROFEN
1175. ICE MAKING PLANT
1176. ICE CUBE PLANT
1177. ICE CREAM OF DIFFERENT FLAVOURS
1178. ICE CREAM STABILIZERS
1179. ICE CREAM & ICE CANDY
1180. ICE CREAM
1181. ICE CREAM CUPS OF PLASTIC
1182. ICE & COLD STORAGE
1183. IDLER ROLLERS FOR CONVEYERS (PLAIN & RUBBER COVERED)
1184. IF/RF COILS
1185. IGNITION CONDENSERS
1186. IGNITION CONDENSER
1187. IMMERSION HEATER
1188. IMITATION JEWELLERY
1189. INDUCTION FURNACE (M.S.
1190. STAINLESS STEEL PATTA
1191. INJECTION WATER & SALINE
1192. INSULATING VARNISH
1193. INJECTION MOULDED PLASTIC ARTICLES
1194. INDUSTRIAL REFRIGERATION
1195. INJECTION & BLOW MOULDED PLASTIC Products
1196. INJECTION MOULDED HOUSE HOLD ITEMS
1197. INSECTICIDES FROM NEEM OIL, LEAVES & NEEM SEEDS
1198. INJECTION MOULDED PLASTIC COMPONENTS
1199. INSTANT FOODS (IDLI MIX, SAMBAR MIX, VADA MIX, GULAB JAMUN, TOMATO SOUP MIX ETC.)
1200. INDUCTION FURNACE BASED C.I. CASTING
1201. INDUCTION HARDENING OF MACHINE COMPOUNDS
1202. INFORMATION MOVING DISPLAY
1203. INJECTION MOULDED PLASTIC COMPONENTS FOR ELECTRICAL/ ELECTRONICS INDL.
1204. INSULATING VARNISH (POLY VINYL BUTYRAL BASED FFC GRADE)
1205. INDUSTRIAL OXYGEN GAS
1206. INTRAVENOUS (I.V.) SET
1207. INDIAN PICKLE
1208. INDIAN MADE FOREIGN LIQUOR (IMFL)
1209. INDUCTION FURNACE

1210. INSULATING VARNISH(DryType)
1211. INTERNAL COMBUSTION ENGINE (for Agricu-ltural Equipments)
1212. INTEGRATED COMPLEX OF EASTERS & ALLIED PRODUCTS (DOP, DBP, ETHYL ACET-ATE, BUTYL ACET-ATE, WIRE ENAM-EL, JELLY CABLE COMPOUNDS)
1213. INSULATING VARNISH & WIRE ENAMEL
1214. INDUSTRIAL KNIFE
1215. INDIGO BLUE
1216. INVESTMENT CASTINGS
1217. INVESTMENT CAS-TINGS OF BRASS
1218. INVERTER
1219. INDUSTRIAL HARD OIL USED IN SOAP MAKING
1220. INDUSTRIAL GLOVES
1221. INVERTER & CONVERTER
1222. INSTANT ICE CREAM MIX
1223. INTEGRATED CIRCUITS
1224. INDUSTRIAL ALCOHOL FROM MOLASSES
1225. INVESTMENT CASTINGS FOR SS & HIGHER ALLOYS
1226. INDUSTRIAL ALCOHOL FROM ETHYLENE
1227. INSTANT TEA & COFFEE
1228. INJECTABLE FOR PHARMACEUTICALS
1229. INSTANT SOUP
1230. INSTANT NOODLES
1231. INSULATING LAGGING OF BOILERS & STEAM TUBES
1232. INTIMATE SCENT, CHEMICALS ETC. FROM ALL TYPES OF FLOWERS
1233. IONES FROM LEMON GRASS OIL
1234. IODIZED SALT
1235. IODIZED SALT (MOISTURELESS-FREE FLOWING)
1236. IRON POWDER FROM MILL SCALE SCRAP ARISING from Iron & Steel Rerolling Mill
1237. IRON TAWA
1238. IRON & STEEL WIRE & NETTING
1239. IRON OXIDE PIGMENT
1240. IRON (WROUGHT) & BRASS STAIRCASE, RODS, RAILING, GATE & GRILL
1241. ISO PROPANOL (ISO PROPYL ALCOHOL)
1242. ISOPRENE & NEOPRENE BASED RUBBER ADHESIVE
1243. I.V. CANNULA
1244. I.V. FLUID
1245. I.V. SET
1246. I.V. PLASTIC BOTTLES
1247. JAM & JELLY
1248. JAM, CHUTNEY, PICKLE & SQUASHES

1249. J-ACID
1250. JASMINE & LILY FLOWER OIL
1251. JACQUARD FABRICS
1252. JAUN DEHULLING FOR BEER INDUSTRY
1253. JEANS & JACKETS (DENIM)
1254. JEAN DYEING & FIXING BY INDIGO BLUE (JIGGER DYE & DIP DYE)
1256. JELLY FILLED CABLES
1257. JELLY & JAM
1258. JEWELLERY (Gold)
1259. JOB WORK UNIT (FOUNDRY & MACHINING)
1260. JUTE TAR FELT
1261. JUTE BAGS
1262. JUTE BATCHING OIL
1263. JUTE WASTE PRODUCTS
1264. JUTE PROCESSING TWIN & GUNNY BAGS
1265. JUTE TWIN INCLUDING COTTON & COIR
1266. JUTE BAGS FROM RAW JUTE
1267. JUTE, COIR, GRASS, ROPE SUTLI MAKING
1268. JUICES (Fruit)
1269. KATECHU (Kattha)
1270. KALI MEHNDI (HAIR DYE)
1271. KATTHA & CUTCH
1272. KATTHA
1273. KANTHAL/NICHRO-ME FURNACE HEATING WIRE
1274. KERNAL (CASHEW NUT KERNAL EXTRACT)
1275. KHANDSARI SUGAR
1276. KIMAM MANUFACTURE
1277. KITCHEN SINK (S.S)
1278. KNITTING FABRICS
1179. KNITTED CLOTH
1280. KRAFT PAPER (FROM WASTE PAPER)
1281. KRAFT PAPER & MILL BOARD
1282. KRAFT PAPER FROM WASTE CARTON BOXES
1283. KRAFT PAPER & SPECIAL PAPER
1284. LAMINATED OF PAPER WARE (CARDS) WITH GLOSSY PP (POLYESTER FILM)
1285. LAUNDRY & DRY CLEANER
1286. LACTIC ACID
1287. LACTIC ACID FROM WHITE SUGAR (BY FERMENTA-TION PROCESS)
1288. LATEX RUBBER THREAD
1289. LAMINATED SAFETY GLASS
1290. LAMINATED SAFETY & TOUGHENED GLASS-
1291. LAMINATED PARTICLE BOARD & HARD BOARD
1292. LATEX RUBBER ADHESIVE
1293. LAUNDRY & WASHING SOAP
1294. LAUNDRY SOAP
1295. LAMINATED HESSIAN BAG
1296. LAMINATED SPRAY BRASS ARTICLES/BADGES
1297. LAMP CAPS
1298. LAMINATED JUTE BAGS
1299. LABORATORY CHEMICAL UNIT
1300. LATEX RUBBER CONDOM
1301. LATHER SHAVING CREAM
1302. LAPTOP COMPUTERS
1303. LAMP FILAMENT
1304. LATEX FOAM PRODUCTS
1305. LADDU
1306. LACTOSE & BYE PRODUCT PROCESSING FROM MILK
1307. LAMINATION OF CO-EXTRUSION, THREE LAYERS-FILM WITH LAMINATION & PRINTING
1308. LAMINATION OF CO-EXTRUSION MULTI LAYER FILM IN ROLL FORM
1309. LAUNDRY FOR '5' STAR HOTEL
1310. LDPE/HDPE FROM ETHYL ALCOHOL
1311. LDPE/HDPE PLANT
1312. LDPE/HDPE PIPES
1313. LEATHER GARMENTS
1314. LEMON GRASS OIL BASED IONES

1315. LEAD CRYSTAL
1316. LEATHER GOODS
1317. LEATHER TANNING & COLOURING
1318. LEATHER SHOE & CHAPPAL
1319. LEATHER BINDER (RESIN BASED)
1320. LEVELING & DISPERSING AGENT
1321. LEATHER STRAPS FOR WRIST WATCHES
1322. LEATHER SHOES
1323. LEATHER BOARD
1324. LECITHIN (SOYA BASED)
1325. LEATHER TANNING
1326. LEATHER GOODS
1327. LETTER PRESS PRINTING
1328. LEATHER AUXILIARIES & CHEMICAL
1329. LEATHER TANNING & LEATHER GARMENTS
1330. LEATHER DYES
1331. LEASING BUSINESS
1332. LEASING & HIRE PURCHASE
1333. LEAD STEARATE
1334. LEMON GRASS OIL
1335. LEAD REFINING USING LEAD DROSS, LEAD SCRAP, LEAD POWDER
1336. LEAD NITRATE
1337. LEATHER GARMENTS, SHOES & CHAPPALS
1338. LEATHER WASHERS
1339. LEAD MONOXIDE
1340. LEATHER SUIT-CASES, BRIEF CASES & TRAVELING BAGS
1341. LEAD EXTRACTION FROM SCRAP BATTRIES
1342. LEAD BATTERY PLATES & BATTERY ASSEMBLY
1343. LEAD PENCILS
1344. LEAD SMELTING
1345. LEAD OXIDE (A) LEAD MONOXIDE (B) REA LEAD (LEAD TETROXIDE) (C) GREY LEAD OXIDE
1346. LEAD EXTRACTION (SECONDARY) FROM SCRAPS (A) BATTERY PLATE (B) PIPES (C) SHEET
1347. LIQUID BINDI & SINDUR
1348. LIQUID GLUCOSE & ITS BYE PRODUCTS FROM MAIZE
1349. LIQUID SOAP
1350. LIQUID DETERGENTS
1351. LIQUID SHOE POLISH PUFF
1352. LITHOPONE
1353. LIQUID GLUCOSE FROM POTATOES
1354. LIQUID OXYGEN BOTTLING
1355 LIGHTNING ARRESTER AND ISOLATOR
1356. LIGHT LIQUID PARAFFIN
1357. LILLY FLOWER & JASMINE
1358. LIQUID SOAP BY PINE OIL
1359. LINK CHAIN
1360. LITMUS PAPER
1361. LIGHT EMITING DIODE (LED)
1362. LIME STONE, DOLOMITE CHIPS & POWDER
1363. LIME STONE CRUSHING, GRINDING AND PULVERISING (FOR MFG. CHIPS & POWDER)
1364. LIQUID DETERGENTS (NON IONIC)
1365. LIME COLOUR/CEMENT COLOUR/SYNTHETIC RED IRON OXIDE USED FOR FLOORING
1366. LIMIT SWITCHES & METAL PLUG SOCKETS
1367. LIQUID DETERGENT
1368. LIPSTICKS
1369. LINSEED OIL
1370. LICHEN (JHYAU) (CHARILA)
1371. LIQUID GLUCOSE
1372. LIST OF 100% EOU/EOU UNIT
1373. LINING MATERIAL FOR FLUID FLOWING PIPE (LIQUID PETROLEUM)
1374. LOW PRESSURE CELLULOSE LIQUID
1375. LOUDSPEAKER
1376. LOOM OIL
1377. LOW TENSILE TRANSFOR-MERS (L.T) upto 400 KVA

1378. LPG STOVE
1379. LPG CYLINDER TESTING CENTER
1380. LPG CYLINDER
1381. LPG GAS REGULATOR
1382. LPG GAS BOTTLING PLANT
1383. LPG GAS STOVE
1384. LPG GAS PIPE
1385. LPG GAS DETECTOR
1386. L.T TRANSFORMER REPAIRING (400 KVA)
1387. LUBE OIL FROM CNSL TO REDUCE FRICTION
1388. LUBE OIL & GREASES
1389. LUBE OIL RECLAMATION
1390. LUBE OIL BLENDING
1391. LUBRICATING OIL & GREASES (BLENDING OF LUBRICATING OILS) & MANUFACTURE OF GREASE
1392. LUBRICANT VISCOSITY INDEX IMPROVERS
1393. LUBRICANT (WIRE DRAWING)
1394. MACARONI & VERMICELLI
1395. MANUFACTURE OF T-SHIRTS WITH KNITTING FABRICS
1396. MANGO PEEL BASED PECTIN
1397. MASALA/SPICES
1398. MATCH BOX MAKING UNIT
1399. MARBLE & GRANITE TILES
1400. MANGANESE ORE CONCENTRATION
1401. MAGNESIUM CARBONATE, MAGNESIUM METAL, CALCIUM CARBONATE FROM DOLOMITE
1402. MAGNESIUM SILICATE (TALC)
1403. MAIZE/CORN STARCH
1404. MALTED MILK FOOD
1405. MARINE CONTAINERS
1406. MANILA ROPES
1407. MALACHITE GREEN
1408. MANGO PULP & MANGO SLICES CANNING
1409. MAIZE STARCH
1410. MAGNESIUM HYDROXIDE POWDER
1411. MAGNESIUM SULPHATE
1412 MAGNESIUM TRI-SILICATE
1413. MAIZE/CORN OIL
1414. MALEIC ANHYDRIDE
1415. MALTING PLANT
1416. MARKING INK FOR FIBER TIP PENS
1417. MACARONI
1418. MANGALORE TILES & BRICKS
1419. MAN POWER EXPORT
1420. MACHINE SCREWS & SELF TAPPING SCREWS
1421. MANGO POWDER
1422. MANGO JUICE
1423. MANGO KERNEL POWDER
1424. MAGNET
1425. MAGNESIUM CARBONATE & BI-CARBONATE
1426. MAGAZINE
1427. MATCH SPLINTERS & INNER BOX MAKING PLANT FROM POPLAR WOOD
1428. MATERIAL HANDLING EQUIPMENTS (HOISTS & CRANES)
1429. MANUFACTURING OF PHARMACEUTICALS-TABLETS, CAPSULES ETC.
1430. MANGO PROCESSING & CANNING (MANGO PULP)

1431. MANGO PRODUCTS, MANGO JUICE, PICKLES, CHUTNEY ETC.
1432. METAL CUTTING DIE DESIGN
1433. MEASURING TAPES (STEEL, METALLIC & PLASTIC)
1434. MENTHOL CRYSTAL & OTHER CHEMICALS
1435. METHANE GAS
1436. METAL SPECTACLE FRAME
1437. MELAMINE CRYSTALS
1438. METTOL FROM HYDRO QUINENE & METHYL AMINE
1439. MEDICAL X-RAY FILM, SLITTING & REPACKING
1440. MEDICAL PLANT EXTRACT
1441. METAL FINISHING
1442. MENTHOL & D.M.O.
1443. MELAMINE CROCKERY
1444. METHYL METHA CRYLATE
1445. MELAMINE FORMALDE-HYDE POWDER
1446. METAL HARDENING
1447. METAL FITTINGS FOR LEATHER GOODS & GARMENTS
1448. METAL CONTAINER
1449. MECHANICAL TOY
1450. MENTHOLCRYSTAL
1451. METAL BONDED DIAMOND IMPREGNATED SEGMENT FOR MARBLE SAWING
1452. METHYLATED SURGICAL SPIRIT
1453. METALLIZED POLYPRO-PYLENE FILM
1454. METAL NAPHTHANATE
1455. METALLIC GASKET (SPIRAL WOUND)
1456. METAL PRE TREATMENT CHEMICALS
1457. MENTHA OIL
1458. METALLIC ACID
1459. MERCURIC OXIDE
1460. METHYL METHACRY-LATE MONOMER & VARIOUS CHEMICAL ADDITIVES FOR PLASTIC BANGLES
1461. METAL POLISH SOAP
1462. METAL HOOKS & CLIP
1463. METALLIC STEARATES
1464. METHYLINE GLUE
1465. METHYL SALICYLATE
1466. MEAT PROCESSING (BUFFALO)
1467. METAL POLISHING BAR
1468. METHYL ETHYL KETONE
1469. M.G. KRAFT PAPER FROM WASTE PAPER
1470. MICRO SCALE STEEL PLANT
1471. MICROWAVE OVEN
1472. MINI CEMENT PLANT (BY ROTARY KILN PROCESS-800 TPD)
1473. MILK PRESERVATION & MARKETING TO WHOLESAL-ERS (IN POUCH)
1474. MILK/DAIRY PRODUCTS
1475. MINI RE-ROLLING MILL
1476. MINI PAPER PLANT FORM JÙTE STICK & WHEAT HUSK/ RICE HUSK
1477. MILK/DAIRY PRODUCTS
1478. MILK CHOCOLATE
1479. MINI STEEL PLANT BY INDUCTION FURNACE
1480. MINI CEMENT PLANT
1481. MICA PAPER FOR ELECTRICAL INSULATION
1482. MINI SUGAR PLANT
1483. MICRO CRYSTALLINE WAX
1484. MINIATURE CIRCUIT BREAKER (MCB)
1485. MINI FLOUR MILL (ROLLER)
1486. MINI FLOUR MILL (PULVERISED)
1487. MINI PAPER PLANT (KRAFT PAPER)
1488. MINI PAPER PLANT FROM SISAL WOOD

1489. MITHAI/NAMKEEN
1490. MICRO CRYSTALLINE WAX FROM SLUDGE OF PETRO CHEMICAL REFFINERY
1491. MINIATURE WATCH BATTERY
1492. MICRO NUTRIENT MIXTURE (SOLID)
1493. MISHRI PEARL SUGAR CANDY
1494. MINI PAPER PLANT FROM EUCALYPTUS WOOD
1495. MILL & KRAFT PAPER FROM WASTE CARTON BOXES
1496. MINI PAPER PLANT (WHITE WRITING & PRINTING)
1497. MINERAL WATER IN POUCHES
1498. MINERAL WATER IN POUCHES & PLASTIC BOTTLES
1499. MIRIT SANJEEVNI SURA
1500. MINI STEEL PLANT
1501. MILK PRESERVATION & MARKETING (MILK CHILLING PLANT)
1502. MICRO NUTRIENTS MIXTURES
1503. MICRO WAVE TUBES USED IN MICRO WAVE OVEN
1504. MILK POWDER
1505. MILD STEEL BOLT
1506. MILD STEEL NUTS
1507. MINI (PERSONAL) COMPUTER
1508. MINIATURE TRANSFORMER
1509. MINI PAPER PLANT USING BAGASSE
1510. MILK POWDER, GHEE & SPICES
1511. MICRO PAPER
1512. MIRROR (GOLDEN, SILVER AND PINK)
1513. MICROVEE & ABSOLUTE FILTER
1514. MICRO MOTORS
1515. MIXERS/GRINDERS (MIXIE)
1516. MILK POWDER & GHEE
1517. MICRO CELLULAR SHEET FOR SHOE SOLE
1518. MILK TOFFEE
1519. MILK CHILLING PLANT & PACKING IN POUCHES
1520. MODERN COSMETIC INDUSTRY
1521. MOSQUITO COILS & MATS
1522. MOULDED CASE CIRCUIT BREAKER (MCCB)
1523. MOTHER BOARD
1524. MONOCHROME MONITOR FOR COMPUTER
1525. MOULDED LUGGAGE
1526. MOULDED LUGGAGE (V.I.P. TYPE)
1527. MOULDED LUGGAGE (CHEAP QUALITY)
1528. MOSQUITO REPELLENT MAT
1529. MOTHER TINCTURE & BIO-CHEMIC MEDICINES
1530. MOTEL/SMALL HOTEL
1531. MOSQUITO COILS
1532. MODERN RICE MILL
1533. MOSAIC TILES
1534. MOTOR START ELECTROLYTIC CAPACITORS
1535. MOSQUITO MAT RECHARGER

1536. MONO CHLORO ACETIC ACID
1537. MOBILE CATERING VAN
1538. MODERN VEHICLE WORKSHOP
1539. MODERN BREAD AND BAKERY UNIT
1540. MONOCHROTOPHOS (TECHNICAL)
1541. MOSQUITO REPELLENT OIL
1542. MOTEL/SMALL HOTEL, BANQUET HALL WITH RESTAURANT
1543. MOSQUITO COILS USING EUCALYPTUS LEAVES
1544. MODERN ADVERTISING AGENCY WITH DTP & FILM STUDIO
1545. M.S. INGOTS (INDUCTION FURNACE)
1546. M.S. WIRE DRAWING PLANT & ANNEALING
1547. M.S. HINGES
1548. M.S. INGOTS & H.R. STEEL STRUCTURES
1549. M.S. WELDING ELECTRODES
1550. M.S. DRUM & FABRICATION OF STORAGE TANK
1551. MUSTARD OIL (EDIBLE OIL)
1552. MULTI PURPOSE SPRAY DRIER
1553. MUSICAL DOOR BELL
1554. MUSHROOM CULTIVATION
1555. MUSHROOM CULTIVATION & PROCESSING WITH CANNING
1556. MULTI LAYER PRINTED CIRCUIT BOARD (PCB)
1557. MULTI PURPOSE COLD STORAGE FOR MEDICINES, FRUITS & VEGETABLES
1558. MULTIPLE RELAY FOR LOW VOLTAGE APPLICATION
1559. MUSHROOM (EOU) CULTIVATION & PROCESSING UNIT (DEHYDRATION & PICKLING OF OYSTER & PADDY STRAW MUSHROOM)
1560. MUTTON TALLOW FOR INDUSTRIAL USE
1561. MUFFLERS & SILENCERS FOR TWO WHEELERS
1562. MUFFLER & SILENCER PIPES FOR FOUR WHEELER
1563. MUSHROOM & PROCESSED FOOD
1564. MUSICAL SOUND GENERATOR
1565. MULTI LAYER FILM
1566. MULTI STOREY COMMERCIAL COMPLEX ALONGWITH RESIDENTIAL & DELUXE FLATS FOR FOREIGN TOURISTS & REVOLVING RESTAURANT
1567. MUSTARD OIL EXTRACTION & REFINING
1568. MURABBA
1569. MULTI LAYER CO-EXTRUSION, THREE LAYERS-FILM WITH LAMINATION PRINTING
1570. NAPHTHALENE BALLS
1571. NAMKEEN & SWEETS
1572. NAIL ENAMEL (NAIL POLISH)
1573. NAMKEEN INDUSTRY
1574. NAPHTHALENE BALLS
1575. NAPHTHA BASED THINNER
1576. NAIL CUTTER WITH FILER & MANICURE
1577. N-ACETYL, L-TYROSINE
1578. N.C. PUTTY
1579. N.C. THINNER USED IN AUTO PARTS
1580. N.C. SENDING SEALERS
1581. NEWS PRINT PAPER FROM RICE STRAW/BAGASSE
1582. NEWS PAPER
1583. NEOPRENE BASED ADHESIVES
1584. NEON SIGN
1585. NEON BULB
1586. NEEM OIL FROM SEEDS
1587. NEON LAMP INDICATORS
1588. NEON INDICATOR
1589. NEEM SEEDS INSECTICIDES
1590. NEEDLE ROLLERS FOR BEARING
1591. NEROL LAUNDRY SOAP
1592. NEWS PAPER FOR CHILDREN (DAILY)-EVENING NEWS PAPER

1593. NITRO CELLULOSE (LACQUER)
1594. NICHROME WIRE
1595. NICHROME/KANTHAL FURNACE HEATING WIRE
1596. NICKEL PLATING BRIGHTNER (PRIMARY OR CARRIER BRIGHTNER AND SECONDARY)
1597. NICKEL SALT
1598. NICKEL/CADMIUM BATTERY
1599. NICKEL PLATING
1600. NICKEL PLATING BRIGTNER
1601. NICKEL LINED SCREENS
1602. NICKEL SULPHATE
1603. NICKEL CATALYST
1604. NICKEL CATALYST FOR HYDROGENETION OF VEGETABLE OIL
1605. NICKEL ELECTROPLATING SALTS (ONLY MARKET SURVEY)
1606. NICKEL CHROMIUM PLATING & HARD CHROMIUM
1607. NICKEL RECLAMATION FROM SPENT CATALYST OF VANASPATI INDUSTRY
1608. NITROGEN & OXYGEN UNIT
1609. NILGIRI OIL
1610. NICOTINIC ACID
1611. NIRMA TYPE DETERGENT POWDER
1612 NITROCELLULOSE
1613. NITRO MUSK
1614. NICOTINE SULPHATE FROM TOBACCO WASTE
1615. NON-STICK KITCHEN WARES (TEFLON COATED UTENSILS)
1616. NON-FERROUS SCRAP MELTING ROD CASTING & WIRE DRAWING
1617. NON-IONIC SURFACTANTS WETTING AGENTS
1618. NOODLES
1619. NON-BASMATI RICE FROM PADDY
1620. NON-IONIC LIQUID DETERGENT
1621. NON-ALCOHOLIC FLAVOUR
1622. NON-CARBONATED SOFT DRINK
1623. NON-FERROUS METAL ALLOY
1624. NON-FERROUS FORGING
1625. NON-EDIBLE & EDIBLE OIL MILL
1626. NOTE BOOK, REGISTER & FILES
1627. NON-WOVEN CARPETS (WADDED WITH POLYESTER FIBER)
1628. NUMBER COMBINATION AUTO LOCKS FOR LUGGAGES
1629. NUT, BOLTS, RIVETS/ WASHER
1630. NURSING HOME
1631. NURSERY SCHO-OL (PRE-NURSERY & NURSERY)
1632. NYLON YARN CRIMPING DOUBL-ING, BLEACHING, DYEING ETC.
1633. NYLON POLYESTER & P.P. ROPE MAKING
1634. NYLON ZIP FASTENERS
1635. NYLON SOCKS
1636. OCTYL ALCOHOL
1637. OFFSET PRINTING PRESS
1638. OFFSET SECURITY PRINTING PRESS
1639. OFFSET COLOUR & TREADLE TYPE PRINTING PRESS
1640. OFFSET PRINTING INK
1641. OIL (COTTON SEED)
1642. OIL (MUSTARD)
1643. OIL (GROUND NUT)
1644. OIL MILL
1645. OIL SEALS
1646. OIL (CASTOR)

1647. OIL (RICE BRAN)
1648. OIL (ESSENTIAL)
1649. OIL BOND DISTEMPER PAINT
1650. OLEORESIN OF SPICES
1651. OLEORESIN FROM CHILLY
1652. ONE TIME CARBON PAPER
1653. ONION POWDER
1654. ONION & POTATO POWDER
1655. OPTICAL GLASS GRINDING
1656. OPTICAL FIBER CABLE
1657. OPTICAL WHITENER
1658. OPEN END SPINNING PLANT
1659. OPTICAL WHITENER
1660. ORTHO BORIC ACID
1661. ORGANIC SOLVENT PURIFICATION PLANT
1662. ORTHO TOLUENE SOLVENT
1663. ORGANIC MANURE
1664. OSSEIN & GELATIN
1665. OSSEIN FROM ANIMAL BONES
1666. OXYGEN GAS
1667. OXALIC ACID
1668. OXALIC ACID FROM WASTE VEGETABLES
1669. OXYGEN & NITROGEN PLANT
1670. OXALIC ACID FROM SAW DUST
1671. OXIDISED WAX
1672. OYSTER MUSHROOMS (CULTIVATION & PROCESSING UNIT)
1673. PAINT INDUSTRY
1674. PACKAGING OF NAMKEEN, BHUJIA, DALMOTH ETC. IN FLEXIBLE POUCHES
1675. PARAFFIN WAX FROM SLACK WAX
1676. PAINT BRUSHES
1677. PAPER BAGS
1678. PALM OIL
1679. PARACETAMOL
1680. PAPPAD PLANT
1681. PAN MASALA IN POUCHES & TIN PACKS
1682. PAPER FROM BAMBOO
1683. PAPER FROM WASTE PAPER (KRAFT PAPER)
1684. PAPER FROM WASTE PAPER (WRITING & PRINTING PAPER)
1685. PAPER FROM BAGASSE
1686. PAPER FROM RICE STRAW
1687. PAPER CONES & TUBES
1688. PAPER & PULP
1689. PAPER FROM EUCALYPTUS
1690. PAPER ENVELOPS
1691. PAPER FROM RICE HUSK & WHEAT HUSK
1692. PAPER FROM PAPYRUS GRASS
1693. PAPER (HAND MADE PAPER)
1694. PAPER CUPS
1695. PAPER PLANT FROM TREE BARK & EUCALYPTUS WOOD
1696. PAPER BASED PHENOLIC SHEET (FOR ELECTRICAL APPLIANCES)
1697. PAPER WASTE RECYCLING
1698. PAPER & PAPER BOARD
1699. PAPER PRODUCTS
1700. PAPAIN
1701. PAPAIN FROM PAPAYA
1702. PAPAYA CULTIVATION
1703. PAPAYA & TOMATO CULTIVATION
1704. PAPAYA CULTIVATION & PAPAIN MANUFACTURE
1705. PARTICLE BOARD
1706. PAPER COATED ALUMINIUM & COPPER WIRES
1707. PANEL, FLUSH DOOR, WINDOWS, OFFICE FURNITURE & HOUSE HOLD FURNITURE
1708. PANEER
1709. PAPER PLATES
1710. PAINT & VARNISH
1711. PARACETAMOL BY PNCB
1712. PARAAMINO BENZOIC ACID

1713. PAINT INDUSTRY (LIME COLOUR, DRY DISTEMPER, OIL BOUND DISTEMPER, ENAMEL PAINT, RED OXIDE PRIMER/RESIN, MICA BASED PAINT)
1714. PAN MASALA & POUCH MAKING PLANT
1715. PARA CHLORO NITRO BENZENE
1716. PASTEURIZATION OF MILK (FLAVOURED MILK)
1717. PARTICLE BOARD FROM RICE HUSK
1718. PAN MASALA, TOBACCO, ZARDA & KIMAM
1719. PAINT-BITUMINOUS BASED CORROSION RESISTANT
1720. PAINT REMOVERS
1721. PALM OIL CRUSHING UNIT
1722. PAPER VARNISH
1723. PAPER FROM AKRA
1724. PARTICLE BOARD WOOD CHIPS
1725. PARTICLE BOARD & BLOCK BOARD WITH SENDING & LAMINATION OF PARTICLE BOARD
1726. PAPER CONES FOR LOUDSPEAKER
1727. PATCHES (TUBE REPAIR MATERIAL)
1728. PAINT INDUSTRY (PRIMER)
1729. PAPER PLANT (KRAFT & WHITE WRITING & PRINTING PAPER)
1730. PAPAIN FROM PAPAYA (PAPAYA LATEX)
1731. PCB SHEETS
1732. PCC ELECTRIC POLES
1733. PCC/RCC PIPES
1734. PEPSI COLA IN POLY TUBES
1735. PETROMAX CONTAINER
1736. PERFUMERY COMPOUND
1737. PERFUMERY COMPOUND, COSMETICS ETC.
1738. PERFUMED PHENYL (PINE OIL DISINFECTANT)
1739. PERFUMERY COMPOUNDS (AROMATIC)
1740. PERFUME (SPRAY)
1741. PERFUMERY COMPOUND (SYNTHETIC AGARBATTI)
1742. PERFUMES (SCENT) FROM LEMON GRASS OIL AND JASMINE OIL
1743. PET BOTTLE/CONTAINERS
1744. PERSONAL COMPUTER
1745. PECTIN BY RAW PAPAYA
1746. PECTIN FROM APPLE POMACE
1747. PECTIN FROM CITRUS, LEMON & ORANGES
1748. PECTIN BY MANGO PEELS
1749. PECTIN FROM ORANGE/ LIME PEELS
1750. PERFUME FOR SOAP, DETERGENT & AGARBATTI (YARA YARA)
1751. PERFUME & SCENTS
1752. PERFUMED PHENYL (THICK)
1753. PETROLEUM COKE
1754. PESTICIDE FORMULATIONS
1755. PETROLEUM JELLY
1756. PESTICIDES (MELATHION, MANCOZEV, COPPER OXY-CHLORIDE, WATTABLE SULPHUR, ZINC PHOSPHIDE)

1757. PEANUT COATING (SPICES, HONEY, CHEESE, CHOCOLATE, SALT)
1758. PENCIL (LEAD)
1759. PELLETIZER PLANT (FOR CATTLE FEED, POULTRY FEED, SHEEP FEED, PIG & OTHER FEED)
1760. PETHA PACKAGING
1761. PEPPERMINT OIL
1762. PHARMACEUTICAL
1763. ALCOHOL FROM NON-MOLASSES BASED
1764. POWER LOOM
1765. POWDER COATING (CHAMBER TYPE)
1766. POUCH FILLING for SAUNF, SUPARI & ELAICHI ETC.
1767. PUBLISHING & PRINTING UNIT
1768. POTATO STARCH
1769. POLYTHENE BAGS & AUTOMATIC PRINTING
1770. PVC FABRIC YARN ON POWER LOOM (TERRYCOT)
1771. PVC CONDUIT PIPE
1772. PVC PIPE & FITTINGS
1773. PHARMACEUTICAL UNITS (TABLETS, CAPSULES, SYRUPS, LOTION, OINTMENT, POWDER INJECTABLE, EYE DROPS & EYE OINTMENT ETC.)
1774. PHENACETIN
1775. PHTHALOCYNINE BLUE & GREEN
1776. PHOTO POLYMER COATING FOR PLATE & BLOCK MAKING
1777. PHOTO GRAVURE & FLEXO GRAPHIC PRINTING INK FOR PLASTIC FILM PRINTING
1778. PHOSPHORIC ACID FOR POLLUTION CONTROL
1779. PHOTO ALBUM ADHESIVES
1780. PHENOLIC RESIN
1781. PHENOLIC FORMALDEHYDE RESIN (PF RESIN)
1782. PHOTOGRAPHIC DEVELOPERS & FIXERS
1783. PHENYL ACETIC ACID
1784. PHOTO DEVELOPER & FIXER
1785. PHENOL
1786 PHOTO ETCHING OF STAINLESS STEEL PLATES
1787. PHOTO TYPE SETTING
1788. PHENYL (BROWN & WHITE)
1789. PHENYL (BLACK) IN LIQUID FORM
1790. PHOSPHORIC ACID FROM ROCK PHOSPHATE
1791. PHOTO COLOUR LAB (QSS)
1792. PHOTO EMULSION FOR ROTARY SCREEN PRINTING
1793. PHOSPHORIC ACID (Purification) FROM CRUDE
1794. PILFER PROOF CAPS & CROWN CAPS
1795. PILFER PROOF CAPS (P.P. CAPS)
1796. PIG IRON
1797. PICKLES, MURABBAS, SAUCES ETC. (VEGETARIAN & NONVEG.PICKLES)
1798. P.I.D. CONTROLLER
1799. PIGMENTS (DYE PIGMENTS)
1800. PISTON ASSEMBLY (ALUMINIUM ALLOY)

1801. PISTON ASSEMBLY (ALUMINIUM ALLOY)
1802. PIGGERY/MEAT/CHICKEN PROCESSING
1803. PINEAPPLE JUICE & CANING
1804. PINE APPLE SLICE CANNING
1805. PIGMENT DYE & DYE INTERMEDIATES
1806. PICKLE & SAUCES
1807. PIGMENT BINDER FOR TEXTILE PRINTING
1808. PIGGERY FARM
1809. PICKLES
1810. PICTURE VARNISH
1811. PLASTIC MOULDED T.V CABINETS
1812. PLASTIC INJECTION MOULDED AUTO COMPONENTS
1813. PLASTIC PRODUCT-AUDIO, VIDEO CASSETTE SHELL)
1814. PLASTIC BUCKETS & DCLI
1815. PLASTIC DRINKING STRAW
1816. PLASTIC FILM CAPACITOR
1817. PLAIN PAPER COPIER
1818. PLASTIC GRANULES (HDPE, LDPE, PP) FROM PLASTIC SCRAPS/WASTE
1819. PLATINUM LABORATORY APPARATUS
1820. PLASTIC SPRAY LAMINATED BRASS ARTICLES/BADGES
1821. PLASTIC TOOTH PICK
1822. PLASTIC I.V. BOTTLES
1823. PLASTIC FILM & SHEETS WITH PRINTING (FLEXO & ROTO) LDPE/HDPE/PP/HM/ PVC
1824. PLASTIC CORRUGATED SHEET & BOXES
1825. PLASTIC BUTTONS FROM POLYESTER SHEET & RODS
1826. PLASTIC ADVERTISEMENT BALLOONS
1827. PLASTIC CONTAINER (BLOW MOULDED)
1828. PLASTIC INJECTION MOULDING PROJECTS
1829. PLASTIC SHEET FROM PLASTIC SCRAPS
1830. PLASTIC CANES
1831. PLASTIC SYRINGE (DISPOSABLE)
1832. PLASTER OF PARIS BANDAGES
1833. PLASTER OF PARIS
1834. PLASTER OF PARIS BANDAGES & COTTON ADHESIVE TAPE
1835. PLASTIC BUTTONS
1836. PLASTIC CONFERENCE BAGS, FOLDERS ETC.
1837. PLASTIC MOULDED FURNITURE
1838. PLASTIC WASTE REPROCESSING
1839. PLASTIC SUTLI
1840. PLANT PROTECTION EQUIPMENTS

EIRI

Areas of Expertise

IDENTIFICATION OR PRODUCT

CONDUCTING MARKET SURVEY

PREPARATION OF PROJECT PROFILES & FEASIBILITY STUDIES

PREPARATION OF TECHNOECONOMIC FEASIBILITY STUDIES

PREPARATION OF FINANCING SCHEME & LOAN APPLICATION

GUIDANCE OF PROCEDURES FOR GOVERNMENT CLEARANCE

TURNKEY SERVICES

TECHNOLOGY TRANSFER

1841. PLASTIC COLLAPSIBLE TUBES
1842. PLASTIC TANKS (WATER STORAGE SINTEX TYPE TANKS)
1843. PLASTIC MOULDED TOYS
1844. PLASTIC WARES
1845. PLASTIC SPRAY LAMINATED ARTICLES
1846. PLASTIC MOULDED ARTICLES
1847. PLY WOOD & PLY BOARD
1848. PLY WOOD
1849. PLY WOOD BOARD
1850. PLY WOOD & PLY BOARD (PHENOL BONDED, BOILING WATER PROOF, TERMITE, RESISTANCE, LAMINATED & COMMERCIAL PLY WOOD & PLY BOARD)
1851. PLASTIC STRIPPABLE COATING MATERIAL
1852. PLASTER OF PARIS (CALCIUM SULPHATE)
1853. POLYSTYRENE MOULDING (EXPANDED)
1854. POTATO POWDER
1855. POLYESTER RESIN
1856. POULTRY & CATTLE FEED
1857. POULTRY FEED
1858. POLYESTER YARN
1859. POUCH PACKING FOR MILK
1860. POWER PLANT
1861. PORK PROCESSING & FARMING
1862. POUCHES FOR OIL & GHEE PACKING
1863. POLYPROPYLENE BOX STRAPPING
1864. POWER SUPPLY (LINER&SWITCHMODE)
1865. POWER TRANSFORMER
1866. POLYURETHANE FOAM FLEXIBLE & RIGID
1867. POTATO CHIPS/WAFERS
1868. POWER SUPPLY (SWITCH MODE)
1869. POTATO GRANULE
1870. PROCESSED FRUITS
1871. POLYPROPYLENE/HDPE BOX STRAPPING
1872. POULTRY & BROILER FARMING
1873. POULTRY & HATCHERY FARMING
1874. POULTRY FARM
1875. POTABLE ALCOHOL FROM GRAINS & ROTTEN FRUITS
1876. POTASSIUM SILICATE
1877. POLY VINYL ALCOHOL
1878. POLY BUTENS FROM CAREFFINATES
1879. POLYESTER HOSIERY LABELS & PATCHES
1880. POLYURETHANE FOAM (P.U. FOAM)
1881. POLYPROPYLENE SPINNING FILAMENT YARN

Price Rs. 2500/- for each "Detailed Project Report" Payable in advance through Draft/Cash/M.O. in favour of "ENGINEERS INDIA RESEARCH INSTITUTE". Or Ask by V.P.P. PH.: 291 8117, 291 6431, 292 0361 Fax: 91-11-291 6431 (24 Hrs.)

1882. PORTABLE TELEVISION
1883. POLYSTER YARN FROM WASTE
1884. POLYSTER BEADING
1885. POUCH MAKING & GRAVURE PRINTING
1886. POWDER COATING
1887. POLY VINYL ACETATE
1888. POLYTHENE PRINTING BAG (P.P & H.M. FLEXIBLE FOUR COLOURS ROTO GRAVURE PRINT)
1889. POWER TRANSFORMERS UPTO 600 KVA
1890. POLYTHENE BAGS & TUBES
1891. POLYESTER RESIN FOR WIRE ENAMEL
1892. PORTABLE GENERATOR SET
1893. POTASSIUM NITRATE
1894. POTASSIUM PERMANGANATE (IN SOLUTION FORM)
1895. POWER COATING PAINT (EPOXY, ACRYLIC & POLYESTER BASIS)
1896. POTATO & ONION POWDER
1897. POTATO CHIPS WITH IMPORTED MACHINERY
1898. POLYURETHANE RIGID FROM MOULDING
1899. POLYURETHANE SOLE
1900. POLYURETHANE FOAM & ITS PRODUCTS
1901. POUCH PACKING FOR MILK
1902. POWER PLANT
1903. PORK PROCESSING & FARMING
1904. POTASSIUM IODIDE
1905. POTATO POWDER AUTOMATIC IMPORTED PLANT
1906. POTABLE LIQUOR
1907. POLYESTER YARN
1908. POLISH (WAX)
1909. POLISH (CAR)
1910. POTASSIUM DI-CHROMATE/BI-CHROMATE
1911. POWER INVERTER
1912. POLYPROPYLENE & MULTIFILAMENT SPINNING YARN
1913. POLYESTER MICRO FIBER
1914. POWER PLANT (HYDRO BASED)
1915. POLYETHENE POUCHES FOR GHEE, BUTTER, OIL, MILK ETC.
1916. POLYTHENE BOTTLES FOR MINERAL WATER, I.V. FLUIDS ETC.
1917. POPLAR PLANTATION
1918. PRINTED TIN CONTAINERS
1919. PRINTING INKS
1920. PRINTING INKS (FLEXO GRAPHIC)
1921. PRINTED CIRCUIT BOARD (PCB)
1922. PROCESSING OF FRUIT & VEGETABLE
1923. PRUSSIAN BLUE
1924. PRINTING PLATE FOR OFFSET PRINTING MACHINE
1925. PROCESSED FOOD (READYMADE)
1926 PRECIPITATED CALCIUM CARBONATE
1927. PROCESSED CHEESE
1928. PRE STRESSED CONCRETE RAILWAY SLEEPER

1929. PRINTING PRESS (LETTER PRESS)
1930. PRINTING PRESS (OFFSET)
1931. PRESSURE DIE CASTING ALUMINIUM
1932. PROTEIN & PROTEIN BASED PRODUCTS
1933. PRECIOUS METAL PLATING & MANUFACTURE OF THEIR SALTS
1934. PRESSURE COOK-ER & ALUMINIUM UTENSILS
1935. PRESSURE COOKER (ALUMINIUM/STAINLESS STEEL) & WATER FILTER
1936. PRESSURE SENSITIVE ADHESIVE TAPES
1937. PRESSURE SENSITIVE ADHESIVE FOR BOPP TAPES (ACRYLIC BASED)
1938. PRECIPITATED CALCIUM CARBONATE FROM BYE-PRODUCTS LIME SLURRY & CARBON DIOXIDE
1939. PRINTING INK (ROTO GRAVURE & FLEXO GRAPHIC)
1940 PRINTING INK (OFFSET)
1941. PROCESSED FOOD & MARINE PRODUCTS
1942. PRINTING INDUSTRY (DTP & OFFSET)
1943. PRESSURE COOKER
1944. PRESSURE COOKER (ALUMINIUM & STAINLESS STEEL)
1945. PRECIPITATED SILICA
1946. PRODUCTS BASED ON INDUSTRIAL WASTE (COVERING TEN PROJECT PROFILES)
1947. PROCESSED FOOD & SPICES
1948. PROCESSED CONTROL TIMER (Electronic Timer)
1949. PRAWN FISH FARMING
1950. P.U. (POLYURETHANE) RIGID FOAM
1951. PUMIC WHITE ABRASIVE CAKE/STICK
1952. PULVERIZED FLOUR MILL
1953. PULSE MILL (DAL MILL)
1954. PULP FROM WOOD, BAMBOO OR GRASS
1955. PULP FROM BAMBOO & WOOD
1956. PUTTY (METAL CASEMENT PUTTY)-ASIAN PAINT TYPE
1957. PUTTY & WATER PROOFING PLANT
1958. PURIFICATION OF CASEIN
1959. PVC INSULATION TAPES
1960. PVC WIRES & CABLES
1961. PVC WIRES/TWIN FLAT CABLE
1962. PVC PIPES & FITTINGS
1963. PVC GRANULES/ COMPOUNDS BY CHEMICAL PROCESS
1964. PVC GRANULES FROM PVC SCRAPS (POLLUTION CONTROL)
1965. PVC GRANULES/ COMPOUNDS BY PLASTIC WASTE
1966. PVC RIGID PIPE
1967. PVC INSULATED CABLES
1968. PVC PROFILES (DOOR & WINDOW)
1969. PVC FOOTWEAR

1970. PVC SOLES FOR LEATHER SHOEUPPERS
1971. PVC STABILIZERS
1972. PVC/XLPE (ARMOURED) CABLES
1973. PVC WIRE & CABLES/PIPES & FITTINGS
1974. PVC CASING CAPING MATERIAL FOR ELECTRICAL FITTING
1975. PVC/PLASTIC/SOFT/RIGID/FILM SHEETS
1976. PVC LEATHER CLOTH
1977. PVC CABLES
1978. PVC FLOOR TILES
1979. PVC ELECTRICAL INSULATION TAPE WITH PRINTING (STEEL GRIP TYPE)
1980. PVC COATING ON LEATHER SHEETS
1981. PVC BATTERY SEPARATOR
1982. PVC PIPES & FITTINGS (RIGID PIPE, FLEXIBLE PIPE, CONDUIT PIPE, ELBOW FITTING, T-JOINTS ETC.)
1983. PVC RULLER
1984. PVC SOLVENT CEMENT
1985. PVC SUCTION HOSES
1986. PVC FLEXIBLE PIPES
1987. PVA BASED ADHESIVES
1988. PVC ON G.I. WIRE
1989. PVC ROOFING SHEET
1990. PVC FILM
1991. QSS COLOUR PHOTO LAB
1992. QUICK LIME
1993. RAILWAY SLEEPERS (PRE STRESSED CONCRETE)
1994. RAISING COMPOUNDS OR EMBOSSING POWDER
1995. RABBIT FARMING
1996. RAINBOW COLOUR ON PVC FILM & SHEET
1997. RAINBOW COLOUR ON METALS
1998. RAZOR BLADE
1999. RCC SPUN PIPES
2000. REACTIVE DYES
2001. READY MADE PROCESSED FOOD
2002. RECTIFIED SPIRIT FROM MOLASSES & MAHUA FLOWER
2003. REROLLING OF SARIYA (TOR)
2004. RESTAURANT
2005. REFINED OILS (COTTON SEEDS, GROUNDNUT, SUNFLOWER ETC.)
2006. RESIN BASED LEATHER BINDER
2007. REROLLING OF STEEL
2008. RECOVERY OF LEAD FROM DISPOSED LEAD ACID BATTERY
2009. REFRIGERATOR & MINI REFRIGERATOR
2010. RESIN CORED SOFT SOLDERING WIRE
2011. RECLAMATION OF TRANSFORMER OIL
2012. RED IRON OXIDE
2013. RE-ROLLING MILL (ALUMINIUM) & UTENSILS
2014. REFINED SUNFLOWER SEED OIL
2015. RESIDENTIAL APARTMENT
2016. RESIDENTIAL & DELUXE FLATS
2017. RECLAMATION OF USED ENGINE OIL
2018. RECLAMATION OF WAX SLUDGES FOR MANUFACTURING OF MICROCRYSTALINE WAX
2019. READY MADE GARMENTS

2020. READY MADE GARMENTS AND HOSIERY
2021. REFINING OF GROUNDNUT OIL
2022. RECONDITIONING OF EMPTY CEMENT JUTE BAG
2023. RED OXIDE PRIMER
2024. REFINING OF CASTOR OIL
2025. RECHARGEABLE TORCHES
2026. READY MADE GARMENTS MERCHANDISE PLANT
2027. RECOVERY OF SILVER NITRATE FROM PHOTO GRAPHIC WASTE FIXERS
2028. REMOTE CONTROL SYSTEMS (FOR STARTING DOOR, OPEN & CLOSE HEADLIGHT ON & OFF FOR CAR)
2029. RECOVERY OF SILVER FROM WASTE FIXTURE BLEACH OBTAINED FROM PHOTO COLOUR LAB BY SULPHIDE PROCESS
2030. RECYCLING OF WASTE CELLULOSE ACETATE INTO CELLULOSE ACETATE SHEETS
2031. RED OXIDE PIGMENTS FROM IRON PICKLING PLANT WASTE
2032. REFRACTORIES
2033. REFINED OIL & GROUNDNUT OIL
2034. REROLLING OF STEEL CUTTING
2035. RED MUD PVC PIPES & FITTINGS
2036. REXINE CLOTH & ALIKE PRODUCTS
2037. RECONDITIONING OF T.V PICTURE TUBE
2038. RECONDITIONING OF FLUORESCENT TUBE
2039. RECTIFIED SPIRIT FOR POTABLE ALCOHOL, INDUSTRIAL ALCOHOL & MEDICAL ALCOHOL
2040. RE-REFINING OF USED LUBRICANT
2041. RECTIFIED SPIRIT FROM RICEPADDY STRAW
2042. RED OXIDE PRIMER (ANTI CORROSIVE)
2043. READY MADE GARMENTS (100% EOU)-STITCHING, WASHING, DYEING, PRINTING & FINISHING ETC.)
2044. REFINED VEGETABLE OILS
2045. REROLLING OF STEEL SECTIONS
2046. REFINING OF MUSTARD OILS
2047. REPACKING OF MEDICINES
2048. READY MADE SALWAR SUITS
2049. RED OXIDE PIGMENTS
2050. RECLAMATION OF HYDRAULIC OIL
2051. RED MIRROR BY ELECTROLESS DIPPING METHOD
2052. REACTIVE DYE M5B DYE
2053. RIGID PVC PIPES & FITTINGS (RIGID PIPES, PIPE FITTINGS LIKE ELBOW FITTINGS, T-JOINTS ETC.)
2054. RE-WINDING OF BURNT ELECTRIC MOTOR
2055. RECLAMATION OF NICKEL FROM SPENT CATALYST OF VANASPATI INDUSTRY
2056. RECLAMATION OF SPENT BLEACHING EARTH
2057. REFRIGERANT ALFA-R134
2058. RESISTORS (WIRE WOUND)
2059. RESIN CORED SOFT SOLDERING WIRE
2060. RESIN COATED SAND (SHELL MOULDING SAND)
2061. RED PHOSPHORUS
2062. RICE HUSK BASED CEMENT
2063. RICE&CORNFLAKE
2064. RICE MILL
2065. RICE FLAKES (CHUDA)
2066. RICE POLISHING AND PACKAGING IN POUCHES
2067. RIGID PVC PIPES
2068. RIGID PVC PIPES & FITTINGS
2069. RICE BRAN OIL
2070. RICE TRADING (BASMATI)
2071. RICE POLISHERS
2072. RIVETS
2073. ROLLING BEARING FORGING OF OUTER/INNER RINGS
2074. ROLLER FLOUR MILL

2075. ROLLING MILL
2076. ROLLING OF STAINLESS STEEL SHEET (PATTA)
2077. ROTARY PRINTING & DYEING ON COTTON/ SYNTHETIC TEXTILE
2078. ROOFING TILES (CEMENT)
2079. ROSIN & TERPENTINE DISTILLATION
2080. ROSE CRYSTALS
2081. ROSE PLANTATION & ROSE OIL EXTRACTION
2082. ROLLER FLOUR MILL & MUSTARD OIL MILL
2083. ROTO GRAVURE PRINTING
2084. ROASTED & FRIED DRY FRUITS, GROUNDNUTS/ PEANUTS WITH PACKAGING
2085. ROUND GLASS MARBLES
2086. ROASTED/SALTED/COATED CASHEWNUT, PEANUT, ALMOND (IMPORTEDAUTOMATIC)
2086A. RIGID & ELASTIC TAPES
2087. RUBBER BALLOONS (DECORATIVE, TOYS & INDUSTRIAL BALOONS)
2088. RUBBER HAWAI CHAPPALS
2089. RUBBER ADHESIVES
2090. RUBBER CHAPPALS & GENTS LEATHER SHOES
2091. RUBBERISED CORK SHEETS
2092. RUBBER SHEET & ALLIED HOSPITAL GOODS
2093. RUBBERIZED COIR FOAM
2094. RUBBER FOAM MATTRESS
2095. RUBBER SHEET FROM USED TYRE
2096. RUBBER SHEET FOR SHOE SOLE
2097. RUBBER LATEX FOAM PRODUCT
2098. RUBBER CONDOM
2099. RUBBER SOLUTION
2100. RUBBER AUTO PARTS
2101. RUBBER LINING
2102. RUBBER GOODS FROM WASTE RUBBER
2103. RUBBING COMPOUND FOR AUTOMOBILE
2104. RUBBER BANDS
2105. RUM FLAVOUR
2106. RUBBER TOYS
2107. RUBBER PLASTIC STAMP & PAD (AUTOMATIC)
2108. RUBBER HOT WATER BOTTLES
2109. RUBBER COTS & APRONS
2110. RUBBERIZED CLOTH
2111. RUST PREVENTIVE (PETROLEUM)
2112. RUBBER COMPOUND TOYS (USING PLASTER OF PARIS)
2113. RUBBER BUSHING
2114. RUBBER HOSE PIPES & RUBBER GLAZING
2115. RUBBER PLANTATION
2116. RUBBER MOULDING & LINING OF RUBBER SHEETING

TERMS

Price Rs. 2500/-

(Rs. Two Thousand & Five Hundred only)

for each

Detailed Project Report

(Market Survey cum Detailed Techno Economic Feasibility Report)

or

US $ 250/-

each for overseas clientele, payable fully in advance through Draft/M.O./Cash in favour of

ENGINEERS INDIA RESEARCH INSTITUTE

New Delhi

or

Ask to send by V.P.P.

(All the mentioned reports herewith are fluently available)

2117. RUBBER ADHESIVE (All PURPOSE)-NEOPRENE & ISOPRENE BASED
2118. RUBBER ADHESIVE
2119. RUBBER ROLLERS
2120. RUBBER ROLLER FOR PRINTING MACHINE
2121 RUBBER ROLLER FOR RICE MILL
2122. RUBBER CONVEYOR BELT
2123. RUBBER HOSE PIPE
2124. RUBBER RECLAMING
2125. RUBBER CAPS FOR PHARMACEUTICAL USE

2126. RUBBER ROLLERS FOR TEXTILE MILLS & PAPER INDUSTRIES
2127. RUBBER ROLLER& EBONITE ROLLER
2128. RUBBER (LATEX) LINED JUTE MATS
2129. RUBBER PROCESS OIL
2130. RUBBER BELTING (FAN/V BELT)
2131. RUBBER (FIELD) CONVERTED TO THE 60% LATEX RUBBER
2132. RUBBER ERASERS (SCHOOL RUBBER)
2133. RUBBER AUTO GASKET
2134. RUBBERISED CANVAS SHOES
2135. RUBBER (SYNTHETIC)
2136. RUBBER HOSES FOR AUTOMOBILE
2137. SAFETY GLASS
2138. SANITARY WARE & WALL TILE/FLOOR TILE
2139. SALINE & INJECTION WATER
2140. SANITARY NAPKIN
2141. SANITARY NAPKIN & DISPOSABLE BABY DIAPERS
2142. SAW MILLS
2143. SAFETY MATCHES (MATCH BOX)
2144. SAND PAPER (ABRASIVE PAPER)
2145. SALT GLAZED STONE WARE PIPES & FITTINGS
2146. SAND LIME BRICKS
2147. SAGOL
2148. SAUSAGED FOOD CASING (100%ECU)
2150. SAFETY PINS
2151. SALINE & INJECTION WATER
2152. SALTED GROUNDNUT
2153. SAGO SEED FROM POTATO & SWEET POTATO (SABOO DANA)
2154. SAFETY MATCH & FIREBOX
2155. SALT LICKS FOR CATTLES
2156. SANITARY NAPKINS (TAB ENDED-TUBE FILLED)
2157. SAFETY BELT
2158. SABOO DANA
2159. SCOOTER TYRE & TUBE
2160. SCREEN PRINTING INKS
2161. SCREEN PRINTING ON PAPER/CARDS
2162. SCREEN PRINTING
2163. SCREEN EMULSION
2164. SCREWS FOR AUDIO CASSETTE
2165. SCENT & PERFUME FOR AGARBATTI
2166. SCENTS/PERFUME
2267. SCENT BY LEMON GRASS OIL & JASMINE OIL
2168. SCENTED SUPARI
2169. SCENT (INTIMATED SCENT, CHEMICALS ETC.)

2170. SCREEN PRINTING ON TEXTILES
2171. SCHOOL
2172. SCOOTER RIMS
2173. SECURITY SYSTEM
2174. SECONDARY LEAD EXTRACTION FROM SCRAPS (A) BATTERY PLATE (B) PIPES (C) SHEETS
2175. SNACK FOOD (CRAX TYPE-ROLL & BALL TYPE)
2176. SNUFF FACTORY
2177. SELF TAPPING STEEL SCREWS
2178. SEWING NEEDLES (FOR USED WITH DOMESTIC/ INDUSTRIAL SEWING MACHINE)
2179. SECURITY OFFSET PRINTING PRESS
2180. SEWING THREADS, REELS & BALLS
2181. SEMI CONDUCTORS FOR TRANSISTORS & DIODE
2182. SEMI CONDUCTOR DEVICES
2183. SESAME OIL FROM SESAME SEEDS
2184. SERVO CONTROLLED STABILIZERS (1-100 KVA)
2185. SEWING MACHINE (PARTS MACHINING & ASSEMBLY)
2186. SEMI AUTOMATIC BRICKS PLANT
2187. SEMI AUTOMATIC CONFECTIONERY PLANT
2188. SEAMLESS M.S. TUBES
2189. SEALING MATERIAL COMPATIBLE TO CERAMIC & NICHROME WIRE
2190. S.G. IRON & MALLEABLE IRON CASTING
2191. S.G. IRON & ALLOY STEEL CASTINGS
2192. SHEET GLASS
2193. SHAMPOOS
2194. SHOE POLISH PUFF
2195. SHOVELS
2196. SHOCK ABSORBERS
2197. SHAMPOOS FOR DOGS
2198. SHAMPOO & CREAM (COLD CREAM, ALL PURPOSE & VARNISHING CREAM)
2199. SHUTTLELESS LOOM
2200. SHAVING CREAM & SHAVING SOAP
2201. SHAWLS (POWER LOOM)
2202. SHOE UPPER
2203. SHOE POLISH (BOOT POLISH)
2204. SHEET METAL PRODUCTS (FERROUS/NON-FERROUS)
2205. SHIP CONTAINERS
2206. SHEEP & GOAT FARMING
2207. SHOE LACES
2208. SHOES, CANVAS AS WELL AS BOOT, RUBBER KNEES, JUNGLE BOOT COMBAT, RUBBER LINED
2209. SHAVING CREAM (LATHER)
2210. SHERBAT
2211. SHOTS & GRITS OF HIGH CARBON STEELS
2212. SHUTTLE COCKS FOR BADMINTON
2213. SHOE TACKS
2214. SHEHNAZ HUSSAIN'S INSTITUTE FOR SKIN, HEALTH & HAIR CARE (HEALTH CLUB CUM BEAUTY PARLOUR TRAINING INSTITUTE)
2215. SILK COCOON CULTIVATION (GROWING OF SILK COCOON FROM SILK WORM)
2216. SILICA GEL
2217. SINGLE SUPER PHOSPHATE (S.S.P)
2218. SILICON COMPOUND
2219. SILICON EMULSION (MOULD RELEASING AGENTS)
2220. SILK SCREEN PRINTING ON SAREES (BLOCK & SCREEN PROCESS)

2221. SILK WASTE PROCESSING & SPINNING
2222. SILK REELING UNIT
2223. SILICA SAND
2224. SILICON RELEASE PAPER
2225. SILVER NITRATE
2226. SILVER DIP (CLEANING SOLUTION)
2227. SIZING OF YARN
2228. SINTERED BUSHES
2229. SINTERED BUSHES (SELF LUBRICATED)
2230. SINTERED METAL PRODUCTS
2231. SHISHAM PLANTATION
2232. SILICON RUBBER NIPPLE/ TEAT
2233. SILENCERS FOR TWO/ THREE WHEELERS
2234. SINGLE CORE TWIN FLAT CABLE
2235. SILICON EMULSION
2236. SILVER EXTRACTION FROM WASTE HYPO SOLUTION BY CHEMICAL PROCESS
2237. SILVER EXTRACTION BY WASTE HYPO SOLUTION, X-RAY FILM
2238. SILVER JEWELLERY & CUTLERY (GOLD PLATED)
2239. SILVER & GOLD JEWELLERY
2240. SINGLE SUPER PHOSPHATE (S.S.P) & SULPHURIC ACID
2241. SILVER & GOLD PLATING ON PVC & NYLON
2242. SILICON
2243. SINDHUR
2244. SILVER DIP (CLEANING SOLUTION)
2245. SILVER PLATED UTENSILS
2246. SINTERED BEARINGS
2247. SILVER JEWELLERY
2248. SILVER BRAZING FOIL
2249. SILK FABRICS (POWER LOOM)
2250. SILICON FROM RICE HUSK
2251. SKIMMED MILK (LIQUID)
2252. SKIMMED MILK POWDER
2253. SKYLATED PHENOL
2254. SKY BAGS
2255. SKIMMED MILK POWDER & GHEE
2256. SMOKELESS COAL
2257. SOFT DRINKS (NON CARBONATED)
2258. SODIUM DICHROMATE & SODIUM SULPHATE
2259. SOLVENT EXTRACTION & REFINING OF SOYA BEAN
2260. SORBITOL
2261. SODIUM TRI-POLY PHOSPHATE
2262. SODIUM THIO-SULPHATE FROM SODIUM SULPHATE
2263. SODIUM SULPHATE
2264. SOLID FUEL CAKE
2265. SODIUM HEXA META PHOSPHATE
2266. SODIUM SULPHIDE FROM AMMONIUM SULPHITE & SODIUM CHLORIDE
2267. SOFT DRINK CONCENTRAT (SACCHARINE BASED)
2268. SOAP COATED PAPER
2269. SODIUM BENZOATE
2270. SOLVENT EXTRACTION PLANT
2271. SOCKS KNITTING
2272. SODA ASH
2273. SODA LIME
2274. SOLAR CELL
2275. SOLAR COOKER
2276. SOLAR PHOTO VOLTAGE MODULES (SOLAR ELECTRICAL CELLS & PANEL)
2277. SOLAR PHOTO VOLTAIC SYSTEM
2278. SOLAR PUMP
2279. SOLAR ELECTRICAL CELLS & PANELS
2280. SOLAR PUMP
2281. SOLAR ENERGY WATER HEATER (GEYSER)
2282. SOLAR POWER EQUIPMENTS

2283. SOLAR MODULES
2284. SOYABEAN PRODUCTS
2285. SOYABEAN BARIYAN
2286. SOFT DRINKS CONCENTRATES & ESSENCES (ORANGE, COLA, LIME, PINE APPLE) FLAVOURS FOR BAKER & SODA WATER
2287. SOLVENT EXTRACTION PLANT FROM COCONUT CAKE
2288. SODIUM BICARBONATES
2290. SOLDERING PASTE
2291. SOYA MILK FROM SOYABEAN
2292. SOYA SAUCE (CHINESE)
2293. SOLDER WIRE (SOFT RESIN CORED)
2294. SOAP RIVETS (HOLLOW TYPE)
2295. SOYABEAN BARIYAN
2296. SOAP FROM SOAP STOCK (SOAP INDUSTRY)
2297. SOFTWARE (COMPUTER)
2298. SOYABEAN OIL
2299. SOLVENT & THINNERS
2300. SOFT DRINK (COLD DRINKS)
2301. SODIUM META SILICATE
2302. SODIUM ACETATE
2303. SODIUM SULPHITE FROM SODIUM DIOXIDE
2304. SODIUM THIO-SULPHATE BY SODIUM SULPHATE
2305. SODIUM SILICATE FROM SILICA SAND
2306. SODIUM SULPHATE (ANHYDROUS)
2307. SODIUM SILICATE FROM RICE HUSK/PADDY HUSK
2308. SODIUM DICHROMATE (BICHROMATE)
2310. SODIUM SULPHIDE
2311. SODIUM SULPHIDE BY BARIUM SULPHATE PROCESS
2312. SODIUM CAFFINATES & CALCIUM CAFFINATES
2313. SODIUM SULPHITE
2314. SODIUM NITRATE
2315. SODIUM NITRITE
2316. SODIUM LAURYL SULPHATE
2317. SODIUM ALUMINATE
2318. SODIUM HYDRO SULPHITE (ZINC REDUCTION PROCESS)
2319. SODIUM HYDRO CHLORITE (BLEACH LIQUOR)
2320. SODIUM NAPHTHOANATE
2321. SODIUM BI-SULPHITE
2322. SODIUM SULPHIDE FROM SALT CAKE
2323. SODIUM PETROLEUM SULPHONATE
2324. SODIUM PERBORATE (TETRA HYDRATE)
2325. SODIUM CYCLAMATE
2326. SODIUM ALGINATE
2327. SODIUM META SILICATE
2328. SODIUM CHROMATE
2329. SODIUM TRI-POLY PHOSPHATE
2330. SODIUM ALUMINIUM SULPHATE
2331. SODIUM FLUORIDE
2332. SODIUM HYPO-CHLORITE (BLEACH LIQUOR)
2333. SODIUM BENZOATE
2334. SODIUM PERBORATE (TETRAHYDRATE)
2335. SODIUM SALT (2,4-D)
2336. S.W.PIPES
2337. SOLVENT EXTRACTION & REFINING PLANT (COTTON SEED OIL
2338. SOFT DRINK ESSENCES
2339. SOFT & HARD FERRITES
2340. SOAP SHOP
2341. SOYA MILK & PANEER
2342. SPONGE RUBBER (LATEX FOAM RUBBER)
2343. SPECIAL STEEL (HIGH ALLOY)
2344. SPRAY DRIED DETERGENT POWDER
2345. SPRAY LAMINATED BRASS ARTICLES/BADGES (PLASTIC)
2346. SPARK PLUGS
2347. SPORT SHOES

Cost
Rs. 2500/-
for each
Detailed
Project Report

2348. SPORT SHOES (IMPORTED) AUTOMATIC PLANT-ACTION, LIBERTY TYPE
2349. SPONGE IRON
2350. SPECTACLE FRAMES (PLASTIC)
2351. SPIRAL WOUND METALLIC GASKET
2352. SPECTACLE FRAMES (METAL)
2353. SPICES (MASALA)
2354. SPRAY DRIER
2355. SPEAKER PARRY RING (FORMULAE)
2356. SPINNING OF VISCOSE STAPLE FIBER INTO YARN
2357. S.S. HINGES
2358. STEP DOWN TRANSFORMER
2359. STEEL DRUM & BARRELS
2360. STENCIL COATING SOLUTION
2361. STARCH & DEXTRIN BASED ADHESIVES
2362. STENCIL PAPER (DUPLICATING)
2363. SOAP JELLY
2364. SPIKENARD (JATAMANSI)
2365. SPRAY PERFUME
2366. SPINDLE OIL
2367. SPICE OILS OR OLEORESINS (EXTRACTION OF ESSENTIAL OILS- CARDAMOM, JEERA, AJWAIN, GINGER OIL & OTHER SPICES)
2368. STARCH (MAIZE/CORN)
2369. STAINLESS STEEL CASTINGS BY INDUCTION FURNACE
2370. STAINLESS STEEL SHEET ROLLING & MANUFACTURE OF STAINLESS STEEL UTENSILS
2371. STAINLESS STEEL PATTA
2372. STAMP PADS & PAD INKS
2373. STAPLES, GEM CLIPS & PAPER PINS
2374. STRAW BOARD & MILL BOARD
2375. STEEL PLANT (EAF-BASED)
2376. STANNOUS CHLORIDE
2377. STEEL ROLLING MILL
2378. STEEL/ALUMINIUM COAST FOR WINDING OF TEXTILE YARNS
2379. STITCHING WIRE
2380. STEEL WOOL
2381. STUFFING JOINT BOX OF PLASTIC
2382. STARCH & ALLIED PRODUCT FROM MAIZE
2383. STEAM IRON (LIGHT WEIGHTED)
2384. STEARIC ACID
2385. STRAW BOARD
2386. STEEL WIRE ROPES
2387. STEEL TUBE/ PIPE
2388. STEEL FOUNDRY
2389. STARCH, DEXTROSE, SORBITOL, VITAMIN - C, ETC. FROM MAIZE
2390. STEARATES MANUFACTURE
2391. STRIPPERS FOR ROTAORY PRINTING EMULTION
2392. STAINLESS STEEL UTENSILS (COPPER BOTTOM)
2393. STEEL BALL BEARINGS
2394. STEEL FURNITURE
2395. STEREO CASSETTE RECORDERS/PLAYERS
2396. STABLE BLEACHING POWDER
2397. STRAW BOARD & GREY BOARD
2398. STEEL CASTING FOR RAILWAYS
2399. STONE CRUSHER
2400. STAINLESS STEEL UTENSILS (COPPER ELECTROPLATED)

Price Rs. 2500/- for each "Detailed Project Report" Payable in advance through Draft/Cash/M.O. in favour of "ENGINEERS INDIA RESEARCH INSTITUTE". Or Ask by V.P.P. PH.: 291 8117, 291 6431, 292 0361 Fax: 91-11-291 6431 (24 Hrs.)

2401. STEEL FORGING (AUTOMOBILE PARTS)
2402. STEEL WIRE HEALDS
2403. STARCH FROM TAPIOCA
3323. STREET LIGHT FITTING
2404. STAMPING HOT FOILS
2405. STEEL REROLLING MILL (STEEL RODS & COILS FROM SCRAPS)
2406. STAINLESS STEEL TIFFIN BOX (LUNCH BOX)
2407. STEEL TAPES FOR CABLE ARMOURING
2408. STICKER MAKING-AUTOMATIC PLANT
2409. STEEL BALLS
2410. STEEL BALLS FOR BALL POINT PENS
2411. STICKER & LABELING PLANT
2412. STAIN REMOVERS
2413. SURAT JARI
2414. STARCH BOOK BINDING CLOTH
2415. STEEL STRIPS (COLD ROLLED)-ELECTRICAL SILI-CON WITH ORIE-NTED GRAINS FOR ELECTRICAL MACHINES & TRANSFORMERS
2416. STARCH BOOK BINDING CLOTH
2417. STEEL TANKS FOR DRIN-KING WATER (WATER STORAGE TANKS OF M.S)
2418. STEEL PLANT (25-T UHF ELECTRIC ARC FURNACE & HOT ROLLING)
2419. STEEL STRIPS (COLD ROLLED)-ELECTRICAL SILICON WITH ORIENTED GRAINS FOR ELECTRICAL MACHINES & TRANSFOR-MERS
2420. STEEL WIRE DRAWING & GALVANIZING
2421. STORAGE BATTERY
2422. STUFF TOYS
2423. STAINLESS STEEL VACUUM FLASK (UN-BREAKABLE)
2424. STARCH FROM WHEAT FLOUR
2425. STAINLESS STEEL KNIFE
2426. STEEL PIPES
2427. STAINLESS STEEL CUTLERY
2428. STEEL INGOTS (GAS FIRE FURNACE)
2429. STARCH & ALLIED PRODUCTS FROM BROKEN RICE, LIQUID GLUCOSE, DEXTROSE ANHYDROUS
2430. STEEL WIRE/ROD
2431. SUNFLOWER PLANTATION
2432. SUBMERGED ARC WELDED PIPES (SAW PIPE)
2433. SUNFLOWER OIL
2434. SUBMERSIBLE PUMP
2435. SULPHUR POWDER FROM SULPHUR CRYSTALS/LUMP
2436. SUGAR CANE WAX FROM PRESS MUD
2437. SURGICAL/ABSORBENT COTTON
2438. SURFACE FLOOR & CAR POLISHES
2439. SUPER ENAMELED COPPER WIRE (COPPER SCRAPS)
2440. SUGAR MANUFACTURING PLANT BY CARBONATION PROCESS
2441. SURGICAL EXAMINATION GLOVES (DISPOSABLE)
2442. SULPHUR CRYSTAL
2443. SUGAR CANE JUICE PRESERVATION
2444. SUNMICA
2445. SURAT ZARI (ZARI MANUFACTURE FOR SAREE)
2446. SURGICAL COTTON & BANDAGES
2447. SURGICAL COTTON AND SURGICAL ADHESIVE TAPES
2448. SULPHUR BLACK DYES

2449. SURGICAL GLOVES FROM LATEX
2450. SURGICAL BANDAGE, SANITARY NAPKINS & ALLIED PRODUCTS
2451. SURGICAL ADHESIVE TAPE ON CLOTH SURFACE
2452. SURGE SUPPRESSER
2453. SULPHUR RECOVERY FROM SLUDGE
2454. SUNFLOWER SEED OIL EXTRACTION
2455. SURGICAL BANDAGES
2456. SUPER ENAMELED COPPER WIRE
2457. SUGAR PLANT
2458. SULPHURIC ACID (H_2SO_4)
2459. SURA
2460. SUGAR CUBES
2461. SUPER ENAMELING FOR WINDING
2462. SURGICAL METHYLATED SPIRIT
2463. SUGAR COATED CASHEWNUT, ALMONDS.
2464. SWITCH MODE POWER SUPPLY (SMPS)
2465. SWEATER, MUFF-LER & KNITTING INDUSTRY
2466. SWITCH BOARD
2467. SWEET AROMA OF BETAL NUT
2468. SYNTHETIC IRON OXIDE (YELLOW)
2469. SYNTHETIC IRON OXIDE (RED)
2470. SYNTHETIC RED & YELLOW IRON OXIDE
2471. SYNTHETIC ASAFOETIDA (HING)
2472. 2-4-D SODIUM SALT
2474. SYNTHETIC ALMOND OIL
2475. SYNTHETIC TALLOW
2476. SYNTHETIC DETERGENT (BLUE POWDER)
2477. SYNTHETIC ADHE-SIVE FOR DECORATIVE LAMINATE BONDING
2478. SYNTHETIC PEARL COATING ON POLYSTY-RENE BEADS
2479. TARTARIC ACID
2480. TAPE DECK MECHANISM
2481. TAB ENDED PULP FILLED NAPKINS (Sanitary Napkin)
2482. TABLET & CAPSULE
2483. TABLET, CAPSULE, SYRUPS, LOTION & OINTMENT
2484. TAMARIND JUICE CONCENTRATE
2485. TARTARIC ACID FROM MALEIC-ANHYDRIDE
2486. TAR FROM PINE WOOD
2487. TABLE FAN
2488. TABLE WARE & CERAMIC TILES
2489. TALCUM POWDER (FACE & TOILET)
2490. TALC (MAGNESIUM SILICATE)
2491. TAPER ROLLER BEARINGS
2492. TAILORS CHOKES
2493. TANTALUM CAPACITOR
2494. TABLE OFFSET & D.T.P
2495. TANNIC ACID
2496. TABLE TENNIS BALL
2497. TALLOW PROCESSING FOR SOAP MANUFACTURING
2498. TABLET, CAPSULE, SYRUP & LOTION
2499. TEA PACKAGING & DISTRIBUTION JOB WORK
2500. TETRA PACK FOR MILK PACKAGING & OTHER LIQUIDS
2501. TENNIS BALL & CRICKET BALL
2502. TEA PLANTATION
2503. TEA INDUSTRY
2504. TEA & COFFEE PROCESS-ING AND PACKAGING
2505. TEAK & MUSHROOM PLANTATION

Price Rs. 2500/- for each "Detailed Project Report" Payable in advance through Draft/Cash/M.O. in favour of "ENGINEERS INDIA RESEARCH INSTITUTE". Or Ask by V.P.P. PH.: 291 8117, 291 6431, 292 0361 Fax: 91-11-291 6431 (24 Hrs.)

2506. TEAK PLANTATION
2507. TEFLON MANUFACTURING
2508. TEFLON COATED ELECTRIC CABLES
2509. TELEPHONE CABLES/CORD
2510. TERELENE PRODUCTS
2511. TENT & TARPAULINE
2512. TEFLON TAPES
2513. TEA PACKAGING
2514. TELEPHONE AMPLIFIER
2515. TEXTURISED POLYESTER YARN
2516. TENNIS BALL
2517. TEFLON COATED UTENSILS (NON-STICKS)
2518. TEXTILE GOLD STAMPING PASTE
2519. TEXTILE PRINTING PIGMENT BINDERS
2520. TELEVISION ANTENNA
2521. TELEVISION (COLOUR AND BLACK & WHITE)
2522. TELEVISION (PORTABLE)
2523. TEXTILE DYEING BLEACHING FINISHING & PRINTING
2524. TERRY TOWEL
2525. TEXTILE AUXILLIARIES & CHEMICALS
2526. TEFLON TAPES & CABLE
2527. TEFLON COATED UTENSILS (NON-STICK)
2528. TEXTILE PRINTING PASTE (GUM)
2529. TELEVISION
2530. TEA PACKAGING & DISTRIBUTION
2531. TERRY TOWELS/TERRY FABRICS WEAVING UNIT
2532. TELEVISION (B/W)
2533. TELEPHONE CABLE (JELLY FILLED)
2534. TEA BAGS
2535. TEA (INSTANT)
2536. THREE STAR HOTEL
2537. THERMOMETER (CLINICAL)
2538. THINNERS
2539. THERMOCOLE MOULDING
2540. THREAD, CUSHION COMPOUND AND VOLCANIZING SOLUTION FORMULATION & MANUFACTURE
2541. THERMO PLASTIC ELECTRICAL SWITCHES & FITTINGS
2542. THERMOCOLE PACKAGING
2543. THERMO COUPLE TIPS
2544. THERMOCOUPLES
2545. THERMOCOLE SHEET & MOULDED PRODUCTS
2546. THERMO PLASTIC POLYURETHANE
2547. THERMOCOLE
2548. THERMOFORMED PACKAGING (BLISTER & POUCH PACKING)
2549. THREE WHEELER ASSEMBLY
2550. THINNER/SOLVENTS & ITS ALLIED PRODUCT
2551. THERMOSTATE FOR REFRIGERATOR
2552. TIN PRINTING & ANODIZING ON ALUMINIUM
2553. TIN CONTAINER
2554. TILES (MOSAIC)
2555. TILES (GLAZED CERAMIC)
2556. TIE ROD ENDS
2557. TITANIUM OXIDE
2558. TITANIUM NITRIDING
2559. TISSUE CULTURE (100% EOU)
2560. TITANIUM DIOXIDE BY CHLORINE
2561. TISSUE & AIR MAIL PAPER
2562. TISSUE & TOILET PAPER ROLL & AIR MAIL PAPER
2563. TISSUE PAPER ESPECIALLY FACIAL PAPER, MOIST TOILETTERIES, CLEANSING TISSUE & RELATED PRODUCTS
2564. TIN PRINTING
2565. TIMBER/WOOD SEASONING
2566. TOMATO POWDER
2567. TOMATO CONCENTRATE
2568. TOYS (PLASTIC)
2569. TOYS (ELECTRONICS)
2570. TOMATO PULP
2571. TOMATO WAFFERS
2572. TOBACCO & ITS PRODUCTS
2573. TOILET PAPER
2574. TOXIC COMPOUNDS EFFECTS ON HUMAN BODY
2575. TOYS (STUFF)
2576. TOILET SOAPS
2577. TOOTH BRUSH
2578. TOOTH PASTE (GEL-COLGATE, CLOSE-UP TYPE)
2579. TOOTH PASTE & POWDER
2580. TOOTH PASTE
2581. TOOTH BRUSH, TOOTH PASTE & POWDER
2582. TOMATO PRODUCT IN POUCHES
2583. TOUGHNED GLASS FOR WRIST WATCH
2584. TORCH & TRI LIGHT UNITS INTEGRATED PLANT INCLUDING MINIATURE BULB & TUBES, ENGINEERING PLASTIC MOULD/DIES MANUFACTURE
2585. TOILET & HERBAL SOAP
2586. TOMATO & PAPAYA CULTIVATION
2587. TOILET PAPER & NAPKIN
2588. TOY BALLOONS, DECORATIVE BALLOONS
2589. TOFFEE (MILK)
2590. TOWEL, SOCKS & HOSIERY
2591. TOMATO PASTE
2592. TOMATO KETCHUP, JAMS, JELLY ETC.
2593. TOGGLE SWITCHES
2594. TONER INK
2595. TOILET SEATS & COVERS
2596. TOUGHENED GLASS & SILVER MIRROR GLASS
2597. TOBACCO TOOTH PASTE FROM TOBACCO DUST
2598. TOBACCO TOOTH PASTE FROM TOBACCO
2599. TRANSPARENT LACQUER (CLEAR) FOR COATING ON BRASS BANGLES TO MAKE IT WEATHER RESISTANT
2600. TREAD RUBBER (CAMEL BLACK)
2601. TRI-PHENYL PHOSPHITE
2602. TRI SODIUM PHOSPHATE
2603. TRICYCLE RIKS-HAW ASSEMBLY
2604. TRI-METHOPRIME
2605. TRI BASIC LEAD SULPHATE
2606. TRANSFORMER OIL RECLAMATION
2607. TRANSFORMER
2608. TRANSFORMER (DISTRIBUTION)
2609. TRANSFORMER OIL
2610. TRAVELLING AGENCY
2611. TRACING PAPER
2612. T-SHIRT & KNITTING FABRIC
2613 T.V. & AUDIO CABINETS & THEIR ASSEMBLING UNIT
2614. TURKEY RED OIL
2615. TUBULAR POLES, TRANSMISSION LINE, HARDWARE & MAIN SWITCH FOR ELECTRICAL TRANSMISSION
2616. TURPENTINE OIL
2617. TURPENTINE OIL FROM EXTRACTIONS OF DIPETROCORPUS TREE
2618. TUTI FRUITY FROM PAPAYA FRUITY
2619. TURMERIC POWDER (EDIBLE GRADE)
2620. TURMERIC OIL OLEORESIN FROM RAW TURMERIC
2621. TUBE VALVES
2622. TUBULAR POLES FOR ELECTRICAL TRANSMISSION
2623. TUNGSTEN FILAMENT
2624. TURPENTINE & ROSIN DISTILLATION
2625. T.V. PICTURE TUBE (B/W) & COMPUTER MONITOR TUBE
2626. T.V CUM VIDEO GAMES
2627. T.V. SIGNAL BOOSTERS
2628. TWISTED YARN (NYLON)
2629. TWO-T 2-STROKE OIL
2630. TWO WHEELERS REPAIR & SERVICE WORKSHOP
2631. TYRE RETREADING
2632. TYRE RETREADING BY COLD PROCESS
2633. TYRE RETREADING (HOT PROCESS)
2634. TYRE & TUBES FOR SCOOTER, MOTOR CYCLE, RIKSHAW, 2/3 WHEELERS
2635. TYRES, TUBES AND FLAP (MOPED TO TRUCK)
2636. 2-4-D SODIUM SALT
2637. U-CLAMPS, U-BOLTS & NUTS
2638. U.J. CROSS & KING PIN
2638. ULTRAMARINE BLUE
2639. UMBRELLA

2640. UNDECYLENIL ACID
2641. UNSATURATED POLYSTER RESINS
2642. UNINTERRUPTED POWER SUPPLY (UPS)
2643. UN ARMOURED, PVC INSULATED CABLES
2644. UTENSILS (SILVER PLATED)
2645. UTENSILS (ALUMINIUM)
2646. UTENSILS (BRASS)
2647. UREA FORMALDEHYDE POWDER
2648. UREA FORMALDEHYDE RESIN
2649. UREA
2650. UREA FERTILIZER PLANT
2651. UREA FORMALDEHYDE & MELAMINE FORMALDEHYDE MOULDING POWDER
2652. UTENSILS (STAINLESS STEEL)
2653. UTENSILS (TEFLON COATED)
2654. U.V. PAINT
2655. VACUUM METALIZING
2656. VANASPATI GHEE
2657. VALVE GUIDES
2658. VARNISH & PAINT UNIT
2659. VASELINE
2660. VARNISH THINNER (SOLVENT)
2661. VACUUM-METALLISING LACQUER
2662. VAT DYES
2663. VACUUM CLEANER
2664. V-BELTS
2665. VCP & VCR
2666. VENETIAN BLIND
2667. VELVET CLOTH BY FLOCKING PROCESS
2668. VEGETABLE OIL REFINING (BY PHYSICAL PROCESS)
2669. VEGETABLE OIL (EXTRACTION & REFINNING)
2670. VELCROW FASTENING TAPE (FASTNER HOOP LOOP TAPE & SYNTHETIC)
2671. VETENERY MEDICINES
2672. VERMICELLI
2673. VERMICELLI & MACARONI
2674. VIDEO & T.V. GAMES
2675. VIDEO & AUDIO CASSETES
2676. VIDEO CASSETES
2677. VIDEO STUDIO
2678. VIDEO & AUDIO MAGNETIC TAPES
2679. VINEGAR & MALT VINEGAR FOR INDUSTRIAL & DOMESTIC USE
2680. VIDEO CASSETE ASSEMBLING & RECORDING
2681. VITAMIN-C FROM POTATO EXTRACT
2682. VISCOSE RAYON YARN FROM COTTON LINIERS
2683. VIDEO CAMERA
2684. VIDEO FILM STUDIO
2685. VIDEO CASSETTES (COMPLETE MANUFACTURING & ASSEMBLING UNIT)
2686. VIDEO TAPE
2687. VIDEO FILM STUDIO TO MAKE FILMS ETC. IN VIDEO CASSETTES & FILM ROLLS
2688. VIDEO CASSETTES LIBRARY
2689. VISCOSE STAPLE FIBRE (RAYON STAPLE FIBER)
2690. VOLTAGE REGULATOR (FOR AUTOMOBILES)
2691. VOLTAGE STABILIZER
2692. VOLTAGE STABLIZER
2693. VODKA FROM WASTE GRAIN
2694. WAX CRAYON
2695. WAX FLOOR POLISH
2696. WASHING & LAUNDRY SOAP
2697. WALL TILES/FLOOR TILES/ SANITARY TILES
2698. WASHING MACHINE (AUTOMATIC ELECTRO COMPUTERISED)
2699. WAX (PARAFFIN)
2700. WAX (MICRO CRYSTALLINE)
2701. WATCH LEATHER STRAP
2702. WALL PAPER PRINTING
2703. WAX EMULSION
2704. WAX FOR PAPER
2705. WATER PROOF CEMENT COMPOUND
2706. WAX EMULSION
2707. WATER FILTER CANDLES
2708. WATER FILTER & PRESSURE COOKER
2709. WASHING MACHINE & GEYSER
2710. WATER PROOFING BITUMINISED COMPOUND
2711. WAX FOR PAPER INDUSTRY
2712. WATCH CASE BUFFING
2713. WATER FOR INJECTION AMPOULES PLANT
2714. WATER PROOF MARKING INK
2715. WATTLE EXTRACT (TANNIN POWDER)
2716. WAX PAPERED MATHC STICK
2717. WATCH GLASS
2718. WAX & CHEMICAL COATED BRAIDED TINSEL WIRE
2719. WALL PAPER
2720. WASHING CAKE, DETERGENT CAKE & POWDER
2721. WATER PROOFING FORMULATIONS FOR PAPER CONES USED FOR SPEAKERS
2722. WATER PROOFING FOR COTTON CLOTH
2723. WATER METER
2724. WATER STORAGE TANK
2725. WATER PROOFING PAINT
2726. WATER (MINERAL)
2727. WATER METER
2728. WATER STORAGE TANK
2729. WATER PROOFING PAINT
2730. WATER (MINERAL)
2731. WASHING POWDER & WASHING SOAP
2732. WELDING FLUXES
2733. WELDING RODS (SPECIAL) & M.S. WELDING ELECTRODES
2734. WELDING BRASS ROD
2735. WETTING OIL
2736. WELDED WIRE MESH
2737. WEET AROMA OF BETAL NUT
2738. WELDING CABLE
2739. WEET AROMA OF BETAL NUT
2740. WELDING CABLE

2741. WELDING ELECTRODES
2742. WELDING WIRE ELECTRODES (CO2)
2743. WHITE CEMENT
2744. WHTIE OIL FROM KEROSENE OIL
2745. WHEAT PUFF
2746. WHEAT PORRIDGE (DALIA)